D0324780

# The Police Officer Exam Cram Sheet

This cram sheet is designed to provide you a quick study guide to refer to just before you take the exam. This quick reference will serve you well if you have worked through the chapters in the book and you review the information listed in this quick reference just before entering the test room.

## FACTS FOR THE POLICE WRITTEN TEST

1. Create an outline of the study material.

2. Take good abbreviated notes. During the exam, time is very important. Do not waste time writing full words. Create your own spellings of common words. As you use these abbreviated words over and over again, you will create your own short-hand.

   For example, you don't have to write People every time you see that word. You can use an abbreviated version such as ppl.

3. Take notes in a consistent pattern. As mentioned in the chapter, you will be required to memorize descriptions of the suspects. If there is a question like that, start memorizing the description from the head and stop at the footwear. If there are several questions about suspect description, use the same method again. By following the same pattern again, your notes will be better organized and easier to remember.

4. When observing or memorizing floor plans, crime scenes, and suspect information, draw diagrams. When allowed to do so, transfer these diagrams from memory to the scratch paper provided during the exam.

5. *Direct routes* are those that require the least amount of time to get from point A to point B.

6. When attempting questions that measure your ability to follow written directions, pay special attention to azimuth.

7. Street grids are street blocks created by streets running east to west and from north to south.

8. In most cities, even number addresses on a street running east and west are on the north side of the street and odd number addresses on the south side of the street. For streets running north and south, even number addresses are on the west side of the street, and odd number addresses are on the east side of the street.

9. Almost all even-numbered interstate highways run east and west, and all the odd-numbered interstate highways run north and south.

10. Forms are very important in police report writing. Expect to see a complete section on filling out forms and reports.

11. Reading the general exam instructions is very important because they specify what you need to do in the entire forms and reports section. Be sure to read them carefully!

12. Follow the question instructions. Do not read too much or too little into the instruction. Most of the time, there are no trick questions.

13. There are two types of questions you are likely to see in the forms and report section of the written exam. In the first type of question, you are given a scenario with a variety of information. You are then expected to fill a form by following the instructions given for the form. In the second type of question, you are given a form with the data already in it. You are to extract the data from the form and answer a series of questions based on the scenario.

14. Good writing skills are an important aspect of police work because you will be required to write many different types of reports.

15. It is important for you to be able to write clearly and effectively. You can do that by keeping your focus on facts and listing them down.

16. Use simple words that are relevant to the situation and avoid jumbled-up sentences.

17. Keep sentences short and simple, and avoid long, complicated ones.

18. It is important for you to proofread whatever you write and try to list things in chronological order.

19. Follow correct grammar rules and make sure that your tenses are correct; you must understand the correct usage of punctuation and other grammar principles.

## GENERAL STUDY GUIDE

1. Prioritize your study tasks.

2. Practice, practice, and some more practice.

3. Manage your time before the test. This includes getting a good night of sleep and eating right the night before and morning of the exam.

4. Use your time management skills during the test.

5. Manage your time during the oral interview.

6. Manage your time during the physical agility test.

7. Try to understand the question completely before answering it.

8. Highlight the keywords.

9. Before you turn in the test to the proctor, always review it.

10. Read all the choices before making a decision. Ignore nothing!

11. When reading the question, look for clues. These clues will help you answer the question.

20. Improve your vocabulary and spelling by writing down new words carefully.

21. Read pronunciation out loud so that it helps you remember the spelling.

22. Try to remember the syllable division of a word for better recall of its correct spelling.

23. You need to have good reading comprehension skills in order to understand test questions in the police officer written test. To increase your reading comprehension, use the following tools:

    • Improve your vocabulary by reading extensively and finding the meanings of words you don't understand by using a dictionary.

    • Read with concentration and understanding, and try to follow a helpful reading technique that you have practiced before.

    • Look at how the information is organized in the text and what method the writer has followed in writing.

    • Try to recognize the purpose for reading the text and at the meaning the writer is trying to convey. Try to anticipate what might come next as you read.

    • Read out loud and review what you have read. Form questions that are answered by the text.

24. Improving memory retention skills will help you to remember facts and recall information for the police officer written test and other related procedures. You can improve your memory by using the following methods:

    • Try to develop an interest in the subject so that you find it easy to remember facts and information.

    • If you understand what you're learning, it will help you improve your recall.

    • Try to link your previous knowledge to newly learned situations so that they make more sense to you and are easy to remember.

    • Try to study at a balanced pace and do not cram at the last moment because that will confuse you and restrict good recall.

    • Making notes will always help you retain information because it requires maximum concentration to summarize and take notes.

    • Generalize or categorize bits of information so that you are able to recall them when your mind gives you a cue for certain information.

## FACTS FOR THE POLICE EXAM: ORAL INTERVIEW

1. Create an inventory of personal and professional accomplishments.

2. Utilize the inventory created in step 1 to create a professional-looking resume.

3. Create a two-minute introduction about yourself, your goals, and your accomplishments.

4. Also, be sure to create a five-minute introduction about yourself, your goals, and your accomplishments in case your interviewer wants more information than a two-minute introduction provides.

5. Practice delivering the statements discussed in step 4 in front of a mirror. You can also practice with a friend or relative.

6. A *structured oral interview* is in an employment interviewing environment in which all the participating candidates are asked the same questions and their responses are evaluated according to a set standard of answers.

7. An *individual interview* is an employment interview with one person, such as with a human resource manager or chief of police.

8. Remember to send thank you letters to your interviewer. If you are interviewed by a board be sure to send a letter to every member.

9. Always use the correct spelling of an interviewer's name and title.

## FACTS FOR THE POLICE PHYSICAL AGILITY EXAM

### Push-Ups

1. Push-ups are physical exercises that require the performer to push his body weight using his upper arms, triceps, and shoulder muscles. Push-ups are used to build upper body strength. As a test, push-ups measure the endurance of the chest, shoulder, and triceps muscles.

2. How to improve your push-up score:

    • Determine the number of correct push-ups you can do in one minute. For example: 52 push-ups in one minute.

    • Multiply the number by .75. This is the number of push-ups that you need to do in each set.

    • The number for the individual set is 52 x .75 = 39.

    • Perform three to five one-minute sets of push-ups, maintaining proper form.

    • Do not rest for more than one minute between the sets.

    • If the last set becomes too difficult to finish, rest long enough to finish the set.

    • Perform this routine three times a week.

    • Increase the number of repetitions by one or two repetitions each week.

### Sit-ups

3. Sit-ups are physical exercises that require the performer to sit up by using his stomach muscles. The exercise is used to build stomach muscles.

4. How to improve your sit-up score:
   - Determine the number of correct sit-ups you can do in one minute. For example: 40 sit-ups in one minute.
   - Multiply the number by .75. This is the number of sit-ups that you need to do in each set.
   - Number for the individual set 40 x .75 = 30.
   - Perform three to five one-minute sets of sit-ups, maintaining proper form.
   - Do not rest for more than one minute between the sets.
   - If the last set becomes too difficult to finish, rest just enough to finish the set.
   - Perform this routine three times per week.
   - Increase the number of repetitions by one or two repetitions each week.

## Running

5. How to improve your running score:

Use the following chart as a guideline to build your endurance.

| Week | Activity | Distance in Miles | Duration in Minutes | Times Per Week |
|------|----------|-------------------|---------------------|----------------|
| 1 | Walk | 1 | 17-20 | 5 |
| 2 | Walk | 1.5 | 25-29 | 5 |
| 3 | Walk | 2 | 32-35 | 5 |
| 4 | Walk/Jog | 2 | 28-30 | 5 |
| 5 | Walk/Jog | 2 | 27 | 5 |
| 6 | Walk/Jog | 2 | 26 | 5 |
| 7 | Walk/Jog | 2 | 25 | 5 |
| 8 | Walk/Jog | 2 | 24 | 5 |
| 9 | Jog | 2 | 23 | 4 |
| 10 | Jog | 2 | 22 | 4 |
| 11 | Jog | 2 | 21 | 4 |
| 12 | Jog | 2 | 20 | 4 |

## Flexibility

6. Flexibility is the capability of a joint to move through a normal range of motion of bending and stretching the muscles surrounding the joint.

7. How to improve your flexibility score:

   The best way to improve flexibility is by proper stretching. Stretching is useful in preventing injury and for treatment of any injury. Add a variety of exercises to your stretching regimen before your workout as a warm-up phase and after your workout as a cool-down process. The best time to increase flexibility is after you have worked out and your body has warmed up. To improve flexibility, think of flexibility training and not just brief stretching periods before workout.

## Sprinting/Fast Speed Running

8. Sprinting is quick or fast speed running.

9. How to improve your sprinting score:
   - Measure the time for your all-out effort for 110 yards.
   - Divide your all-out time by .80 to determine your training time.

     For example: 40 x .80 = 32 seconds.
   - Adhere to the following schedule and gradually increase your speed and short distance endurance:

| Weeks | Distance in Yards | Reps | Training Time in Seconds | Rest Times | Times per Week |
|-------|-------------------|------|--------------------------|------------|----------------|
| 1–2 | 110 | 10 | 32 | 2-3 seconds | 2-3 |
| 3–4 | 110 | 10 | 32 | 2-3 seconds | 2-3 |
| 5–6 | 110 | 10 | 32 | 5-6 seconds | 2-3 |
| 7–8 | 220 | 8 | 64 | 2-3 seconds | 2-3 |
| 9–10 | 220 | 8 | 64 | 4 seconds | 2-3 |

## Vertical Jumps

These basic exercises, if performed on regular basis, will help build leg muscles and increase your explosiveness.

## Lunges, Squats, Calf Raises, Step ups, Knee Bends Jumping Rope

Below is a sample workout.

### Warm Up

Start out with a set of warm-up exercises. Stretching and jumping rope are excellent choices for a warm-up activity. Perhaps 10-15 minutes of jumping rope with stretching afterwards.

### Workout

I like to keep my workouts simple and easy to follow on a regular basis. I like to do three exercises per body muscle and keep my body guessing.

### Monday

3 set of 10 reps Lunges
3 set of 10 reps Step Ups
3 set of 10 reps Knee Bends

### Wednesday

3 set of 10 reps Squats
3 set of 10 reps Calf raises
3 set of 10 reps Step Ups

### Friday

3 set of 10 reps Lunges
3 set of 10 reps Step Ups
3 set of 10 reps Knee Bends

EXAM CRAM™

# Police Officer
# Exam

BRIDGEVIEW, IL 60455

que®
CERTIFICATION

# Police Officer Exam Cram, Second Edition

ISBN-10: 0-7897-4224-1
ISBN-13: 978-0-7897-4224-7

Library of Congress Cataloging-in-Publication data is available upon
request.

Printed in the United States of America

First Printing: September 2009

## Trademarks

## Warning and Disclaimer

## Bulk Sales

Que Publishing offers excellent discounts on this book when ordered
in quantity for bulk purchases or special sales. For more information,
please contact

**U.S. Corporate and Government Sales**

**1-800-382-3419**

**corpsales@pearsontechgroup.com**

For sales outside the U.S., please contact

**International Sales**

**international@pearsoned.com**

**Publisher**
Paul Boger

**Associate Publisher**
Dave Dusthimer

**Acquisitions Editor**
Betsy Brown

**Senior Development Editor**
Christopher Cleveland

**Managing Editor**
Patrick Kanouse

**Project Editor**
Seth Kerney

**Indexer**
Ken Johnson

**Proofreader**
Bethany Wall

**Technical Editors**
Robert Ladd
Tim Brennen

**Cover Designer**
Gary Adair

# Contents at a Glance

# Table of Contents

# Part I  Written Exam

## Chapter 2
## Reading Comprehension

## Chapter 3
## Memory Retention

## Chapter 4
## Geographical Orientation

## Part III  Physical Agility

### Chapter 8
### Physical Agility......................................................................**145**

## Part IV  Maximizing Test Scores

### Chapter 9
### Time Management......................................................................**163**

# About the Author

Rizwan Khan is a 22-year veteran of law enforcement. He began his career in law enforcement in 1986 with the Indiana University Police Department at Indianapolis as a Cadet Officer. After completion of Indiana University Police Academy in 1987, he was commissioned by the Indiana Law Enforcement Training Board as a police officer for the university. Rizwan received a B.S. in public affairs from Indiana University–Purdue University at Indianapolis in 1989. After finishing his degree, he was employed by the Indianapolis Police Department. After completing the Indianapolis Police Department Training Academy program, Rizwan was commissioned for the second time by the same board as a police officer for the city of Indianapolis. Rizwan held a variety of positions for the Indianapolis Police Department, including uniform patrol officer, evidence technician, detective, and warrant service officer. While working as a detective, Rizwan investigated burglaries, larcenies, aggravated assaults, shootings, traffic accidents, and hit and run cases.

Rizwan has attended numerous law enforcement training classes offered by the Indianapolis Police Department and other outside agencies, including Basic and Advanced Detective School and Evidence Technician.

Currently, Rizwan works as a detective for the North District of the Indianapolis Police Department.

Pamela Rich Hahn currently works as an independent contractor providing technical and other writing and editing services. Prior to her freelance career, Pamela worked in law enforcement for 10 years. Pam has authored or co-authored more than 10 technical and general non-fiction books, including *How to Use Microsoft Access 2000* and *Alpha Teach Yourself Grammar and Style in 24 Hours*, and *The Everything to Improve Your Writing Book*, and she has been a contributing writer and editor to a number of others.

Pam has published several hundred general interest and technical articles in local, national, and online publications. Pam also designs and maintains several Web sites, among them her personal site (www.RiceHahn.com), The Blue Rose Bouquet online magazine (www.blueroses.com), GenealogyTips (www.GenealogyTips.com), and Cooking With Pam (www.CookingWithPam.com).

# About the Technical Editors

**Timothy Brennan and Robert Ladd** are both peace officers currently employed as Gang Investigators. Tim Brennan is a veteran police officer with 27 years' experience who currently works for the Los Angeles County Sheriff's Department. Robert Ladd has been a police officer for 26 years, and he is currently working for the Garden Grove Police Department in Orange County. Both officers are experienced in the field of gang violence and gang-related crimes.

For several years, Tim and Robert were partners assigned to the Compton Police Department's Gang Intelligence/Investigations/Homicide Unit. This specialized unit was tasked with investigating gang violence, gang-related crimes, and homicides. They are members of the California Gang Investigators Association and attend monthly meetings to discuss current trends, rivalries, gang-related investigations, and gang-enforcement strategies.

Tim and Robert experienced first-hand the early days of gang warfare in Compton with the "Gangster Rap" industry that began in the 1980s, including the rise and fall of Death Row Records, the well-known 1992 Los Angeles/Compton Riot, the 1993 murder of two Compton police officers, the 1993 Mexican Mafia Edict, the 1994 El Rey Theatre murder of Rapper DJ Quick, and many other Gangster Rap murders. Tim was instrumental in the 1987 parole revocation of Suge Knight.

Tim and Robert have provided gang training to schools, businesses, community organizations, federal and local police, prosecutors from across the country, U.S. military personnel, and police from several European countries. They have provided gang-related intelligence and evidence for prosecution to law enforcement and prosecuting agencies across the country, traveled throughout California, Texas, Nevada, Illinois, Oklahoma, Louisiana, and Washington on gang-related investigations, attended world heavyweight boxing title fights in Las Vegas as gang expert consultants to the local police, and have had portions of gang affidavits and gang investigations published in national newspapers, magazines, books, as well as featured on several television programs.

In their spare time, they work on their Web site, www.comptonpolice-gangs.com, and spend time with their families.

# Dedication

*In Memory of all the soldiers, sailors, marines and airmen of the United States armed forces who gave their lives for our freedom and for all the soldiers who are currently serving overseas so that we can sit here in the comfort of our homes and do our daily routine. This book is also dedicated to all our brothers and sisters in law enforcement who put their lives on the line everyday.*

—Rizwan Khan and Pamela Rice Hahn

# Acknowledgments

I would like to thank my late parents and my sister for providing me life instructions. I would also like to thank my wonderful wife Shaheena for supporting me in writing this book and my daughters, Nida, Hira, Hania and Zarah, for letting me cut into their time while I was writing.

Thanks to Pamela Rice Hahn for providing the sample questions, composite sketches, and other input.

Thanks to Acquisitions Editor Betsy Brown and Senior Development Editor Christopher Cleveland for staying with me on this book allowing me to miss a few deadlines. I would also like to thank technical editors, Robert Ladd and Tim Brennan of Compton Police Gangs for providing all the constructive criticism.

—Rizwan Khan

In addition to acknowledging the help and assistance of the others who worked on this book, I would like to acknowledge John Corder and Paul Wright of Smith & Wesson Identi-Kit Solutions (www.identikit.net, 1-866-414-9286, 14500 N. Northsight Blvd., Suite 116, Scottsdale, AZ 85260). The Smith & Wesson Identi-Kit Solutions software was used to create the majority of the composite sketches for this book. Designed with the assistance of public safety officers, Identi-Kit.Net's menus and tool buttons allow you to shape, shade, and scale every facial feature. Composite sketches are created online with a Web browser, which allows for collaboration with other law enforcement agencies and easy addition of new information as it is discovered. The program has tools to create wanted posters instantly that can be circulated worldwide via the Web and email. In addition, I would also like to thank Lizz Matheson of IQ BIOMETRIX INC. for the use of that company's Faces software to create other composite sketches for the book. Faces facial composite technology is used by thousands of police agencies worldwide, including the FBI and CIA. For more information, please see www.iqbiometrix.com.

For their help and support, I would further like to thank my friends and associates at www.ProudPatriots.com; my daughter Lara Sutton; my grandkids Taylor, Charlie, and Courtney; my mother Pat Rice; Ann, Andrew, and Tony Rice; and David Hebert.

—Pamela Rice Hahn

# We Want to Hear from You!

As the reader of this book, *you* are our most important critic and commentator. We value your opinion and want to know what we're doing right, what we could do better, what areas you'd like to see us publish in, and any other words of wisdom you're willing to pass our way.

As an Associate Publisher for Pearson, I welcome your comments. You can email or write me directly to let me know what you did or didn't like about this book—as well as what we can do to make our books better.

*Please note that I cannot help you with technical problems related to the topic of this book. We do have a User Services group, however, where I will forward specific technical questions related to the book.*

When you write, please be sure to include this book's title and author as well as your name, email address, and phone number. I will carefully review your comments and share them with the author and editors who worked on the book.

Email:   scorehigher@pearsoned.com

Mail:    Dave Dusthimer
         Associate Publisher
         Que Publishing
         800 East 96th Street
         Indianapolis, IN 46240 USA

# Reader Services

Visit our website and register this book at www.examcram.com/register for convenient access to any updates, downloads, or errata that might be available for this book.

# Introduction

Welcome to *Police Officer Exam Cram!* This book is designed to prepare you for the police officer selection exam. But before it goes into the details of the exam, the book talks about the job of a police officer. A detailed job description is given in Chapter 1. Take a good look at the job description. You are getting ready to commit to a noble profession. The book discusses the training and requirements of becoming a police officer, including a description of the testing environment and a discussion of test-taking strategies.

Chapters 2 through 6 are designed to introduce different sections you will be tested on during the written portion of the police exam. Chapter 7 covers the oral interview section of the police exam. The oral interview is one of the most important phases of the whole selection process. Chapter 8 provides you information on the physical agility test. This test is demanding and you will need plenty of preparation time. Chapters 9 and 10 cover topics such as time management and test-taking strategies during the written and oral portion of the exam.

The three practice tests at the end of the book should give you a reasonably accurate assessment of your knowledge on the topics covered in the test. You have been provided the answers and explanations to the tests. Be sure to review any weak spots you found you had on the practice exams as well. Revisit the chapters that cover your weak spots and also visit the "Need to Know More?" appendix at the end of the book to find other resources you can visit for extra practice and review in your weak areas. In all, if you read the book and understand the material, you'll stand a very good chance of scoring high on all portions of the police officer selection process.

*Exam Cram* books help you understand and appreciate the subjects and materials you need to score high on the police officer selection exam. *Exam Cram* books are aimed strictly at test preparation and review. They do not teach you everything you need to know about a topic. Instead, you will be presented questions and problems that you're likely to encounter on a test. I have worked to bring together as much information as possible about the police officer selection exam.

Nevertheless, to completely prepare yourself for the police test, I recommend that you begin by taking the self-assessment immediately following this introduction in this book. The self-assessment tool will help you evaluate your readiness to become a police officer. Based on what you learn from the self-assessment, you might decide to make some adjustments in your lifestyle that will be conducive to performing well on the police exam.

All police officer selection exams are completely closed book. In fact, you are not permitted to take anything with you into the testing area, but you will be given a blank sheet of paper and a pen. I suggest that you immediately write down on that sheet of paper as much test information you've memorized as possible.

# What This Book Will Not Do

This book will *not* teach you everything you need to know about becoming a police officer. However, this book will teach basic concepts that will help you score high on your police officer selection exam.

This book uses a variety of teaching and memorization techniques to analyze the exam-related topics and to provide you guidance and techniques that have been proven successful to obtain high scores in police officer exams. Once again: This book will *not* make you a police officer or teach you everything there is to know about being a police officer.

# What This Book Is Designed to Do

This book is designed to teach you basic concepts and techniques that will, if followed, help you obtain high scores on the police officer selection exam.

# Chapter Formats

Each *Exam Cram* chapter follows a regular structure, and provides graphical cues about especially important or useful material. The structure of a typical chapter is as follows:

- ▶ **Opening hotlists**—Each chapter begins with lists of the terms you'll need to understand and the concepts you'll need to master before you can be fully conversant with the chapter's subject matter. I follow the hotlists with a few introductory paragraphs, setting the stage for the rest of the chapter.

- ▶ **Topical coverage**—After the opening hotlists, each chapter covers the topics related to the chapter's subject.

- ▶ **Exam Alerts**—Throughout the topical coverage section, I highlight material most likely to appear on the exam by using a special Exam Alert layout that looks like this:

## EXAM ALERT

This is what an Exam Alert looks like. An Exam Alert stresses concepts, terms, or activities that will most likely appear in one or more police exam questions. For that reason, I think any information found offset in Exam Alert format is worthy of unusual attentiveness on your part.

Even if material isn't flagged as an Exam Alert, *all* the content in this book is associated in some way with test-related material. What appears in the chapter content is critical knowledge.

▶ Notes—Also, in this book you will find note elements that expand on topics being discussed. See below for an example:

## NOTE

A note is an aside piece of information that is related to the regular content flow, but is not really suitable to be in the regular flow of content. These are good for giving you extra information about police work and life that doesn't necessarily have much to do with the exam, but is good to know nonetheless.

▶ **Tips**—I provide tips that will help you to build a better foundation of knowledge or to focus your attention on an important concept that will reappear later in the book. Tips provide a helpful way to remind you of the context surrounding a particular area of a topic under discussion.

▶ **Practice questions**—This section presents a short list of test questions related to the specific chapter topic. Each question has a following explanation of both correct and incorrect answers. The practice questions highlight the areas we found to be most important on the exam.

▶ **Need to Know More?**—Every chapter ends with a section that is represented in an appendix titled "Need to Know More?" This section provides pointers to resources that we found to be helpful in offering further details on the chapter's subject matter. If you find a resource you like in this collection, use it, but don't feel compelled to use all these resources. I use this section to recommend resources that I have used on a regular basis, so none of the recommendations will be a waste of your time or money. These resources might go out of print or be taken down (in the case of Web sites), so I've tried to reference widely accepted resources.

The bulk of the book follows this chapter structure, but there are a few other elements that I would like to point out:

▶ **Practice tests**—The practice tests, which appear in Chapters 11, 13, and 15 (with answer keys in Chapters 12, 14, and 16), are very close approximations of the types of questions you are likely to see on police officer selection exam.

- ▶ **Answer keys**—These provide the answers to the practice tests, complete with explanations of both the correct responses and the incorrect responses.

- ▶ **Glossary**—This is an extensive glossary of important terms used in this book.

- ▶ **Cram sheet**—This appears as a tear-away sheet inside the front cover of this *Exam Cram* book. It is a valuable tool that represents a collection of the most difficult-to-remember facts and numbers I think you should memorize before taking the test. Remember, you can dump this information out of your head onto a piece of paper as soon as you enter the testing room. These are usually facts that I've found require brute-force memorization. You need to remember this information only long enough to write it down when you walk into the test room. Be advised that you will be asked to surrender all personal belongings before you enter the exam room itself.

You might want to look at the cram sheet in your car or in the lobby of the testing center just before you walk into the testing center. The cram sheet is divided under headings, so you can review the appropriate parts just before each test.

# Contacting the Author

I've tried to create a real-world tool that you can use to prepare for and obtain high scores on your police officer selection exam. All the tips and techniques and information I have presented in the book, I have used myself. In 17 years of law enforcement experience, I have taken the police officer selection exam three times. Each time I scored high on the exam and was interviewed by the agency and offered employment. Just like anything else, some of the information might or might not work for you. But I assure you that after you've read this book, you will develop your own plan of tackling the police officer selection exam. I'm interested in any feedback you would care to share about the book, especially if you have ideas about how I can improve it for future brothers and sisters to be in law enforcement. I'll consider what you say carefully and will respond to all reasonable suggestions and comments. You can reach me via email at rizwanskhan@hotmail.com.

Let me know if you found this book to be helpful in your preparation efforts. I'd also like to know how you felt about your chances of passing the exam *before* you read the book and then *after* you read the book. Of course, I'd be glad to hear from you when you succeed in your endeavor to become a police officer.

Thanks for choosing me as your guide in becoming a police officer. I hope you enjoy the book as much as I enjoyed writing it. I wish you luck on the selection exam. I'm sure that if you read through all the chapters and work with the exam questions and the concepts presented, you will score high and pass with flying colors.

# Self-Assessment

A self-assessment has been included in this *Exam Cram* to help you evaluate your readiness for becoming a police officer.

## The Job

A police officer never knows what will happen next, and the only thing to be expected is the unexpected. Police officers have a wide range of duties. These duties involve protection of life and property, enforcement of laws and ordinances, criminal investigation, crime prevention, suppression, case preparation, and testimony. In addition to these duties, the job requires exceptional customer service skills and a dedication to public service.

## Do You Have What It Takes?

The following subsections detail some facts and some questions that you need to assess truthfully. Answer these items to judge your readiness for taking the challenge of becoming a police officer.

### The Basics

The following bulleted list gives you some facts about pursuing a career as a police officer. Pay careful attention to these items because some of these indicate requirements that you must meet before attempting to join a police force.

▶ A police officer candidate must be 21 years of age.

▶ A high school diploma or GED is required; however, a college degree is preferred.

▶ A candidate must not have felony convictions, including expunged convictions.

▶ You must possess a valid operator's driver's license and have an acceptable driving record.

▶ You must successfully pass a comprehensive background investigation, including polygraph testing and psychological evaluation.

▶ You must successfully pass state-certified law enforcement training.

# Take a Quick Self-Assessment

The following series of questions and observations is designed to help you figure out how ready you are to become a police officer.

**Basic Qualifications**

1. Are you a United States citizen?

(Yes or No)

2. Do you have a valid driver's license?

(Yes or No)

3. Do you have any felony convictions?

(Yes or No)

**Educational Background**

4. Are you a high school graduate?

(Yes or No)

5. Have you completed any college credits?

(Yes or No)

**Physical Requirements**

6. Do you have any known physical conditions that would prevent you from performing strenuous physical activity?

(Yes or No)

7. Do you have health conditions that would prevent you from performing your job effectively?

(Yes or No)

## Work Requirements

**8.** Are you a self-motivated individual who can work with minimal supervision?

(Yes or No)

**9.** Are you dependable and accountable?

(Yes or No)

**10.** Do you follow rules and regulations?

(Yes or No)

**11.** Do you have strong verbal and written communication skills?

(Yes or No)

**12.** Do you have exceptional problem-solving skills and sound judgment?

(Yes or No)

**13.** Police work involves a certain amount of personal danger. Are you apprehensive about verbal or physical altercation?

(Yes or No)

**14.** Police officers are often required to be quick thinkers and to have the ability to be fair. Can you be fair without any biases?

(Yes or No)

**15.** Working as a police officer requires dealing with high stress situations. The job could involve dealing with children and the elderly as victims of crimes. Do you have the ability to be objective, mask your personal feelings, and keep your mind to the task at hand?

(Yes or No)

**16.** A police department is a close-knit, highly efficient team of professionals. Are you a team player?

(Yes or No)

**17.** Do you have obligations that would prevent you from leaving home for training? This training period can last as long as 24 weeks.

(Yes or No)

**18.** Shift assignment can be negotiated when you are employed, but always be prepared for changes. Do you have any commitments that would prevent you from working a specific shift?

(Yes or No)

19. Being a police officer can be a stressful and challenging job for the family as you bring work home from time to time. Do you think some of your personal obligations might create stress for you as you try to fulfill your duties as a police officer?

(Yes or No)

20. Because at times your shift might be lengthened due to an emergency or a late call for help, do you have the ability to work more than eight hours during your shift?

(Yes or No)

Compare your results to the answer sheet at the end of this assessment. If your results are not close to the answers, some challenges lie ahead of you as you move toward one of the most rewarding careers available (in this author's opinion).

# Answers to Self-Assessment

The following answer sheet gives the most preferred answers to the self-assessment questions you answered earlier. These are preferred answers because these answers show a candidate who is most ready to take on the process of becoming a police officer.

| | | | |
|---|---|---|---|
| 1. Yes | 6. No | 11. Yes | 16. Yes |
| 2. Yes | 7. No | 12. Yes | 17. No |
| 3. No | 8. Yes | 13. No | 18. No |
| 4. Yes | 9. Yes | 14. Yes | 19. No |
| 5. Yes | 10. Yes | 15. Yes | 20. Yes |

# 1

## CHAPTER ONE

# Police Officer
# Selection Process

Many say being a police officer is one of the most rewarding—as well as challenging—careers you can choose. With the current job outlook, when a variety of positions in other professions are being outsourced, being a police officer might be one of the most secure jobs available. Police departments all across the country are constantly looking for qualified people to fill the gap being created by retirements, promotions, and transfers.

Figure 1.1 shows a Monster.com listing for vacant police officer jobs. As you can see, at the time of this screenshot, 292 jobs were listed in various jurisdictions.

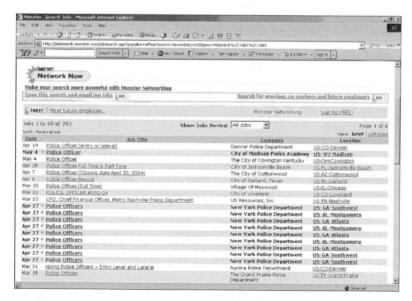

**FIGURE 1.1**   A web page that shows various open police positions.

# Job Outlook

In 2006, there were 861,000 police officers and detectives working in the United States. Out of this number, 680,190 officers worked for the local municipalities, while 180,810 officers worked for federal and state agencies. According to the United States Department of Labor's statistics for 2006, there will be 11 percent growth in police and law enforcement-related jobs during the next 10 years. The reason for this is that people are concerned about safety and security; the employment of police officers is expected to increase about as fast as the average for all occupations through 2016.

Consider the following statistics from the U.S. Bureau of Labor Statistics's 2008[nd]09 Occupational Outlook Handbook:

▶ In May 2006, median annual earnings for police and sheriff's patrol officers were $47,460. The middle 50 percent earned between $35,600 and $59,880. The lowest 10 percent earned less than $27,310, and the highest 10 percent earned more than $72,450. Median annual earnings were $43,510 in federal government, $52,540 in state government, and $47,190 in local government.

▶ In May 2006, median annual earnings of police and detective supervisors were $69,310. The middle 50 percent earned between $53,900 and $83,940. The lowest 10 percent earned less than $41,260, and the highest 10 percent earned more than $104,410. Median annual earnings were $85,170 in federal government, $68,990 in state government, and $68,670 in local government.

▶ In May 2006, median annual earnings of detectives and criminal investigators were $58,260. The middle 50 percent earned between $43,920 and $76,350. The lowest 10 percent earned less than $34,480, and the highest 10 percent earned more than $92,590. Median annual earnings were $69,510 in federal government, $49,370 in state government, and $52,520 in local government.

Overall, opportunities in local and state police departments will be excellent for individuals who meet the requirements. There will be more competition for jobs in federal agencies than for jobs in local police agencies. Competition is less for smaller agencies that provide lower pay than for larger agencies in large metropolitan cities. Competition and requirements are tougher for federal agencies, where the chances of advancement are higher and bring with it a higher salary scale. Most federal jobs require a minimum of a bachelor's degree with several years of law enforcement, or a master's degree with some law enforcement experience, to stay competitive.

Figure 1.1 shows a Monster.com listing for vacant police officer jobs. As you can see, I did a search on Monster.com for police officer jobs posted in the last 60 days. There are a total of 170 jobs posted, in a variety of jurisdictions ranging from local to federal. In the current economic conditions, that is not too bad.

Becoming a police officer is not an easy task. If you've ever tested and applied for a police position, you know that the police officer application process is much lengthier than similar processes for other occupations.

Succeeding in the process and becoming a police officer requires extensive academic training in a controlled environment and on-the-job training in a field setting, called the *Field Training Officer (FTO)* program. There are several phases to the FTO program, and they are unique to individual police agencies. Each of these training phases can take anywhere from 8 weeks to 22 weeks.

The majority of police departments keep their newly appointed police officers on probation for a period of one year. During the probationary period, any disciplinary problem might be considered conduct unbecoming a police officer, and will quite possibly cost you your position. It is after this probation period that you can truly call yourself a police officer.

> **NOTE**
>
> Being appointed as a police officer is similar to joining the military as an officer. If any of you reading this book have previous military experience, you'll see many similarities in the process and training.

The text of this book is designed to take you through each step of the process of becoming a police officer, but let's first learn a little about the actual job of a police officer.

# Police Officer Job Description

As a police officer, you'll be required to perform a variety of tasks. A police officer responds to crimes in progress, investigates traffic accidents, enforces traffic laws, prepares police reports, and takes appropriate action including but not limited to arresting suspects, interviewing victims and witnesses, collecting evidence, issuing traffic citations, preparing cases for court, and much more. In my personal opinion, there is no other job more diversified than a police officer's. Your primary job as a police officer, as the motto goes, is "To Serve and Protect" the residents of your community. Here are some key tasks that a police officer performs:

- ▶ Patrols assigned area in a vehicle, bicycle, or on foot by using proper patrolling techniques, and maintains high visibility to prevent crime.

- ▶ Receives and responds to emergency runs and nonemergency runs from 911 police dispatch. Operates proper emergency equipment when responding to emergency runs. Upon arrival, evaluates situation to determine what's needed to resolve the incidents. Subdues violent subjects using physical force, if required.

- ▶ Responds to scenes of traffic accidents with injury and without injury to render assistance as needed, including first aid, CPR, and any immediate medical assistance. Requests advance medical assistance or fire rescue as needed. Prepares traffic accident reports, including diagrams, photographs, and other physical evidence.

- ▶ Enforces state criminal and traffic laws and city ordinances by apprehending violators and by issuing traffic citations.

- ▶ Investigates crimes by gathering all the pertinent information and interviewing all parties present including suspects and witnesses.

- ▶ Prepares appropriate reports, such as incident reports, probable cause affidavits, arrest warrants, and search warrants.

- ▶ Collects necessary evidence, draws the crime scene diagram, checks for fingerprints, and takes photographs.

- ▶ Assists detectives in their criminal investigation by providing information from the officer's assigned patrol area.

- ▶ Assists district attorneys in preparation and prosecution of criminal cases by testifying in court as a state witness.

- ▶ Serves arrest warrants, search warrants, and summonses issued by criminal courts.

- ▶ Attends community and block watch meetings. Meets and talks to community residents to provide information on safety and crime prevention. Develops better ways to resolve community problems by using creative problem-solving skills.

The job description of a police officer has not changed in recent years; however, it has become more challenging. Officers are being held to much higher standards. With the advances in technology, it is becoming easier to identify a police officer's mistakes in handling different situations. With the increased availability of video cameras and cell phone cameras, it is quite common to be caught on tape and fall under the scrutiny of the general public through the media. Most of the time, the media show only enough to sell the story, ignoring the full circumstances that led to the police action.

# Television Image Versus Reality

Unlike television portrayals, crimes in real life are not solved in an hour. Solving crimes takes hard work and long hours. It requires talking to a great number of people, sifting through a great deal of information, pulling pertinent pieces of information from the pile, and fitting together these pieces of information into a solution—sort of like sorting and assembling a jigsaw puzzle. Police work is not about kicking doors and arresting people all the time. In this job, you are around children as well as adults. Not everyone that you come in contact with is a criminal. While responding to calls for help, you'll come in contact with victims just as much as suspects. The job requires compassion, attention to detail, and a self-motivating personality. Police work requires being out when it is raining or when the temperature is either 100 degrees or –10 degrees. Criminals don't care about the time of day or weather conditions. When a crime occurs, the people of the community expect their law enforcement officers to be out investigating and fighting the crime.

Investigative television programs such "CSI" and "Law and Order" have also affected the job of a police officer. Citizens expect more from a responding officer, and many times these expectations are unreasonable for the type of crime being investigated. For example, the number of resources available for a property crime investigator are extremely limited when compared to those available for a crime against a person, such as homicide and robbery. Some citizens expect that a property crime investigator should be able to perform a DNA analysis from a cigarette butt or body fluids found on the scene of the crime. The reality is that these types of analyses are expensive and mostly reserved for homicide and rape cases.

# Odd Hours

Be prepared to work odd hours. As a uniformed police officer, you will for the most part have an assigned eight-hour shift. Most police departments have three shifts: day shifts, afternoon shifts, and night shifts. Some of the larger departments also have tactical shifts, which overlap the regular shifts. For example, there might be a day tactical shift that overlaps the day and afternoon shifts, and a late tactical shift that overlaps the afternoon and night shifts. These tactical shifts are designed to provide support when primary shifts are going through a shift change. These shifts are also designed to provide extra support during peak hours of street activity in the city. Research has shown that a large number of crimes occur between dawn and dusk. That is why most police departments beef up their patrol assignment during these hours.

If you advance your career and reach the position of detective, you'll be more likely to work odd hours than uniformed officers. The type of cases you're investigating will dictate the hours you work. One case might require long surveillance hours or talking to witnesses who are available only during certain hours. Other cases, such as your lieutenant handing you a new case just as you are about to leave for the day, might involve giving up planned time off. Case assignments like these don't happen often because other detectives are available to take the case, but the potential is there. If you're assigned a major crime case, such as homicide, robbery, or rape, the possibility of losing time off is even higher. There's also the possibility of being paged during time off and being required to respond to investigate.

> **CAUTION**
>
> Be aware that the odd hours you could potentially work might cause a big strain on your personal life. As an officer of the law, expect to be working when your friends and family are celebrating birthday parties, family functions, and so on. Be sure that your family will understand this reality as you pursue your career.

## Working Holidays

Law enforcement is a 24-hour operation. Even though it's Christmas or Thanksgiving for everybody else, someone must be out there minding the street. Criminals do not stop for holidays! In fact, during the holiday season, you will get more calls on family disputes than at any other time of the year. Most officers learn to celebrate holidays a day before or a day after the actual holiday. Are you ready to give up your holidays with your family?

## Quick Lunches

A police officer's time is never completely his own. One of the things that you acquire quickly is the ability to eat quick lunches. Even though lunch breaks are normal, from time to time you end up skipping lunch or eating a very quick lunch. Most of the time, however, a colleague fills in for you during lunch breaks.

> **NOTE**
>
> Expect to miss many lunch breaks due to emergencies, such as homicides, fatal accidents, and natural disasters.

## Not Getting Rich

A police officer is not one of the highest-paid professionals. You will be making a comfortable salary, depending upon where you are working, but your salary will not make you rich. Many police officers moonlight as private security officers for businesses. Depending on the agency they work for, they might or might not be able to use the uniform or the equipment provided to them by the department. Many police officers purchase a different uniform to wear while working for a business. During their career, many police officers also obtain a private detective license and own or work for private investigation businesses. With the stringent requirements, background investigation, and amount of training it takes to become a police officer, obtaining a private detective license is much easier for a police officer than for an ordinary citizen.

### NOTE

Most police departments offer good benefit packages. This includes medical benefits and tax-deferred annuities. A tax-deferred annuity is like an IRA to which you contribute pre-tax dollars while working and from which you draw after your retirement. A young officer should really plan a sound retirement plan at the very beginning and take advantage of these benefits.

# Requirements

Most of the requirements for becoming a police officer are established at the state level. There is usually a state regulatory board that sets the minimum standards in training and the requirements to become a police officer. This regulatory board certifies and conducts training for all the law enforcement officers in the state. Many large departments prefer to have their own academies to train their officers according to their department guidelines, although they always operate under the umbrella of the state board. The training provided by a state-level training academy will be more generic in nature than departmental academy training. Most small police departments send their officers to state academies for training and then have some type of field training program upon their return. After an officer has been certified by the state law enforcement training board or standards board, he or she can work in any jurisdiction within the state.

### CAUTION

Some smaller police departments require applicants to be already certified by the state board before allowing them to apply for a job.

Many police officers who desire to work in large police agencies use lateral transfers to their advantage. They start out at a small- to medium-sized police department to get the experience and training they need, and then they eventually seek a position in a larger police department.

The police training provided by the state law enforcement training academy is specifically for police officers. To be admitted in the program, an individual must be employed by a law enforcement agency. A private citizen cannot simply pay a fee and take the course. Training for reserve officers is usually conducted at the department level.

> **NOTE**
>
> Many states, such as California, send their reserve officers to an academy to get the same training as a full-time officer.

The following list gives some of the basic qualifications needed to become a law enforcement officer:

- ▶ Must be a resident citizen of the United States
- ▶ Must be 21 years old to apply
- ▶ Must have a high school diploma or GED certificate
- ▶ Cannot have a felony conviction
- ▶ Must possess a valid driver's license from the applicant's state of residence
- ▶ Must be a resident of the county or city where the prospective officer is applying
- ▶ Cannot have a dishonorable discharge from the military
- ▶ Must pass a mandatory drug screening test

In addition to the basic qualifications, some departments have requirements specific to their departments.

Even though the minimum requirement to become a police officer is a high school diploma, don't let that fool you! In today's job market the competition level is high. When going through the selection process, you'll see a high number of applicants having an associate degree or even a bachelor's degree in a variety of fields. You will also see police candidates with a master's degree. When comparing two applicants who have scored the same on all phases of the selection process, it may be inferred that selection boards have a tendency to lean toward applicants with the higher level of education.

> **CAUTION**
>
> Applicants having an associate, bachelor's, or even a master's degree often have an edge in the application and promotional process over those who do not have a post-secondary degree of some level.

# A Most Rewarding Job

Now that I've given you a realistic picture of what it is to be a police officer, let me give you the positive side. In my experience, being a police officer is one of the most rewarding jobs available. When you arrive at a location, you are in charge of the scene. Citizens rely on your training and experience and expect that you will help them with their problem at that moment. Children will look up to you as a role model. When you respond to a call in which violence is involved and the victim comes to you and thanks you, it makes this job worth it. You will feel a sense of achievement that you made a difference in someone's life, and that is much more than most people accomplish in a lifetime.

# Educational Opportunities

While employed as a police officer, you'll have a variety of opportunities to advance your education. Several colleges offer credits for the education that you receive while in the police academy. Some of these credits include criminal law, public safety, first aid, and public relations. Numerous police agencies offer tuition reimbursement programs to encourage their officers to finish their college education and offer higher pay for each year completed. Local colleges and universities often offer law enforcement specialization programs and, if taken advantage of, such programs lead to promotion with higher ranks and pay. Other educational opportunities within the police department are technical courses, such as detective training, crime scene investigator, and accident investigator. These courses can help you advance your career as well.

# Private Police Training Programs

Outsourcing and certification seem to be the keywords in this millennium. Certifications are available in all types of fields, from computers to nursing. A person starting in a particular field can take education classes and then pass a certification exam. After passing the certification, candidates can show prospective employers that they have certain knowledge in the field. Some employers may send employees for additional training in the skill set they are seeking, or that are perhaps unique to the organization. Similarly, a growing number of states have "outsourced" Police Officer Basic Training to community colleges or small police training organizations. To ensure that these institutions comply with the minimum requirements, an advisory board is established and oversees that minimum requirements are being met before an institution is certified to provide the training. This creates a win-win situation for both the training institution, which gains a new profit revenue stream, and for the state, which then doesn't have to maintain a law enforcement training academy and training staff. After completing the classroom training program, individuals are sometimes required to pass a state-controlled standard knowledge exam. After passing the exam, the law enforcement training board certifies the individual as a law enforcement officer.

A private training program also benefits the police agency. The agency doesn't have to pay the officer a salary for three months, or pay for his training with room and board. When the agency hires an officer, he is ready to go. He has a proven training record from a certified training provider and has passed a state-provided certification exam. All the new agency has to do is train the officer with *on-the-job training (OJT)*, perhaps regarding its processes and its way of doing things, with a week of classroom training and a FTO program.

New Jersey, Illinois, Missouri, New York, Ohio, and California are just a few of the states in which individuals can complete a state-required police officer basic training program without being employed first by a law enforcement agency. This means that individuals pursuing a career in law enforcement can set themselves up to succeed, while gaining a competitive edge over other candidates in the selection process.

Police officer basic training programs are available at the following locations:

- Somerset County Police Academy; New Jersey (Raritan Valley Community College)
- Police Training Institute; University of Illinois at Urbana-Champaign
- Law Enforcement Training Institute; University of Missouri
- Central Ohio Technical College; Newark, Ohio
- Police Academy Network; Kent State University, Ohio
- Monroe Community College; Rochester, New York
- State University of New York; Canton, New York
- David Sullivan-St. Lawrence County Law Enforcement Academy
- Stanislaus County Sheriff's Department; Modesto, CA
- Fresno City College; Fresno, CA

# Admission Requirements

The admission requirements for these programs are as follows:

- Be a citizen of the United States
- Have a valid driver's license

- ▶ Have no felony convictions
- ▶ Have no domestic violence convictions

# Course Cost

Police Officer Basic Training at a private police academy will cost anywhere from $2,500 to $5,000, depending on the state and length of the program.

# Curriculum and Course Length

Police Officer Basic Training is approximately 24 weeks long, again depending on the state. The course includes a variety of more than 100 topics, including criminal law and first aid. The training is a combination of military and college training. The environment is very challenging and requires a commitment to excellence.

A sampling of the topics covered during the Police Officer Basic Training includes the following:

- ▶ Criminal law
- ▶ Criminal procedure
- ▶ Traffic law
- ▶ Traffic enforcement
- ▶ Traffic accident investigation
- ▶ DWI enforcement techniques
- ▶ Human relations
- ▶ Cultural diversity
- ▶ Patrolling techniques
- ▶ Criminal investigations
- ▶ Physical conditioning
- ▶ First aid/first responder
- ▶ Basic firearms
- ▶ Advance firearms
- ▶ Defensive driving
- ▶ Defensive tactics/subject control
- ▶ Domestic violence

- ▶ Crisis intervention
- ▶ Child abuse and neglect
- ▶ Ethics and professionalism
- ▶ Human behavior
- ▶ Community problem solving
- ▶ Community policing
- ▶ Crime prevention
- ▶ Stress management
- ▶ Health, fitness, and nutrition
- ▶ Report writing
- ▶ Physical training

# General Course Completion Requirements

To complete Police Officer Basic Training, you must meet the following requirements:

- ▶ Attain a grade of "C" or better in all Academy courses
- ▶ Receive a satisfactory grade in the following required areas:
  - ▶ First aid
  - ▶ Defensive tactics/subject control
  - ▶ Firearms
  - ▶ Evasive driving
- ▶ Meet program physical fitness standards
- ▶ Not miss more than the allowed time for absences

# Chances for Advancement

An advantage of working for a larger police department is the opportunity for advancement in rank or specialization. After working for a period of time in uniformed patrol, an officer might choose to transfer into a more specialized unit; for example, homicide, robbery, or narcotics. If the officer has a desire to go higher in rank, promotional exams are offered. These exams are offered on a voluntary basis. Some officers choose to spend their entire career working in uniform as a district officer. Others aspire for the rank, greater pay, and additional responsibilities of a sergeant or a lieutenant.

The following is a list of most common ranking structures for police officers:

- ► Officer
- ► Corporal
- ► Sergeant
- ► Lieutenant
- ► Captain

**NOTE**

In many agencies, field training officers and specialized positions such as evidence technicians or traffic accident investigators are given a rank of corporal.

Captain is the highest merit rank available as a police officer. There are ranks of major, deputy chief, assistant chief, and chief of police, but these are appointed ranks. That means these positions are politically appointed by the chief of police, who is appointed by the mayor of the city. As the political administration changes, these officers are relieved of their rank and returned to the rank they held prior to their appointment.

# Selection Process

The police officer applicant screening process is a multi-phased process. Those phases include the following:

- ► Written exam
- ► Oral interview
- ► Physical ability
- ► Employment application
- ► Background investigation
- ► Psychological evaluation
- ► Polygraph test
- ► Medical and drug screening

Each of the phases is explained briefly in the following sections and detailed in later chapters.

# Written Exam

Table 1.1 provides a breakdown of time allocated for each task.

| Table 1.1    Time Allotments for Activities During a Police Candidate's Written Exam | |
| --- | --- |
| **Time** | **Activity** |
| 15 minutes | Instruction for study session |
| 2 to 3 hours | Study session |
| 1/2 hour | Break |
| 15 minutes | Exam instruction |
| 1 1/2 to 2 hours | Exam |

# Oral Interview

In this phase of the selection process, you'll be faced with an interview board comprised of high-ranking officers, immediate supervisors, and veteran officers. This portion of the selection process will test your decision-making ability, common sense, and how well you perform under stress. Oral interviews can have a variety of approaches, which will be discussed in Chapter 7.

# Physical Ability

Being a police officer is a physically demanding job. In this phase, the human resource department screens the incoming applicants for any physical limitations, such as inability to lift items or stand for long periods of time. Chapter 8 covers in detail what police departments look for in their applicants and how you can improve your score in this phase of the selection process.

# Long Employment Application

As a part of the selection process, you'll be required to fill out a long, paper-based application. The application format varies for each police agency. The purpose of this long application is to gather complete information about the applicant. In the application, be prepared to give the following information:

- ▶ Name, current address, and telephone number.
- ▶ Address, date, and duration of stay for all your previous residences. If you've lived overseas, this information—including postal codes—is still required.

- ► Educational accomplishments.

- ► Names and addresses, including the ZIP code, of your current employer and all previous employers.

- ► Personal information such as date of birth, Social Security number, bank location and address, telephone number, and account numbers.

- ► Banking information and credit obligations.

- ► Personal references.

- ► Business references.

It is a good idea to gather all the information on a separate piece of paper before you begin completing the application form. It is also a good idea to gather all the necessary documents and have them ready instead of searching for them at the last minute.

The original documents you'll need are as follows:

- ► Birth certificate

- ► Educational diplomas

- ► Social Security card

- ► Driver's license

- ► Marriage license

- ► Divorce decree

- ► Naturalization certificate (if you're a naturalized citizen)

- ► Military form DD214 and honorable discharge certificate

Part of the application requires you to a give a set of fingerprints. This is not something you can do ahead of time. Large departments like to use their own identification department to collect these fingerprints. These fingerprints will then be sent to the individual, local, and state police and Federal Bureau of Investigation for classification and background check.

# Background Investigation

Each applicant is assigned a background investigator who is responsible for putting together an information packet about you. This packet will be seen by a variety of people in the department, such as the chief of police, human resources commander, and perhaps even someone in the mayor's office or a city/county council person. Most large police departments even have a hiring board that approves all applicants before their appointment.

When you are scheduled to meet your background investigator, it is more than likely that it will be in the form of an interview. This interview might last from 30 minutes to 2 hours or more, depending on the agency, its processes, and how much information the investigator needs from you. It is important to treat this meeting just as you would any other employment interview. You will be meeting agency representatives whose input will count in the final hiring decision. Furthermore, dress for this interview like you would for another job interview and arrive 10–15 minutes earlier than the scheduled time.

Your background investigator will be interested in your working habits. He will talk to all your employers. The investigator will want to know whether you stole anything from your employers. How many times did you call in sick? How well did you get along with your co-workers? Were you a team player or did you do your own thing? Did you have credit problems from overextending your credit or did you know to live within your means?

One of the most important things that the investigator will determine is whether you have any criminal background. Have you ever stolen anything? Have you ever been arrested? What was the disposition of the case? Did you pay a fine or do time? What were the charges? Was it a crime against person or crime against property?

One piece of advice when it comes to the background investigation: be completely honest about everything! You need to be honest because sooner or later the background investigator will find out what you failed to mention. As an actual police detective, the investigator has access to more information about you than you realize. When negative facts arise during the investigation that you have not admitted in advance, it does not say good things about you. No one is expected to be perfect, just honest.

---

### CAUTION

Just as in any other job, if you show deception when filling out the written application, you automatically disqualify yourself from becoming a police officer. The police department assumes that if you lie on your application, you would probably lie about other things. Also, be aware that if you fail one background investigation, you might be red flagged. That means if you apply again with the same police agency or another, the other background investigator will find out.

---

Your personal references will also be checked. It is always best to list people as personal references who have favorable things to say about you. It is also a good idea to let the individuals know that you've listed them as personal references.

From time to time, the background investigator might ask for things from you. Providing those things will be very beneficial to you and will serve you in many ways. First, it shows the background investigator that you are enthusiastic about the position. Second, it helps you meet all the application requirements for the position. The background investigator can really help you attain the position of police officer. Most large departments rely on the feedback that the background investigator provides to his boss and, after the investigation has been completed, to the approval board.

The job of a police officer is a position of public trust. As a police officer, you will be held to higher standards, both on- and off-duty, by the citizens of your community and the upper echelon of the police department. The background investigation is a process to insure that you meet certain criteria. The background investigation also reveals any automatic disqualifiers that will prevent you from becoming a police officer. If any of the following criteria apply to you, you will be automatically disqualified:

- ▶ You are not a United States citizen.

- ▶ You have been dishonorably discharged from any branch of military service.

- ▶ You have a felony conviction.

- ▶ You have a misdemeanor conviction related to domestic violence, or any conviction that will preclude you from carrying a firearm. (This criterion may vary from state to state.)

- ▶ You have falsified any information on the employment application.

- ▶ Most police agencies also take the adult use of an illegal drug within one year prior to the application process seriously.

# Psychological Evaluation

Before being hired by a police department, you will be required to undertake a psychological evaluation. This could be anything from submitting a personal inventory questionnaire to a more structured questionnaire, such as the Minnesota Multiphasic Personality Inventory (MMPI). After the exam, you might also be required to speak to a psychologist. The purpose of this personal interview is to clarify any questions that the police psychologist has about you.

## A Little More About the MMPI

The MMPI is the most frequently used clinical test. It is employed quite often to provide personality information on criminals. Now, you are probably wondering why you have to take a test that is commonly used for criminals. In addition to criminals, this test is also very frequently used to indicate a mental disorder. The MMPI test is designed to evaluate the thoughts, emotions, attitudes, and behavioral traits that comprise your personality. The results of the test show an individual's personality strengths and weaknesses and can identify certain personality disorders. There are 567 questions in the full version of the test. There is also a short version of the test, which contains 370 questions. For the long version, the time limit is 60 to 90 minutes.

> **EXAM ALERT**
>
> Many of the questions in the MMPI are repeated and put into another form to test the validity of your answer. The test can be tiring and tricky at the same time. Read the questions carefully before you answer.

# Polygraph Test

A *polygraph test*, also known as a *lie detector test*, determines the trustworthiness of an individual. The *polygraph examiner* is the individual who administers the test for the police department. The polygraph instrument collects physiological data from the human nervous system. A chest strap measures and records respiratory activity. Two small metal finger-plates measure perspiration and a blood pressure cuff measures and records changes in your blood pressure.

There are two types of polygraph instruments in use today: the analog instrument (where you can see the ink jets moving over the chart), and the more advanced computerized polygraph instrument.

A polygraph examination involves three phases:

1. Pre-test interview
2. Test phase
3. Post-test interview

## Pre-Test Interview

The pre-test phase consists of the polygraph examiner completing all the necessary forms and explaining the test process. The examiner usually discusses the questions he will ask you during the test. A short introduction about the machine will also be given. During this time, the examiner will be able to answer any of your questions about the test questions. You will not be allowed to ask questions during the test.

## Test Phase

In the test phase, you will be hooked up to the machine with data-gathering probes. A series of questions will be asked, and the results will be gathered on the chart. The actual test questions are divided into different categories. Each police department has its own version of these questions, but you should expect questions to be asked in the following areas:

- ▶ Drug activity
- ▶ Usage and trafficking
- ▶ Theft and/or employee theft
- ▶ Any type of criminal activity
- ▶ Spousal battery (hitting, scuffling, or any type of physical altercation with the spouse)
- ▶ Perjury
- ▶ Job attendance
- ▶ Allegiance to communist and anti-American organizations

Following the data-gathering or test phase, the examiner will analyze the chart and come up with an opinion of your trustworthiness or possible deception.

## Post-Test Interview

The examiner might ask you to clarify some of your answers and could even decide to give you the test again using some of the same questions and comparing your responses to the results of the first test.

After the post-test interview, a final decision will be made; that is, whether you've attempted to be deceptive in answering the questions presented. The overall period for the three phases will last from two to three hours.

**NOTE**

Even after you are hired as a police officer, you may still be required to submit to a random or annual polygraph exam based on the type of job. It is quite common for narcotics detectives or jobs, where officers handle large quantities of money, to take biannual polygraph exams.

# Medical and Drug Screening

Be prepared to fast for 12 hours before going to a medical examination. Depending on the agency to which you are applying, there will likely be a detailed physical examination and screening. The medical exam is very similar to the military one. In addition to the medical screening discussed earlier, there also will be a screening via urinalysis. The drug screen goes beyond the application process. After you've become a police officer, drug screening becomes a part of meeting other qualifications and requirements of your position. From time to time, at random, you will be selected to submit for a urinalysis. Most of the time, the testing is done during the shift you are working. When you are told to go, *you are required to go directly to the medical facility being contracted to perform these tests for you without any delay*. At the facility, you will be constantly monitored prior to giving the sample and also during specimen deposit.

**NOTE**

Even after you are hired as a police officer, you may still be required to submit to a random drug screening process.

# Ride-Along Program

If you really want to learn about the police officer's job, many large police departments have a ride-along program. In this program, you ride with a full-time, certified police officer and watch him perform his daily duties. Individual ride-along policies differ from one police department to the other, but most of them allow the rider to go wherever the officer goes. Participating in such a program enables you to observe the job of a police officer firsthand. This is a great way to see whether the job is for you, so try to take more than one ride-along to get better perspective. The more officers you talk to and see in action, the more you learn about your new career.

Another good learning approach is to join a volunteer police section. Most large police departments have reserve and volunteer police officers. These jobs are mostly unpaid positions. However, most of the departments provide uniforms and training. These types of programs are very beneficial for individuals who are planning to become a police officer down the road or are finishing their educational goals. Reserve police officers are trained just like full-time merit officers. They work with full-time officers on a regular basis and are held to the same standards and guidelines as regular officers. When looking to fill a full-time position, many police agencies look through their reserve ranks. It is also considered favorably if you mention during your oral interview phase that you have reserve police officer experience. The oral interview will be covered in Chapter 7.

# A Typical Day in the Life of a Police Officer

This section gives you a general look at a typical day in the life of a police officer. You will read about taking calls, paperwork, and other general items that a typical officer deals with. Table 1.2 breaks down for you the assignment, location, and time.

| Table 1.2 A Police Assignment | |
| --- | --- |
| Assignment: | Late shift |
| Beginning tour of duty: | 2130 |
| Ending tour of duty: | 0530 |
| Beat assignment: | Adam 50 sector |
| Neighborhood Info: | Low-income neighborhood |
| | High in narcotics traffic and vehicle thefts; also has a high number of domestic disturbances |

You report to the district office for a roll call and to receive the most up-to-date information on what has occurred in your district during the previous shift. After a 15- to 20-minute briefing, the duty sergeant gives you your assignment and your assigned vehicle for the night. Before you can get on the radio to tell the dispatcher where you will be working, the police radio starts blaring, "Shots fired, shots fired, 1900 Minnesota Street." This call is not in your beat, but in the beat next to you. The beat officer next to you and another officer get the run, but you decide to start heading to the area, just in case these officers need help. You rush to your assigned car and start loading it with your equipment. As soon as the vehicle is loaded, you rush to the area. The other officers conduct the investigation. You assist them in securing the crime scene and containing the witnesses. 45 minutes later, the investigation is complete and you are ready to receive other calls.

15 minutes later, you get a call for a domestic disturbance between a boyfriend and a girlfriend. You know from your training and experience that domestic disturbances are one of the most dangerous calls that you will ever take. You meet up with your backup officer and decide to go together to the house for officer safety. You arrive and the female half of the disturbance is

bleeding from the head. You assess the situation for your and your partner's safety and call an ambulance. While waiting for the ambulance, you interview the female half of the disturbance, while your partner interviews the male half. She tells you that her boyfriend assaulted her with a telephone receiver. The argument was over some financial difficulty the couple was going through. While the ambulance staff is giving medical treatment, you meet with your partner to discuss the male half's version of the story. The law in your state dictates that anyone who assaults a live-in spouse must be arrested for battery. You place the male half under arrest. Your partner is gracious enough to transport the prisoner for you, so you process the paperwork in your vehicle while you wait for another call.

The radio seems to be quiet, so you decide to patrol your assigned area. Going up and down the street slowly, just a little bit faster than jogging speed, you patrol the area looking for suspicious activity. In your second or third round, you see a vehicle disregard a traffic light at a busy intersection. You stop the violator. He gives you no reasonable explanation as to why he did not stop at the traffic light. You decide to give a traffic ticket. The driver gets upset with you. Upon returning to your vehicle, the sergeant calls you on the police radio and asks you to meet at the intersection of 10th and College. You rush to that location and learn that a narcotics detective intends to serve a warrant in your beat and wants the beat officer and other uniform officers present for safety. The narcotics detective serves the warrant. Large amounts of marijuana and cocaine are recovered. Thank heavens! You don't have to do the paperwork, but the sergeant rails you for not taking care of your beat.

The whole shift goes by in a flash. You barely had time to eat and take a coffee break. It is almost time to head home. You have one last report left to write. You rush to get it done. Finally, at 0530, your shift is over.

Do you think you can handle nights like this when you are so busy that you don't have time to eat or take a break? Are you a person who can do several things at one time? For example, can you drive a car, listen to your police radio, pay attention to traffic and where you are going, and look for suspects all at the same time? Are you the type of person who likes to help people and are you compassionate about their problems? Are you creative and resourceful in problem solving? If you answered yes to all of these questions, I think you have a very rewarding career ahead of you in serving the people of your community.

# PART I
## Written Exam

C H A P T E R  T W O

# Reading Comprehension

## Terms You'll Need to Understand:

✓ Approach for the exam
✓ Law definitions
✓ Operating procedures
✓ Run scenarios
✓ Sample questions

## Concepts You'll Need to Master:

✓ Create outline
✓ Take good abbreviated notes
✓ Take notes in a consistent pattern

The next section on our police test preparation schedule is reading comprehension. This section evaluates your ability to understand and remember the ideas and facts defined within a written sample. As a police officer, you'll come in contact with a variety of information. You'll receive this information in the form of field interviews, legal bulletins, case laws, department rules and regulations, and investigative procedures and guidelines. You will be accountable for this information and will be expected to apply it in your daily responsibilities and while completing reports. This test is designed to test your ability to do just that.

In this section of the test, you will be provided short essays and bits of information about police work. You must read and learn these pieces of information as well as answer a series of questions based on the information provided. When answering the questions, you will be expected to apply what you just learned in the text. This exam can take two positions. Some of the information will be given to you in the form of text appearing just before the questions you must answer successfully. The other way you will be tested in the reading comprehension section is to be provided text in a pre-exam study guide; you will be expected to remember it from the study session to successfully answer questions on the exam.

# Approaching the Reading Comprehension Section of the Exam

Even though the content of each exam is unique to the police agency, here are some general suggestions on how to approach this section:

▶ Read the instructions carefully before answering questions.

▶ The questions are to be answered based on the information provided in the essays.

▶ Read all the short essays carefully to learn all the facts and principles presented in the paragraph.

▶ It's often helpful to take notes on important ideas and facts. You cannot use these notes in the exam, but writing an outline will help you memorize the information found in the text passages you read. Before you start taking notes, it's a good idea to organize your thoughts and then the information. If you create your own standard style of taking notes, it will make the task much simpler and the information easy to remember.

**NOTE**

Almost all police officers carry some type of notebook. In fact, in some departments, it is mandatory to carry a field notebook just as you would carry a flashlight or your sidearm. In this notebook, the officer takes notes in the field. These notes are then referenced when completing police reports, relaying information to the detective, or testifying in court.

**EXAM ALERT**

If the time given to prepare for the exam is very limited, al least read the passages several times. You'll learn more and retain better every time you read.

▶ Be an **active learner**. By *active learner*, I mean someone who takes an aggressive approach toward learning the test material. Simply reading the material once or twice might not be enough. Make an outline from the material, read it over and over again, use a highlighter to mark key points and keywords, and write out questions that you think might be on the exam. Most police departments offer some type of candidate guide to inform candidates about what to expect during the selection process. This candidate guide, among other information, also includes some type of written exam preparation guide. This guide is an abbreviated version of the actual guide and sample questions. You'll find this material to be very easy compared to the actual test. You can use these guides to develop your own active learning system.

The following is a sample of an active learning system:

1. Read the material
2. Read the material a second time and highlight items of interest
3. Read the material a third time and develop an outline
4. Review the outline as necessary
5. Create questions and possible answers
6. Practice creating this outline from memory
7. Practice questions and answers

▶ During police exams, you might not have time to do all this within the limited time provided before the test. You can modify this sample of active learning outline for your exam need.

For example:

1. Read the material and underline or highlight key points

2. Write an outline based on key points

3. Review the outline as needed

4. As soon as the exam begins, create an outline from memory

▶ In addition to taking notes and organizing your thoughts to increase your comprehension level, read as much material as possible. Read about things that interest you, regardless of whether you're reading fiction or nonfiction, material related to the job, a newspaper, or a magazine. As you read, try to get the main idea of what you're reading. Try to identify the main points and principles.

By improving your reading comprehension, you'll also increase your vocabulary and writing skills—they are very important for police work. Your ability to describe and record what happened during a crime is the key to obtaining search and arrest warrants or conviction during case proceedings. Writing skills are discussed in more detail in a later chapter.

Now that you have some understanding of the basic skills related to the reading comprehension portion of the police exam, let's examine the types of questions you might see on this section of the police officer exam. You'll also discover some of the possible approaches you can take for successfully answering these questions.

# Potential Topic Areas for the Police Exam Reading Comprehension Exam

As I mentioned previously, each agency may have its own version of a reading comprehension section. But research has shown that some topics are quite common. For example, you might see questions about law definition, policies, and extracting data from memos and police reports.

This portion of the test is designed to test how well you read and apply written material like law statutes and policy and report narratives.

# Law Definition

Law definitions or codes are basically elements of crime written for the police officer to use in the field. Officers refer to these codes from time to time while enforcing laws or investigating crimes and to properly charge an individual if a violation is determined. Large police agencies print a pocket-size version of these codebooks for their officers to use in the field.

## Robbery

A person who knowingly or intentionally takes property from another person or from the presence of another person

(1) by using or threatening the use of force on any person; or

(2) by putting any person in fear, commits robbery—a Class C felony. However, the offense is a Class B felony if it is committed while armed with a deadly weapon or results in bodily injury to any person other than a defendant. The offense is a Class A felony if it results in serious bodily injury to any person other than a defendant.

## Burglary

A person who breaks into and enters the building or structure of another person, with intent to commit a felony in it, commits burglary—a Class C felony.

However, the offense is a Class B felony if

(A) It is committed while armed with a deadly weapon or

(B) The building or structure is a

    (i) Dwelling

    (ii) Structure used for religious worship

The offense is a Class A felony if it results in

(A) Bodily injury

(B) Serious bodily injury to any person other than a defendant

Based on the definitions listed here and the scenarios that follow, answer the questions after each scenario.

---

> **NOTE**
>
> You might wonder what the difference is between robbery and burglary. *Robbery* is a crime against a person. The perpetrator has human interaction while committing this crime. For example, a robber might point a handgun, demand money, and threaten to harm the victim if the perpetrator's demands are not met. On the other hand, *burglary* is mostly crime against a property. Burglars usually do not have human interaction. They mostly target homes and businesses when they are unoccupied.

---

## Scenario 1

On May 1, 2009, at approximately 2200 hours, Officer Jones and Officer Smith were dispatched to the Internet Deli, located at 5600 North Illinois Street, on an armed robbery in progress. On their arrival, they observed a white male inside the business. The white male held a handgun. When the robber saw the officers, he decided to surrender. An apprehension was made without any acceleration of force. Officer Smith interviewed the deli manager to find out what transpired prior to the officers' arrival. The manager told the officer that the suspect walked in the store, brandishing a handgun, and demanded money. The suspect made threats that in case of failure to comply with his demands he would shoot the manager.

1.  Based on the law definition provided earlier, the suspect can be charged with which of the following?

    **A.** Robbery, a Class A felony

    **B.** Robbery, a Class B felony

    **C.** Burglary, a Class C felony

    **D.** None of the above

**Answer B is correct.** The suspect knowingly and intentionally attempted to take money from the Internet Deli while armed with a handgun.

Answers A, C, and D are incorrect.

2.  If the suspect were not armed, would he be charged differently?

    **A.** Robbery, a Class A felony

    **B.** Burglary, a Class B felony

    **C.** Robbery, a Class C felony

    **D.** None of the above

**Answer C is correct.** Being armed with a handgun is the key factor. If the suspect were not armed with a handgun, this would have been a Class C felony. The robbery statute states that "the offense is a Class B felony if it is committed while armed with a deadly weapon."

## Scenario 2

On May 24, 2009, Officer Tom and Officer Rogers were dispatched to 234 S. Main Street, an unoccupied residence, on a burglary in progress. As they arrived on the scene, they saw a black male coming out of the residence, carrying a television. The officers identified themselves and the suspect surrendered without any acceleration of force. The suspect was arrested and charged.

1. Based on the law definition provided earlier, the suspect can be charged with which of the following?

    **A.** Robbery, a Class A felony

    **B.** Burglary, a Class B felony

    **C.** Burglary, a Class C felony

    **D.** Theft, a Class D felony

**Answer C is correct.** A person who breaks into and enters the building or structure of another person, with intent to commit a felony in it, commits burglary—a Class C felony.

2. If the building were a church instead of a residence, the suspect could be charged with which of the following?

    **A.** Robbery, Class A felony

    **B.** Burglary, Class B felony

    **C.** Burglary, Class C felony

    **D.** Burglary, Class D felony

**Answer B is correct.** A person who breaks into and enters the building or structure of another person, with intent to commit a felony in it, commits burglary—a Class C felony. However, if the structure is a place of religious worship, the crime becomes a Class B felony.

TIP

A sample outline based on the law definition given earlier might look something like this:

**Robbery**

| | | |
|---|---|---|
| Takes belongings | With Force or Fear | C |
| | Armed | B |
| | Injury | A |

**Burglary**

| | | |
|---|---|---|
| Breaks and enters | | C |
| | Armed | B |
| | Religious | A |

# Policies and Procedures

Another topical area that reading comprehension questions might come from is policies and procedure. Don't worry, you will not be expected to know the police agency's policies. Sample policies will be provided to you in the exam.

Policies and procedures are designed to bring uniformity within the police department. Without policies and procedures, any organization would be in total chaos. Policies in police agencies are created to provide guidance to officers in their work and to outline a standard way of doing things. For example, let's consider evidence handling. If everyone started doing what they think is a proper way of handling a piece of evidence, a police agencies might have hundreds of ways to process evidence—some good and some bad. If proper procedure is not followed when preserving evidence, it could be detrimental to the case in court. For that reason, policies and procedure are very important for any organization.

This section of the test is designed to test how well you read and interpret departmental procedures and guidelines. Let's start practicing this with the next section, "Suspected Drug Operating Procedure."

NOTE

Policies and procedures are also known as *SOP* or *standard operating procedure*.

## Suspected Drug Operating Procedure

When the arresting officer recovers narcotics during an arrest, certain procedures have to be followed to ensure proper handling of the evidence, analysis of suspected drug, and proper disposal. See the sample guidelines from Shore City Police Department.

**Shore City Police Department Narcotics Handling Guidelines**

1. The recovery officer should conduct a field test of the suspected narcotic.

2. The recovery officer fills out a field test form.

3. The recovery officer is responsible for transporting the suspected contraband to the property room.

4. A property slip must be filled out by the recovery officer.

5. The narcotic is put in a plastic heat-sealed bag.

6. A copy of the field test form and a copy of the property slip are attached to the heat-sealed bag.

7. The narcotic is then dropped in a narcotic vault.

# Scenario 3

Officer Rider and Officer Jack, while on routine patrol assignment, observed a car being driven at high rate of speed. They stop the driver for speed violation. As they approach the car, they observe smoke inside the vehicle. From their training and experience, they suspect the smoke to be burned marijuana. After additional investigation, the driver of the vehicle was arrested for narcotic offenses. During a search, Officer Jack found a plastic bag with a green, leafy substance.

Based on the information given in the scenario and the procedures listed above answer following questions:

1. Which of the officers is responsible for conducting the field test?

    **A.** Recovery officer's supervisor

    **B.** Officer who recovered the narcotic

    **C.** Property officer

    **D.** Transporting officer

**Answer B is correct.** The recovery officer should conduct a field test of the suspected narcotics.

2. Which one of the officers is responsible for transporting the contraband to the property room?

A. Property officer

B. Transporting officer

C. Recovery officer's supervisor

D. Officer who recovered the narcotic

**Answer D is correct.** The recovery officer is responsible for transporting the suspected contraband to the property room.

## Scenario 4

Officer Mack and Officer McDonald, while on routine patrol assignment, observed a vehicle failed to stop at a four-way stop sign. Officers stopped the vehicle for this violation. During the investigation, the driver of the vehicle was arrested for an outstanding warrant. During a search of the vehicle, Officer Mack found a plastic bundle with a yellowish rocky substance. From his training and experience, he suspects this to be rock cocaine.

Based on the information given in the scenario and the narcotic procedures discussed earlier answer the following questions:

1. In addition to the property slip, what other form must be filled out?

   A. Narcotics recovery form

   B. Recovery slip

   C. Field test form

   D. Transportation slip

**Answer C is correct.** The recovery officer fills out a field test form.

2. What type of bag is used to store the contraband?

   A. Plastic heat-sealed bag

   B. Plastic bag

   C. Brown paper bag

   D. Any grocery bag

**Answer A is correct.** The narcotic is put in a plastic heat-sealed bag.

# Vehicle Towed Operating Procedure

During an investigation a police officer might be required to tow a suspect vehicle. To ensure proper handling, storage, and release of the towed vehicle, the officer is required to follow a standard procedure. Let's look at another sample procedure from the Shore City Police Department.

**Shore City Police Department Vehicle Tow Procedure**

1. The primary officer is responsible for filling out a vehicle tow form.

2. The assisting officer is responsible for conducting inventory search of the vehicle.

3. If a high-value property is found, the property must be taken to the property room by the primary officer for safekeeping.

4. The assisting officer orders the contract tow truck.

5. The assisting officer notifies central communication of the year, make, model, plate number, and vehicle identification number (VIN) of the vehicle being towed.

6. The primary officer adds the vehicle to the vehicle section of the report as "towed vehicle."

## Scenario 5

While on routine patrol, Officer Eaton stopped a vehicle for disregarding a traffic signal. Officer King assisted Officer Eaton in this investigation. The driver was arrested for driving while his license is suspended and his vehicle was towed for safekeeping.

Based on the information given in the scenario and the procedures listed, answer the following questions:

1. Which of the following officers is responsible for notifying central communication when a vehicle is towed?

    **A.** Reporting officer

    **B.** Assisting officer

    **C.** Primary officer

    **D.** Shift supervisor

**Answer B is correct.** The assisting officer notifies central communication of the year, make, model, plate number, and vehicle identification number (VIN) of the vehicle being towed.

2. Which of the two officers is responsible for filling out the tow form?

   **A.** Primary officer

   **B.** Shift supervisor

   **C.** Reporting officer

   **D.** Assisting officer

**Answer A is correct.**

# Scenario 6

You, as the primary officer, were dispatched to the scene of a personal injury accident at 2345 Main Street. The victim was transported to the hospital via ambulance. Officer Jones assisted you in the investigation.

Based on the information given in the scenario and the procedures listed, answer following questions:

1. Who is responsible for conducting the inventory search of the vehicle?

   **A.** Shift supervisor

   **B.** Primary officer

   **C.** Assisting officer

   **D.** Reporting officer

**Answer C is correct.** The assisting officer is responsible for conducting inventory search of the vehicle.

2. If a high-priced item is found in the vehicle, which of the two officers is responsible for taking the property to the property room for safekeeping?

   **A.** Shift supervisor

   **B.** Primary officer

   **C.** Assisting officer

   **D.** Reporting officer

**Answer B is correct.** If a high-value property is found, the property must be taken to the property room by the primary officer for safekeeping.

# Extracting Data

Another topic you might see in the reading comprehension section of the exam is *data extraction*. Police reports are one of the main sources of information for the investigative officer. Even as a uniformed officer, you rely on police reports for your information. These reports might be written by you. As a uniform officer, you will have to refer to some of your old reports and extract a variety of information. This information could be for the investigative detective, prosecuting attorney, judges, or even a jury. It is very important for a police officer to accurately extract necessary information from a police report.

This section of the exam tests your ability to accurately extract data from a sample police report narrative. Let's practice extracting data with the following police report.

## Police Report 1

On May 1, 2009 at approximately 1950 hours, Officer Jones and Smith were dispatched to 2367 N. Indianapolis Boulevard, Apt. 2a, to investigate a residential burglary. At approximately 1952 hours, both officers arrived at the scene. On their arrival, they met with Mr. Michael Snyder. Mr. Snyder informed both officers that he was away at work between 0900 and 1900 hours. Upon returning home at 1930 hours, he saw his front door apparently kicked open. He entered the apartment and found that the whole house had been ransacked.

Mr. Snyder provided both officers a list of all the items that had been taken in the burglary, along with the serial numbers and brands of the electronic items.

The following is the list of items that were taken in this burglary:

| Item | Brand | Serial Number |
| --- | --- | --- |
| Laptop computer | Toshiba | 99123476 |
| iPhone | Apple | 47623 |
| Scanner | HP | 3489087 |

Jar of coins, value of at least $50.00

Mr. Snyder also told the officer that the lady living in Apt. 2b, right across from his apartment, was usually home during the day. Also, the man in Apt. 2e worked evenings, so he remained home a lot during the day, too.

Both officers walked through the house. Evidence Technician Officer Walker was requested to the scene to gather evidence, if any. Officer Walker was able to get a good set of fingerprints from a drinking glass, which appeared to be used by the suspect or suspects, and a good photograph of a footprint from the front door that was kicked in. While Officer Walker was looking for the evidence, Officer Smith went to Apt. 2b and Officer Jones went to Apt. 2e to locate any possible witnesses.

Officer Smith was able to find a resident and obtain a good suspect description. The resident also believed that she had seen the suspect in the area before, possibly working as a maintenance man. Officer Jones, however, was not that lucky. The resident of Apt. 2e was not home. Officer Jones left a business card for the resident to call. Both officers gathered all the necessary information and completed a police report.

Based on the information given, answer following questions:

1. What was the brand name of the laptop taken in the burglary?

   A. Toshiba

   B. Compaq

   C. Gateway

   D. Dell

**Answer A is correct.**

2. What was the address where this burglary occurred?

   A. 2637 N. Indianapolis Boulevard, Apt. 2a

   B. 2367 N. Indianapolis Boulevard, Apt. 2a

   C. 7623 N. Indianapolis Boulevard, Apt. 2a

   D. 2367 S. Indianapolis Boulevard, Apt. 2a

**Answer B is correct.**

3. What was the time when the officers were dispatched to investigate the burglary?

   **A.** 1950 hours

   **B.** 2100 hours

   **C.** 1700 hours

   **D.** 1930 hours

Answer A is correct.

4. Which of the officers was able to find a good description of the suspect?

   **A.** Officer Snyder

   **B.** Officer Smith

   **C.** Officer Jones

   **D.** Officer Talbot

**Answer B is correct.**

# Police Report 2

On June 6, 2009, at approximately 1400 hours, Officer Clyde and Officer James were dispatched to 1902 Main Street to investigate a disturbance between two neighbors. On their arrival at the scene, both officers saw two white males arguing in the street, on the verge of a fistfight. Both officers separated the males. Further investigation revealed that Mr. Henderson, resident of 1902 Main Street, accused Mr. Talbot, resident of 1906 Main Street, of playing loud music at all hours of the day. Basically, the fight began the night before when Mr. Talbot was playing a stereo until 0200 hours. At that time, Mr. Henderson had called the police on a complaint of loud music. Officer Smith and Officer Reed had responded and asked Mr. Talbot to turn down the stereo. This afternoon, when Mr. Talbot saw Mr. Henderson working in the yard, both subjects began arguing.

Officer Clyde spoke with Mr. Henderson to get his side of the story and Officer James spoke with Mr. Talbot to get his side of the story. Mr. Henderson told Officer Clyde that Mr. Talbot was a nuisance to the neighborhood by playing loud music all the time. He held parties at all hours of the night. His visitors hung around in his yard talking loudly and being rowdy.

Officer James got a different version from Mr. Talbot. According to Mr. Talbot, he worked evenings and on returning home, liked to relax and play some music. He explained that the music was never loud. Mr. Talbot suggested that Officer James should talk to the other neighbors and get their opinion. So that is exactly what Officer James did. Officer James walked over to 1903 Main Street. The resident told Officer James that he had never heard loud music in the vicinity. As far as people talking loudly in Mr. Talbot's front yard, that indeed happened when Mr. Talbot had some guests over. But when Mr. Henderson complained, Mr. Talbot took corrective action and asked his guests to go inside the house.

Both officers took notes of all the necessary information and made a report on the disturbance.

Based on the information given, answer following questions:

1. What was the address where this incident occurred?

    **A.** 1209 Main Street

    **B.** 9201 Main Street

    **C.** 1902 S. Main Street

    **D.** 1902 Main Street

**Answer D is correct.**

2. What was the relation of the parties involved in the disturbance?

    **A.** Friends

    **B.** Relatives

    **C.** Neighbors

    **D.** Spouse

**Answer C is correct.**

3. Which officer talked to the other neighbors?

    **A.** Officer Smith

    **B.** Officer James

    **C.** Officer Clyde

    **D.** Officer Talbot

**Answer B is correct.**

**4.** What was the address of the witness in this case?

   **A.** 1902 Main Street

   **B.** 1903 W. Main Street

   **C.** 1903 Main Street

   **D.** 1901 Main Street

**Answer C is correct.**

# Taking Notes on Reading Comprehension Passages

The best approach in questions like the preceding ones is to take good notes. Place yourself in the situation of the officers and create notes. Based on the given scenario, your field notebook might look something like the sample that follows. As you can see, I've given headings. After you've formed a habit of taking notes in a certain order and have done it repeatedly, you don't need to use headings. When noting someone's personal information—such as name, address, and date of birth—always use the same order every time, regardless of that person's involvement in the scenario.

For example:

- ▶ Status (the person's involvement in the scenario):
- ▶ Name:
- ▶ Address:
- ▶ ZIP code:
- ▶ Date of birth:
- ▶ Social Security number:
- ▶ Home phone number:
- ▶ Hours:
- ▶ Work phone number:
- ▶ Hours:
- ▶ Cell phone number:

The following is an example of how your notes might look like as you prepare for the exam:

**Run 1**

- ▶ Call number or case number:
- ▶ Dispatched to:
- ▶ Arrived:
- ▶ Victim:
- ▶ Witness 1:
- ▶ Witness 2:
- ▶ Suspect:
- ▶ Narrative:
- ▶ Assisting officer:

**Run 2**

- ▶ Call number or case number:
- ▶ Dispatched to:
- ▶ Arrived:
- ▶ Complainant:
- ▶ Person involved:
- ▶ Witness:
- ▶ Narrative:
- ▶ Assisting officers:

# Exam Prep Questions

While on routine patrol, Officer Matthew and Officer Black of the Big City Police Department observed a vehicle go left of center. The driver of this vehicle then righted the vehicle and the vehicle proceeded southbound on Main Street at a high rate of speed, where it sideswiped another vehicle parked on the west side of Main Street, just north of Elm Street. Officers Matthew and Black got in position to stop the vehicle and followed it for two blocks, at which time the vehicle pulled into the Little Italy Food Mart located on Main Street, where it stopped and parked directly under a streetlight on the east edge of the parking lot. The driver of the vehicle then exited the vehicle and attempted to flee on foot, westbound through the parking lot. Officer Matthew radioed station personnel to advise them of the situation. While the officers were in pursuit of this subject, Street Sgt. Meyer arrived on location in Unit C to assist in the arrest.

Officers Matthew and Black subsequently apprehended the suspect driver and escorted him back to his vehicle. While doing so, Officer Matthew detected a strong odor of alcohol about the suspect's person. Therefore, on arrival at the vehicle and with the assistance of Sgt. Meyer, as the primary officer, Officer Matthew conducted field sobriety tests of the suspect while Officer Black inspected the suspect's vehicle.

On his approach to the driver's side of the vehicle, Officer Black noticed a bag of a green leafy substance on the passenger side of the front seat of the suspect's vehicle. He further observed what was later determined to be a laptop computer in a leather case on the driver's side of the backseat of this vehicle.

After placing the suspect under arrest for driving under the influence of drugs or alcohol, and for fleeing the scene of an accident, Sgt. Meyer assisted Officer Matthew as he placed the suspect in the back seat of Officers Matthew's and Black's patrol unit. As they did so, Officer Black secured the laptop computer in the trunk of the patrol unit.

Officers Matthew and Black then transported the suspect to the Big City Police Department while Sgt. Meyer remained at the scene until the wrecker called to impound the vehicle arrived.

Based on the information given in this chapter, answer the following questions:

1. Which officer conducted a field test of the green leafy substance found in the front seat of the suspect's vehicle?
   - ❏ A. Officer Matthew
   - ❏ B. Officer Black
   - ❏ C. Sgt. Meyer
   - ❏ D. Not enough information is provided to answer this question

2. Which officer is responsible for completing the towed vehicle portion of the field report?
   - ❏ A. Officer Matthew
   - ❏ B. Officer Black
   - ❏ C. Sgt. Meyer
   - ❏ D. Not enough information provided to answer this question

3. Which officer is responsible for securing the laptop computer in the property room?
   - ❏ A. Officer Matthew
   - ❏ B. Officer Black
   - ❏ C. Sgt. Meyer
   - ❏ D. Not enough information provided to answer this question

4. Which officer ordered the contract tow truck?
   - ❏ A. Officer Matthew
   - ❏ B. Officer Black
   - ❏ C. Sgt. Meyer
   - ❏ D. Not enough information provided to answer this question

5. Which officer advised central communication of the pertinent information about the vehicle being towed?
   - ❏ A. Officer Matthew
   - ❏ B. Officer Black
   - ❏ C. Sgt. Meyer
   - ❏ D. Not enough information provided to answer this question

6. In most exam situations, you're given paper on which to write notes; however, you aren't allowed to retain those notes during the exam. Why then are such notes important?
   - ❏ A. They help you isolate important points of the information.
   - ❏ B. They help you organize that information in a manner that's easiest for you to retain.
   - ❏ C. They help you pinpoint which information might be pertinent to the test.
   - ❏ D. All of the above.

# Exam Prep Answers

1. **Answer B is correct.** The drug operating procedure information on page 29 of this chapter advises that "the recovery officer should conduct a field test of the suspected narcotic." In this case, the recovery officer is Officer Black; therefore, answers A, C, and D are incorrect.

2. **Answer A is correct.** According to the vehicle towing operating procedure on page 31 of this chapter, the "primary officer adds the vehicle to the vehicle section of the report." In this case, the primary officer is Officer Matthew, therefore, answers B, C, and D are incorrect.

3. **Answer A is correct.** According to the vehicle towing operating procedure on page 31 of this chapter, "if high-value property is found, the property must be taken to the property room by the primary officer for safekeeping." In this case, the primary officer is Officer Matthew; therefore, answers B, C, and D are incorrect.

4. **Answer B is correct.** According to the vehicle towing operating procedure on page 31 of this chapter, the "assisting officer orders the contract tow truck." In this case, the arresting officer is Officer Black; therefore, answers A, C, and D are incorrect.

5. **Answer B is correct.** According to the vehicle towing operating procedure on page 31 of this chapter, the "assisting officer notifies central communication of the year, make, model, plate number, and vehicle identification number (VIN) of the vehicle being towed." In this case, the assisting officer is Officer Black; therefore, answers A, C, and D are incorrect.

6. **Answer D is correct.** Answer A is correct because you isolate information when you underline or highlight it. Answer B is correct because you organize that information when you create an outline. Answer C is correct because when you use your reasoning abilities to discern which information is important, you pinpoint that information that is pertinent to the test. Therefore, answer D, "All of the above," is the correct answer.

CHAPTER THREE

# Memory Retention

---

## Terms You'll Need to Understand:

✓ Observation

✓ Memorization

✓ Retention

✓ Information organization

✓ Notes

---

## Concepts You'll Need to Master:

✓ Being a skilled observer

✓ Maximizing information retention

✓ Organizing information effectively

✓ Taking effective notes

✓ Observing and memorizing floor plans, crime scenes, and suspect information

# Ability to Observe Detailed Information

The ability to observe is marked as a key trait of a skilled police officer. In your daily routine as a police officer, you will come in contact with numerous people, both victims and suspects, and you will be expected to recall their faces and other factual information about them. You also will be expected to recall information when you prepare your reports, when you give information to the detectives who do follow-up investigations on your case, and when you talk to the prosecuting attorney and testify in court as a witness on behalf of the state. Having a keen power of observation and the ability to recall visual information are very important qualities. That is why police officer selection exams are designed to test an applicant's ability to recall information after a brief observation period.

Even though the test format varies among police agencies, most current approaches in police applicant testing give a booklet to all applicants immediately before the exam. The booklet covers a variety of information. Applicants are given equal timeframes to look over the material. At the end of this period, the applicants are tested for their ability to recall information covered in the booklet.

Another approach is to give the booklet to applicants two to four weeks before the test. Applicants can read and memorize the contents of the booklet during this period, and the test covers the material in the booklet. Both approaches test applicants' ability to recall the information in the booklet. The booklet contains a variety of photographs and sketches. Questions are based on what can be observed in the crime scene. The questions focus on the criminal activity itself, not, for example, on the price of a candy bar or soda in the store.

# Maximizing Information Retention

Working as a police officer is sometimes like working with a jigsaw puzzle. As a police officer, information is one of your key assets. Your ability to observe, retain, and recall a key piece of information can make or break a case for investigators and prosecutors alike. I am sure there are some gifted people who can retain mounds of information, but in my opinion, it is a learned skill. In your daily routine, you can develop habits that will help you observe, retain, and recall information as needed. In the section that follows, we will cover two basic techniques that you can use to prepare yourself for the police officer exam. The following are two techniques that will help you retain information for the exam:

- ▸ Organize the information
- ▸ Create notes from memory

# Organize the Information

Organizing and ordering information can significantly improve retention of information. For example, if you are asked to memorize 100 randomly generated letters in a particular order, it will be difficult to retain and recall this information. On the other hand, if the same randomly generated letters make a sentence that you can understand, or you construct some meaning and make links to existing knowledge, it will be very easy to retain this information. Apply the same principle when you study for the test. This approach can be applied not just to the police officer test, but also to any academic test. Organizing and adding meaning to the test material makes storage and retrieval of the information easier. The following strategies will help you organize information to increase your understanding of the material. You can organize this material on paper, similar to making an outline, or simply organize the material in your memory bank.

## Create Notes from Memory

During the study session, you will be given some loose sheets of paper for note taking. You will not be allowed to keep these notes in the class, but you can use these sheets to create an outline of all the information being provided in the study guide. After this outline has been created, it will be a much shorter document to remember than the complete exam guide. When you are ready to take the test, the testers will provide additional scrap pieces of paper. Even though you are not allowed to keep your outline, you will be allowed to create the outline based on what you remember. So, as soon you enter the exam after the study session and the break, you can perform a memory dump and create an outline of everything you studied in the study session.

Because you now have some idea of how you should approach the study material, let's see how you can apply some of these principles to the police officer test exam in particular.

# Exam Information

The memory section of the exam tests your ability to observe and recall information. During the study session of the exam, you will be given a variety of information to learn and memorize in a booklet. This is a total memory section. Unlike other sections, in which the information is given to you again, scenario information from this section will not be repeated for you on the test. The information will be presented to you in the form of scenarios or short stories similar to the way a police officer receives a call for help. You will be expected to remember the key pieces of information about each of these scenarios and images.

Most of the times the scenario will be from the following three categories.

▶ Crime scenes

▶ Suspect information

▶ Building floor plans

# Crime Scenes

In the crime scene section of this memory test, you will be given a scenario. That scenario will include one or two images. After you have looked at the images and read the scenario, there will be a series of questions about the scenario. These questions cover both the image and the information given in the text.

Let's take a look at an example of a test-like scenario and a series of questions that are dependent on the scenario.

## Scenario 1

You have been dispatched to 1200 E. 46th Street on the possibility of an armed robbery in progress. The suspect is described as a white male, armed with a handgun. Upon arrival to the scene, you see this:

Based on the scenario just given, let's answer some of the following questions:

1. When you first arrived at the scene, how many vehicles were parked in the parking lot?

2. How many customers were inside the business?

3. Was the robber a black male or a white male?

4. In which hand was the suspect holding the gun?

5. What was the street address to which you were dispatched?

## Scenario 2

While working on night shift, you and Officer Jones have been dispatched to the scene of a residential burglary in progress at 3421 Central Avenue. A black male has been seen entering a window on the south side of the house. Upon arrival on the scene, you see the following:

Based on the scenario just given, let's answer the following questions:

1. When you first arrived on the scene, were there any cars parked in the driveway?

2. Did you see anyone run away from the scene?

3. What was your dispatch time for the call?

4. Which other officer was dispatched to the scene?

---

**TIP**

Organize information in the form of zones. For example, you can easily divide the armed robbery crime scene into outside and inside the business zones. Then further divide these zones. For instance, you could divide the outside into "people and vehicles," and divide the inside into "customer area and employee area" or "in front of the counter" or "behind the counter." When you have divided your crime scene into zones, concentrate on each zone. For example, for your outside zone, you can look for the following:

▶ Who is outside?

▶ How many cars in the parking lot?

▶ Is someone driving away?

▶ Are there any people sitting inside the vehicle?

Then concentrate on the inside of the business. Some of the following questions might help your breakdown of the business's inside:

▶ How many people are inside?

▶ Is the suspect still inside the business?

▶ How many suspects?

▶ Are there weapons or no weapons?

▶ Description of the suspect?

If the image is clear enough, organize your suspect description. Start from the top of the head and end at the feet. Use the following as a guide when observing a suspect:

▶ Head gear

▶ Hair

▶ Face

▶ Shirt

▶ Pants

▶ Shoes

▶ Age

▶ Height

▶ Weight

You can use a similar approach to any type of crime scene. When you have gathered all the required information, take notes and draw a quick outline.

---

# Suspect Information

As a police officer, you will come across numerous people in your professional life. These people could be victims, witnesses and, most of all, suspects. In addition to meeting people while working your designated area, you will also receive information in various forms. One such form will be a *wanted bulletin*. These bulletins usually have the wanted subject's photo and the charge that the person is wanted for. In the memory section of the test there is a portion that tests your ability to remember peoples' faces and what they are wanted for. The idea is to replicate a wanted bulletin.

Let's practice this idea. The following four scenarios give you subject faces that are associated with different crimes. After the fourth scenario, there will be questions that rely on your observations of the information provided in all four scenarios.

## Scenario 1
The following three subjects are wanted for conspiracy to commit murder:

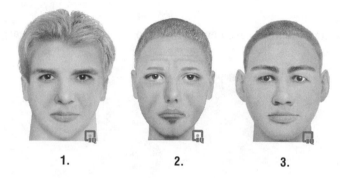

1.                    2.                    3.

## Scenario 2
The following two individuals are wanted by the financial crimes branch for check fraud:

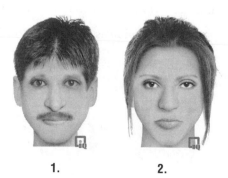

1.                    2.

## Scenario 3

The following individual is wanted for domestic violence:

1.

## Scenario 4

The following individuals are being sought for firearms-related charges:

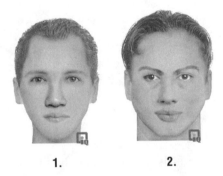

1.                2.

Based on the preceding scenarios, answer the following questions:

1. Which of the following individuals are wanted for domestic violence?

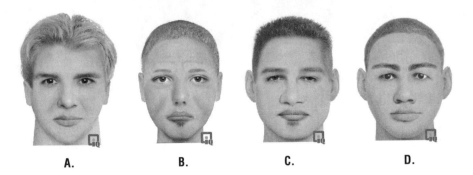

A.            B.            C.            D.

2. Which of the following individuals are wanted for conspiracy to commit murder?

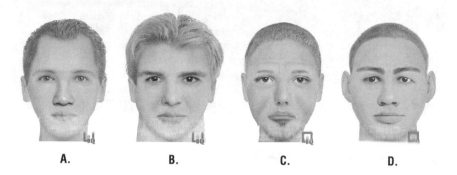

   A.              B.              C.              D.

3. Which of the following individuals are wanted for firearms-related charges?

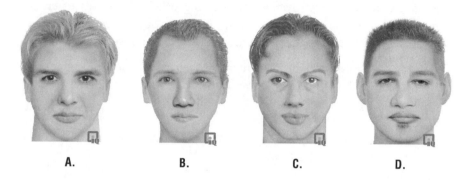

   A.              B.              C.              D.

4. Which of the following individuals are wanted for check fraud?

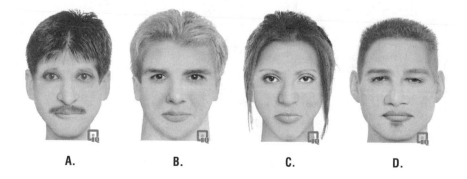

   A.              B.              C.              D.

# Building Floor Plan

From time to time in your career as a police officer, you will be required to serve arrest warrants, search warrants, or call for a more-specialized unit, such as a SWAT team. Members of SWAT teams rely mainly on the information provided to them by the first arriving officer. One area of crucial information is the layout of the building. By using this correct information, specialized teams can better execute search plans and arrest plans.

Let's practice observing floor plans further. Scenarios 1 and 2 give you some floor plans. Based on these plans, answer the questions that follow.

## Scenario 1

Let's look at layout number 1. Figures 3.9 and 3.10 show the first and second floors, respectively, for this layout.

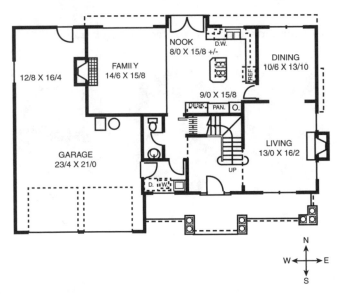

**FIGURE 3.9** First floor.

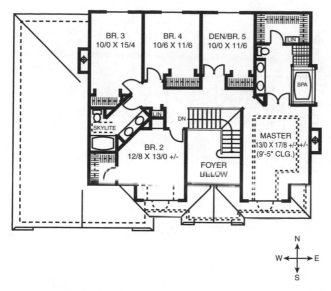

**FIGURE 3.10**  Second floor.

You and Officer Brown have been dispatched to 2347 Naomi Street to serve a felony warrant. You entered the residence and searched the house. The wanted subject has not been found. You suspect that the subject might be hidden in the attic. At this point, you decide to call the SWAT team. Upon SWAT's arrival, the SWAT team leader wants to know the layout of the house. Based on this scenario, answer the following questions:

1. Does this house have a basement?

2. How many rooms are on the first floor?

3. How many rooms are on the second floor?

4. How many windows on the first floor face the north side of the house?

5. Which corner of the house has the master bedroom? Was it E, W, N, S, NE, NW, SE, or SW?

**Answers**

1. No

2. Four

3. Six

4. Three

5. Southeast

## Scenario 2

Let's look at layout number 2.

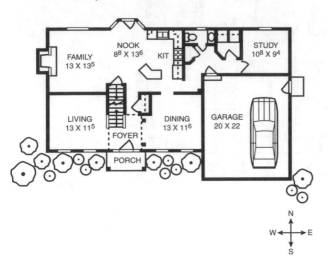

**FIGURE 3.11**    First floor—scenario two.

**FIGURE 3.12**    Second floor—scenario two.

You have been dispatched to a domestic disturbance. You have made an arrest. Now the prosecutor, who is unable to make it to the scene at the time of the arrest, wants to know the layout of the house. Based on this scenario, answer the following questions:

1. Which room of the house is located in the southwest corner of the first floor?

2. Which room of the house is located in the northeast corner of the second floor?

3. How many bathrooms are in this house?

4. How many fireplaces are in the house?

5. Does this house have a garage?

Answers

1. Living room

2. Bedroom number 2

3. Three

4. One

5. Yes

**EXAM ALERT**

Take an organized approach to observing layouts. Start from the front door and imagine that you are walking though the house. Compare the layout with another house that you have visited or even your own house. Use the legend and azimuth that ate provided. Pay special attention to the direction of north. North will not always be toward the top of the page. After you have determined the direction of north, all the other directions fall into place.

**EXAM ALERT**

Do a memory dump on exam day. As soon as you get the opportunity during the test, draw a diagram while the layout is fresh in your mind. If you remember the legend items, outline them on the paper. There could be several questions, for a single layout. Your diagram will be useful and help you answer the questions.

# Exam Prep Questions

You have been dispatched to the scene of a reported armed robbery in progress at the Creative Carets Jewelry Store at 325 West Main. For five minutes, study the drawing of area as it appears on your arrival. After five minutes, set the drawing aside and answer the following questions.

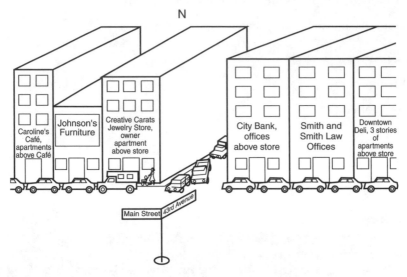

Crime scenario.

1. Upon your arrival at the scene, the perpetrator has already left the store. When canvassing the area for witnesses, from which office locations with windows would somebody most likely have seen the perpetrator leaving the area?
   - ○ A. Northeast floors above city bank
   - ○ B. Northwest floors above Creative Carets jewelry store
   - ○ C. Northwest floors above Smith and Smith Law Offices
   - ○ D. Northwest floors above City Bank

2. To what address were you dispatched?
   - ○ A. 325 West Main
   - ○ B. 335 West Main
   - ○ C. 325 East Main
   - ○ D. 325 North 43rd Avenue

3. What vehicle is observed pulling out into traffic on North 43rd Avenue?
   - ○ A. Four-door sedan
   - ○ B. Pickup truck with cab
   - ○ C. Two-door sedan
   - ○ D. Pickup truck
4. Which business is directly to the west of Creative Carats Jewelry Store?
   - ○ A. Caroline's Café
   - ○ B. Johnson's Furniture Store
   - ○ C. City Bank
   - ○ D. Smith and Smith Law Offices

For five minutes, study the four wanted posters. Be sure to pay attention to both the mug shot drawings and the additional information that accompanies the posters.

Wanted poster 9.

Wanted – Escaped Prisoner
Name: Greg Fox
Age: 24
Height: 6'3"
Eyes: Blue
Scars: Appendectomy scar
Race: White
Weight: 215
Hair: Blonde, curly
Facial hair: None
Tattoos: Numerous prison tattoos, including L-O-V-E on the fingers of his left hand and H-A-T-E on the fingers of his right hand.

Subject, who was serving a 15–20 year sentence for armed robbery, is considered likely to be armed and dangerous. Subject was known to let his hair grow for almost a year prior to his escape, so it is likely he's altered his appearance by cutting his hair; upon his arrest two years ago, he had a buzz cut.

Wanted – Escaped Prisoner
Name: Rupert "Mad Dog" Hinckley
Age: 29
Height: 5'9"
Eyes: Brown
Scars: Surgical scar, bullet removed from right shoulder
Race: White
Weight: 165
Hair: Light brown
Facial hair: None
Tattoos: A snake coiled around (and above) each bicep

Wanted poster 10.

Subject was serving a 3–5 year sentence for possession of drugs with intent to sell and possession of stolen property. He is a chronic drug user, and known to abuse prescription painkillers. Subject also has a partial plate for his two missing front teeth.

Wanted – Escaped Prisoner
Name: Jonathon Bentley Radcliff
Age: 46
Height: 6'2"
Eyes: Hazel
Scars: None
Race: White
Weight: 180
Hair: Brown
Facial hair: None
Tattoos: None

Wanted poster 11.

Subject was serving a 5–10 year sentence for embezzlement. Subject is also known to have numerous international contacts, and might attempt to flee the country.

Wanted – Escaped Prisoner
Name: Jackson Williams
Age: 56
Height: 6 '
Eyes: Green
Scars: None
Race: White
Weight: 220
Hair: Gray
Facial hair: None
Tattoos: None

Wanted poster 12.

Subject, who was serving a 20-year to life sentence for serial rape, is an alcoholic. Subject dresses well, and has been known to loiter in hotel bars and at community meetings in search of victims.

After five minutes, set the posters aside and answer the following questions:

5. Which subject has snake tattoos?

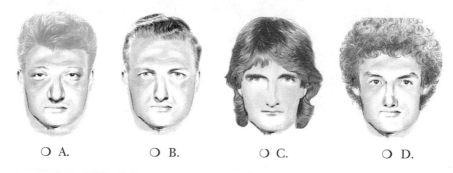

   ○ A.       ○ B.       ○ C.       ○ D.

6. Which subject is known to loiter in hotel bars?

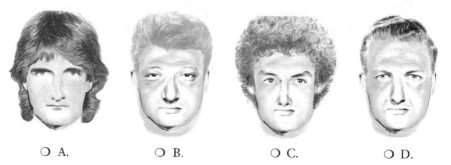

   ○ A.       ○ B.       ○ C.       ○ D.

7. Which subject has prison tattoos?

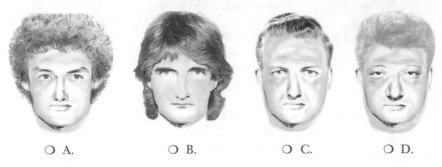

    ○ A.          ○ B.          ○ C.          ○ D.

8. Which subject is suspected of possibly attempting to leave the
country?

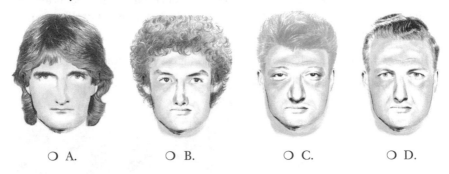

    ○ A.          ○ B.          ○ C.          ○ D.

You are to serve a search warrant at a residence located at 7653 Briarwoods
Road. Study the picture of the house and floor plan drawings for five minutes.

Cambridge.

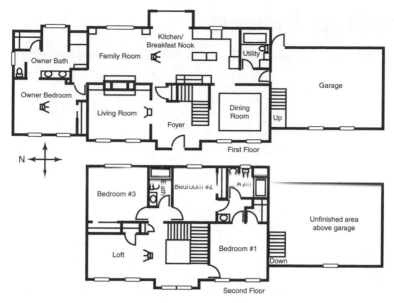

Floor plan.

Set aside the drawings and answer the following questions, choosing all correct answers that apply:

9. The house has stairways leading to the following:
   - ○  A.  The basement
   - ○  B.  The second floor
   - ○  C.  The unfinished third floor
   - ○  D.  The garage attic

10. What is the address of the home to which you are to serve the search warrant?
   - ○  A.  2347 Naomi Street
   - ○  B.  7653 Briarwoods Road
   - ○  C.  7653 Naomi Street
   - ○  D.  2347 Briarwoods Road

11. The garage is at which end of the house?
   - ○  A.  North
   - ○  B.  South
   - ○  C.  East
   - ○  D.  West

12. How many bathrooms are in this house?
   - ○  A.  2
   - ○  B.  3
   - ○  C.  2 1/2
   - ○  D.  3 1/2

# Exam Prep Answers

1. D
2. A
3. D
4. B
5. C
6. B
7. A
8. D
9. B, C, D
10. B
11. B
12. D

CHAPTER FOUR

# Geographical Orientation

## Terms You'll Need to Understand:

✓ Direct routes

✓ Following written directions

✓ Landmark orientation

## Concepts You'll Need to Master:

✓ Street grid

✓ Address placement

# Importance of Geographical Orientation in Police Work

A successful police officer must be able to find an address quickly. This skill can be easily developed over a period of time after understanding the basic principles of street layout in your assigned patrol area. *Global Positioning System (GPS)* devices are now very common and affordable. Furthermore, the majority of patrol cars are equipped with *Mobile Data Terminals (MDTs)*. When an emergency call is dispatched, the dispatcher will usually broadcast the call over the police radio so that officers can start heading in the direction where the help is needed. The dispatcher then sends the details of the call on the MDTs. MDTs are mostly ruggedized laptop computers mounted on specially designed mounts for police cars. Along with the capability to receive call details from central dispatch, some of these laptops also have integrated GPS devices.

GPS devices allow dispatch to know your location at all times, which is a great advantage to officer safety. In police work, it's very important to know where you are located at all times. You might wonder why you still need to be aware of your location at all times with all this advancement in technology—this is important for two reasons:

▶ If you need help from backup officers in case of an emergency, you might not have time to look at your portable GPS device to know your location, or you might be out of your vehicle and not have access to the GPS device. If you know where you are, you can easily tell the other officers your location.

▶ If you are given an emergency run, you will be able to figure out promptly where you need to go, and the fastest way to get there.

---

**TIP**

Although GPS technology can greatly improve your overall navigation, it's still important to know your directions; in other words, know north, south, east, and west, from your location at all times. This might sound like silly and simple advice, but at night it's harder to know where you are and have directional sense—especially in a high-speed pursuit. During those times when every second counts, knowing intuitively which direction you're going improves your effectiveness and can even save lives.

---

In police work, it's also important to know your jurisdiction. If you're out of your jurisdiction, you may or may not be able to enforce laws or make an arrest. Most of the time, law enforcement agencies work together and at times overlap in jurisdiction.

Also important is your assigned area of patrol. Because you are assigned to this area, you are responsible for the calls for help in that area. If the dispatcher dispatches a run, you should be able to recognize by the address whether it is in your assigned area of patrol and volunteer to take the run. This tells your supervisors that you are not just taking care of your district, you are also listening and paying attention to what is going on in and around your area of patrol.

The geographical orientation portion of the test is designed to test your ability to find your target location in a reasonable amount of time.

> **NOTE**
>
> Having *beat integrity,* or handling your assigned area, shows your peers and supervisors that you are a hard worker. When you start your job as a police officer, everyone will be watching you; this is a good opportunity to show everyone that you're a sharp officer who is willing to work and be a team player.

# Basics of Street Layout

Before we get into the details of exam questions and approach you can take to maximize the score, let's cover some basics of street layouts.

Most of the larger cities, and even smaller ones, are divided into *grids*. These grid lines are mostly city streets, dividing the city in small blocks. The street grid generally has a street that runs north and south and divides the city in east and west halves. Similarly, there is usually a street that runs east and west and divides the city into north and south halves. It is using these grid lines, or streets, that the street address numbering scheme is created. All the addresses that are located on the west side of the dividing line will have a *west* directional attribute associated with the address; for example, West 25th Street or West 19th Street. Similarly, the east side of the dividing line will have an *east* attribute associated with the address; for example, East Washington Street or East 42nd Street. The same principle is applied to north and south addresses.

Let's take the grid organization a step further. In most major cities, if a street runs north and south, all the house or building addresses on the west side of the street are even numbers, and odd numbers are on the east side of the street. Similarly, if the street runs east and west, all the even addresses are on the north side of the street and odd addresses are on the south side of the street.

**TIP**

Learning this numbering system will make your life as a police officer easier. Let's say you get a call that involves a man with a gun. Wouldn't you want to know which side of the street he is on before you get there? Little things like this could save your life or your partner's life. This is certainly something to remember as a working police officer.

Let's refer to the diagram in Figure 4.1 and apply the principles covered in the earlier paragraphs. This is a sample street layout we will use throughout this chapter. It is a six block street grid. Washington Street runs east to west and divides the grid into north and south quadrants. Meridian Street runs from north to south and divides the grid into east and west quadrants.

As you can see, Meridian Street runs north and south while dividing the sample city into east and west halves. Washington Street runs east and west, and divides the city into north and south halves, resulting in our four quadrants. That means all the residences or buildings that are east of Meridian Street will have an *east* attribute associated with the address and those houses and buildings that are south of Washington Street will have a *south* attribute associated with the address.

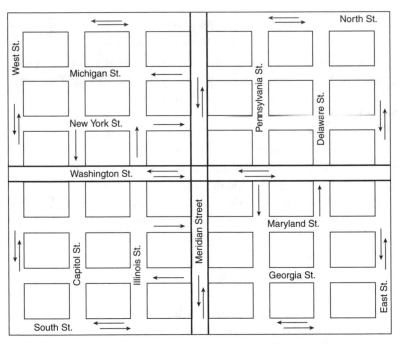

**FIGURE 4.1** Sample street layout.

> **TIP**
>
> When you visit another city, take time to learn a little about how the streets are laid out in the city. Determine what the dividing streets are and how the addresses are laid out within the scheme just discussed.

# Applying Geographical Orientation to the Police Exam

Now that you have an understanding of how the streets are laid out, let's take a look at the exam and how to approach geographical orientation questions.

In the exam, expect to see the following three most common geographical orientation type questions:

- ▶ Determine the most direct way of getting from point A to point B, while obeying all the traffic laws

- ▶ Follow the written directions to get from point A to point B

- ▶ Identify a landmark based on compass location

> **EXAM ALERT**
>
> Read the directions carefully. Know exactly what is being asked. Also be sure to make full use of the legend provided.

# Direct Route Questions

In direct route questions, you're required to head from one location using the most direct route, while following all the traffic laws. For example, you will not be allowed to make a right-hand–turn or a U-turn. In this type of question, you are given a scenario that describes your location and a location where you are headed. There might be some additional information, such as road closing, high water, or traffic jam problems. You are given multiple-choice answers to choose from. Let's take a look at a couple of scenario questions to practice direct route questions.

# Scenario 1

You and Officer Jones are at the intersection of Delaware Street and North Street. You both get a call for a person shot at the intersection of Capitol Street and Georgia Street.

Time is of value. You have to drive with emergency equipment and are required to take the most direct route to the crime scene. When answering the following question, refer to Figure 4.2. It is a six-block street grid. Washington Street runs east to west and divides the grid into north and south halves. Meridian Street runs from north to south and divides the grid into east and west halves. As you can see, north has been given for you. Based on this information, you need to determine other directions. Also given are your starting and stopping positions.

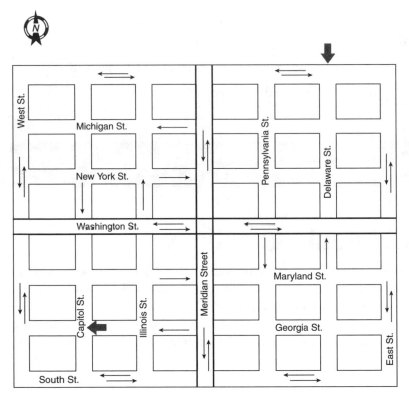

**FIGURE 4.2**  Six-street grid for a crime scene.

1. Which one of the following describes the most direct route?

    **A.** Go west on North Street to Pennsylvania Street, and then south on Pennsylvania Street to Georgia Street. Then go west on Georgia Street to Capitol Street.

    **B.** Go south on Delaware Street to South Street, and then go east on South Street to Capitol Street.

    **C.** Go south on Illinois Street to Georgia Street.

    **D.** Go south on East Street to Georgia Street and then west on Georgia Street.

**Answer A is correct** because Pennsylvania Street is the first street that allows you to travel southbound. Even though you are standing by Delaware Street, you cannot travel south because the street is one way going north. Therefore, you will see that answers B and C are incorrect because no southbound traffic is allowed on Delaware and Illinois streets. Choice D is also incorrect because it is not a direct route. Even though you will get there following the directions, it is a much longer route than answer A.

## EXAM ALERT

During the exam, you might be given multiple diagrams that might all look similar. Make sure that you are using the right diagram for each question.

# Scenario 2

You are at the intersection of Georgia Street and Delaware Street. You get a personal injury accident call at the intersection of Michigan Street and Capitol Street.

First off, remember that time is of value. You will have to drive with emergency equipment and are required to take the most direct route to the accident scene. Figure 4.3 is similar to Figure 4.2. It has been modified to fit scenario 2 so that the starting point and stopping point are different. It, too, is a six-block street grid. Washington Street runs east to west and divides the grid into north and south halves. Meridian Street runs from north to south and divides the grid into east and west halves. When answering the following question, refer to Figure 4.3. As you can see, north has been provided for you. Based on this information, you need to determine the other directions.

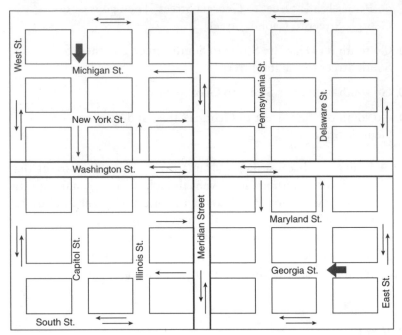

**FIGURE 4.3**  Six-street grid for an accident scene.

1. Which one of the following describes the most direct route?

   **A.** Go south on Delaware Street to South Street. Then go east on South Street to Capitol Street. Then go north on Capitol Street to Michigan Street.

   **B.** Go south on Capitol Street to South Street. Then go east on South Street to Delaware. Then go north on Delaware Street.

   **C.** Go west on Georgia Street to Illinois Street. Then go north on Illinois Street to Michigan Street. Then go west on Michigan Street to Capitol Street.

   **D.** Go north on Delaware street to Michigan Street. Then go east on Michigan Street to Capitol Street.

**Answer C is correct** because this choice gives you the most direct route. Answer A is incorrect because it asks you to go south on Delaware to South Street and then east on South Street to Capitol. If you refer to Figure 4.3, Capitol Street is west of Delaware Street. Answer B is incorrect because it asks you to go south on Capitol. If you follow these directions, it takes you away from your target location. Answer D is incorrect because it asks you to go north on Delaware Street and then east on Michigan Street. Michigan Street is one-way westbound. No eastbound traffic is allowed.

> **EXAM ALERT**
>
> Remember that most of the questions will require you to follow all traffic laws. That means that you cannot go the wrong way on a one-way street.

> **EXAM ALERT**
>
> For questions related to direct route, there is usually more than one route that may be taken from one location to another. It is very important to consider all options before making your final choice.

# Follow the Path

In these types of questions, you're given a set of directions to go from point A to point B. You are to follow these instructions to go to the target location. At that location is some type of landmark. Let's practice these types of questions in the following scenarios.

## Scenario 1

You and Officer Smith are dispatched to an area. The 911 caller does not know the address. When you arrive at the scene, you are to notify central communication of the address. Refer to Figure 4.4 when answering questions for scenario 1 and 2.

### Instructions

You are located at West Street and New York Street. You are to travel east on New York Street, turn south onto Meridian Street to South Street, and then turn east on South Street to East Street.

What is the address of the church located closest to you?

- **A.** 50 N. Alabama Street
- **B.** 300 W. South Street
- **C.** 220 E. South Street
- **D.** 200 E. New York Street

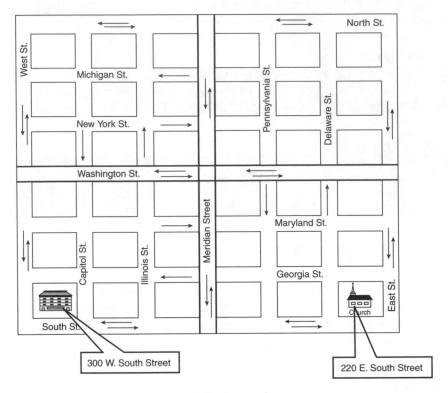

**FIGURE 4.4**   Six-block street grid for following a path.

**Answer C is correct.** Follow the street with your finger while following the direction. Answer A is incorrect because the object is not located on Alabama Street. Furthermore, Alabama Street is not even on the map. Answer B is incorrect because the test asks you to travel east of Meridian. Knowing the numbering scheme, we know that all addresses east of the north and south dividing line will have an east attribute. Choice D is incorrect because the instruction says to travel south onto Meridian Street from New York Street. There is no possible way that the address could be on New York Street.

# Scenario 2

You and Officer Jones are dispatched to an area. The 911 caller does not know the address. When you arrive at the scene, you are to notify central communication of the address.

**Instructions**

You are located at North Street and Capitol Street and travel south on Capitol to Maryland Street. You then turn east on Maryland Street, south on Pennsylvania Street, and then turn west on South Street to West Street.

What is the address of the office building closest to the intersection?

**A.** 50 N. Alabama Street

**B.** 200 E. New York Street

**C.** 100 W. Ohio Street

**D.** 300 W. South Street

**Answer D is correct.** If you follow the street lines with your fingertip while reading the instruction, you will travel south on Capitol Street to Maryland Street. To travel east of Maryland, you will take a right turn. To travel south on Pennsylvania, you will make another right turn. To travel west on South Street, you will make another right turn, taking to you to 300 W. South Street. Answer A is incorrect because Alabama Street is not even on the map. Answer B is incorrect because the instruction asks you to travel south on Capitol Street to Maryland Street. As you can see on the map, Maryland Street is south of Washington Street. As you travel to Maryland Street, you pass New York Street. Answer C is incorrect. Similar to answer B, you pass Ohio Street as you travel towards Maryland Street.

**EXAM ALERT**

There are no shortcuts to answering these questions. You have to follow the path with either a pencil or your fingertip to determine the route.

As you are following the instructions given, imagine yourself driving the vehicle. Making a left or right turn might be different as you look at the exam sheet compared to actually driving on the given street.

# Landmark/Spatial Orientation Questions

In these types of questions, you are given a location. At the location, you'll be asked to identify a landmark in any given direction. For example, you could be given an intersection. When you arrive at the intersection, you are required to identify a landmark to the east, west, north, south, southeast, southwest, northeast, or northwest of an intersection. The landmark could be some type of building, or an object such as a mailbox, fire hydrant, or street sign.

# Scenario 1

Figure 4.5 is similar to Figure 4.4. It is a six-block street grid. Washington Street runs east to west and divides the grid into north and south halves. Meridian Street runs from north to south and divides the grid into east and west halves. When answering both of these questions, refer to Figure 4.5. As you can see, north has been provided for you. Based on this information, you need to determine the other directions.

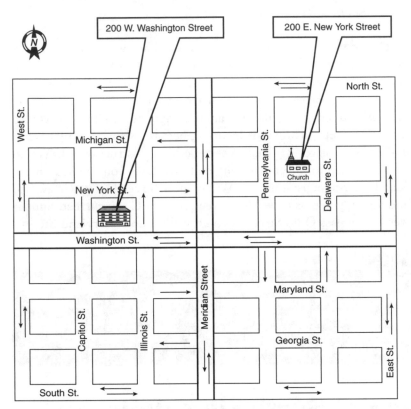

**FIGURE 4.5**    Six-block street grid for landmark location.

1. If you are at the intersection of Pennsylvania Street and New York Street, what is the address of the building located in the northeast quadrant?

   **A.** 200 W. South Street

   **B.** 200 W. Washington Street

**C.** 200 E. New York Street

**D.** 100 N. Illinois

**Answer C is correct.** If you face north, east will be on your right side, west on your left, and south behind you. Based on these directions, there is a church located in the northeast quadrant with the caption 200 E. New York Street.

2. If you are at the intersection of Capitol Street and New York Street, what is the address of the building located in the southwest quadrant?

**A.** 200 E. New York Street

**B.** 200 W. South Street

**C.** 100 N. Illinois

**D.** 200 W. Washington Street

**Answer D is correct.** If you face north, the east will be on your right side, west on your left, and south behind you. Based on these directions, there is an office building located in the southwest quadrant with the caption 200 W. Washington Street.

**EXAM ALERT**

Know your directions. If only north is given and other directions are needed, fill in the other directions. In most exams, you will be allowed to write on the exam sheet. Make full use of this privilege. Draw a compass, if needed.

Understanding the principles just discussed, use the "Exam Prep Questions" section to practice for the exam.

# Exam Prep Questions

Refer to Figure 4.6 and the following instructions to answer questions 1 through 8.

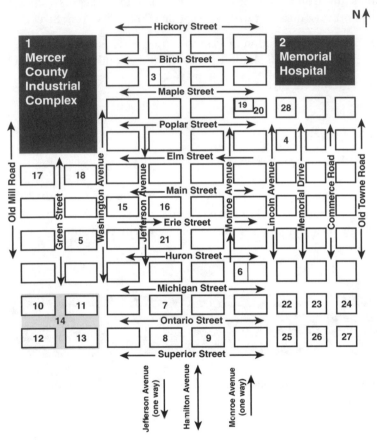

**FIGURE 4.6**

Figure 4.6 is a map of the fictional town of Flagtown, Ohio. Points of interest include

1. Mercer County Industrial Complex

2. Memorial Hospital

3. Jefferson Grade School

4. Lincoln Grade School

5. Washington Grade School

 **6.** Monroe Grade School

 **7.** Jefferson Middle School

 **8.** Memorial High School

 **9.** Memorial Football Stadium

**10–13.** Flagtown Medical Complex

 **14.** Private Parking (Abandoned Streets)

 **15.** Safety Building

 **16.** Municipal Building

 **17.** Water Treatment Facility

 **18.** Power Plant

 **19.** Flagtown Municipal Swimming Pool

 **20.** Founder's Park

 **21.** Post Office

 **22.** Senior Towers Apartments

 **23.** Blue Rose Apartments

 **24.** Country Chef Supermarket

 **25.** Senor Manor Apartments

 **26.** Richfield Manor Apartments

 **27.** Old Towne Shoppes Plaza

 **28.** Founder's Towers Apartments

The Mercer County Industrial Park and the sides of the streets bordering that park are outside the city limits and are in the jurisdiction for the Mercer County Sheriff's Department. Otherwise, the city limits extends to the east side of Old Mill Road, the south side of Hickory Street, the west side of Old Towne Road, and the north side of Superior Street. Note the following jurisdictional exception: Old Towne Road north of Main Street is State Route 683, and is handled by the Ohio State Highway Patrol. All other state routes that coexist on city streets are handled by the Flagtown Police Department.

The emergency entrance and exit for Memorial Hospital is on the north side of Maple Street.

The gray area (marked 14) in the Flagtown Medical Complex indicates abandoned streets that are now private parking for the complex.

1. Officer Brewster, who is eastbound on Huron Street, receives a report of four juveniles doing some acts of vandalism to the northwest corner of Monroe Grade School. As she approaches the school, she observes Juvenile #1 run north on Monroe Avenue, Juvenile #2 run east on Huron Street, Juvenile #3 run west on Huron Street for a block and then run north on Hamilton Avenue, and Juvenile #4 run south on Monroe Avenue. Which youth is most likely to be found hiding in the shrubbery near the gates to Memorial Football Stadium?

   ❑  A.  Juvenile #1
   ❑  B.  Juvenile #2
   ❑  C.  Juvenile #3
   ❑  D.  Juvenile #4

2. A pedestrian walks eastbound on Main Street from the southeast corner of the power plant for a block and then turns left. He continues in that direction for four blocks. Where is the Flagtown Municipal Swimming Pool in relation to the pedestrian's final location?

   ❑  A.  Northeast
   ❑  B.  Northwest
   ❑  C.  Southeast
   ❑  D.  Southwest

3. An accident occurs on Old Towne Road at the northwest corner of Elm Street between two vehicles both traveling southbound on Old Towne Road. Which law enforcement agency should respond to this accident?

   ❑  A.  Flagtown Police Department
   ❑  B.  Ohio State Highway Patrol
   ❑  C.  Mercer County Sheriff's Department
   ❑  D.  Unable to determine from the information given

4. In which direction is a vehicle traveling on Lincoln Avenue from Main Street toward Maple Street headed?

   ❑  A.  North
   ❑  B.  South
   ❑  C.  East
   ❑  D.  West

5. Fearing that an altercation is about to break out over an accidental injury incident inside the Mercer County Industrial Park, the rescue squad requests officers respond to that location to handle crowd control. Which agency should respond?
   - ❏ A. Flagtown Police Department
   - ❏ B. Ohio State Highway Patrol
   - ❏ C. Mercer County Sheriff's Office
   - ❏ D. Unable to determine from the information given

6. An officer is needed for traffic control on Superior Street until a wrecker can remove his disabled vehicle. Which agency should respond?
   - ❏ A. Flagtown Police Department
   - ❏ B. Ohio State Highway Patrol
   - ❏ C. Mercer County Sheriff's Department
   - ❏ D. Unable to determine from the information given

7. Officer Baxter's patrol unit is headed westbound on Elm Street from Hamilton Avenue when he receives a call to respond to the emergency entrance at Memorial Hospital where an altercation is in place. Based on the information given with the map, and obeying all traffic laws (in other words, no U-turns), what would be his most logical route to the hospital?
   - ❏ A. West on Elm Street, north on Jefferson Avenue, and then east on Maple Street until he reaches the emergency entrance
   - ❏ B. West on Elm Street, north on Jefferson Avenue, east on Maple Street, and then north on Lincoln Avenue until he reaches the emergency entrance
   - ❏ C. West on Elm Street, north on Washington Avenue, east on Maple Street, and then north on Lincoln Avenue until he reaches the emergency entrance
   - ❏ D. West on Elm Street, north on Washington Avenue, and then east on Maple Street until he reaches the emergency entrance

8. A report is received that the drivers involved in a traffic accident that occurred in the parking lot of the Flagtown Medical Complex are involved in a fight. Which agency should respond?
   - ❏ A. Flagtown Police Department
   - ❏ B. Ohio State Highway Patrol
   - ❏ C. Mercer County Sheriff's Department
   - ❏ D. None; the accident took place on private property

The following is the key you need to follow for questions 9 and 10:

⬠    Moving vehicle.

⬛    Parked vehicle.

◯    Pedestrian at a stationary location.

⯅    Pedestrian on the move; arrow indicates direction in which the pedestrian is walking.

9. Upon investigating a motor vehicle accident, Officer Connelly ascertains that an eastbound vehicle on Commerce Street west of Ash Street ran the stoplight, made a left turn, and then attempted to make a right turn, subsequently causing his vehicle to be struck by a southbound and a westbound vehicle. Which diagram accurately portrays the direction of travel and subsequent accident?

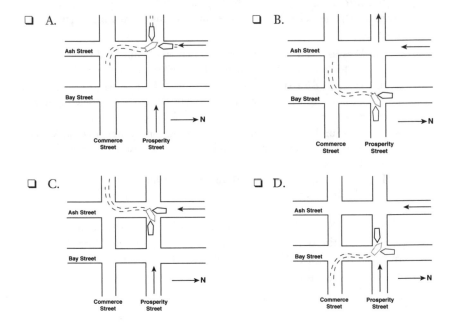

10. While walking west on Unity Street and about to cross 5th Street, which is a one-way street for northbound traffic, Linda Turner observed the driver of a vehicle north of her fail to stop at the stop sign on Grant at 5th Street. As that vehicle continued to travel westbound on Grant, it broadsided a vehicle that had the right of way and was headed north on 5th Street. Another witness, who was standing at the northwest corner of 5th and Unity Streets and waiting until it was safe to cross the street on foot, further corroborated this account. Which sketch is an accurate portrayal of the accident scene?

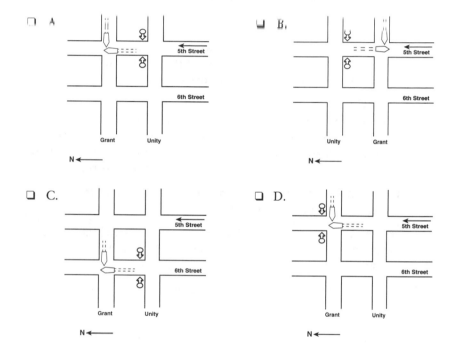

# Exam Prep Answers

1. **Answer D is correct.** The Memorial Football Stadium (9 on the map legend) is southwest of Monroe Grade School. The juveniles described in answers A, B, and C are running away from the stadium.

2. **Answer C is correct.** Properly following the directions, the pedestrian will walk eastbound on Main Street from the southeast corner of the power plant and then head north on Jefferson Avenue for four blocks. (It doesn't matter that Jefferson is a southbound one-way street because this is a pedestrian.) The pedestrian will end up at Jefferson Avenue and Beech Street; the Flagtown Municipal Swimming Pool (19 on the map legend) is at the northwest corner of Maple Street and Monroe Avenue, which is southwest of the pedestrian's final location. Answers B, C, and D are incorrect because they name incorrect directions.

3. **Answer B is correct.** The northwest corner of Elm Street and Old Towne Road is north of Main Street, which means that the accident occurred on State Route 683, which is the Ohio State Highway Patrol's jurisdiction. Therefore, answers A, C, and D are incorrect.

4. **Answer A is correct.** Maple Street is north of Main Street; therefore answers B, C, and D are incorrect.

5. **Answer C is correct.** The Mercer County Industrial Park is outside the city limits and in the Mercer County Sheriff's Department's jurisdiction; therefore answers A, B, and D are incorrect.

6. **Answer D is correct.** The north side of Superior Street is in the city limits, which is in the jurisdiction of the Flagtown Police Department, and the south side of Superior Street is outside the city limits and under the jurisdiction of the Mercer County Sheriff's Department. Answers A, B, and C are incorrect because the exact location of the vehicle on Superior Street is not given.

7. **Answer D is correct.** Answer A is incorrect because Jefferson Avenue is a one-way southbound street, therefore Officer Baxter cannot travel north on that street. Answer B is incorrect for the same reasons that A is incorrect. In addition, it isn't necessary for Officer Baxter to travel northbound on Lincoln Avenue because the emergency room entrance is on Maple Street. Answer C is incorrect because despite Officer Baxter traveling west of the one-way street to take a two-way street (Washington Avenue) northbound, it also has him traveling north on Lincoln Avenue from Maple Street when he should have continued traveling east on Maple until he reached the emergency entrance.

8. **Answer A is correct.** Answers B and C are incorrect because the Flagtown Medical Center is located in the city limits and is under the jurisdiction of the Flagtown Police Department. Answer D is incorrect because officers are responding to a fight complaint, not to the traffic accident.

9. **Answer C is correct.** Answer A is incorrect because the vehicle at fault is shown traveling westbound on Commerce Street, and both vehicles struck are shown to have been traveling the wrong way on one-way streets, which would have put those vehicles in violation as well. Answer B is incorrect because the vehicle at fault is shown to have begun travel from a location east of Ash Street instead of west of it, and the accident is shown at the wrong intersection. Answer D is incorrect because the vehicle at fault is shown to have begun travel from a location on Commerce Street that is east of Bay Street instead of west of Ash Street; the intersection of the collision is also incorrect.

10. **Answer A is correct.** Answer B is incorrect because Grant is shown as a street that's south of Unity when it should be north of it. The pedestrians are therefore at the wrong location and the vehicle shown traveling on 5th Street is headed the wrong way for the one-way traffic, which would mean it was at fault as well and did not have the right of way. Answer C is incorrect because the pedestrians and vehicles involved in the accident are shown at the wrong intersections. Answer D is incorrect because the pedestrians are shown at the wrong intersection.

CHAPTER FIVE

# Forms and Reports

## Terms You'll Need to Understand:

✓ Police reports

✓ Evidence inventory and analysis forms

✓ Charging information forms

## Concepts You'll Need to Master:

✓ What's on the test

✓ Filling forms

✓ Extracting information

✓ Forms and police work

One of the most important tasks for a police officer is filling out report forms completely and accurately. In police work, there are forms for everything. The reason forms are so common is because it standardizes the information. It does not matter how experienced or inexperienced you are, forms force you to give certain specific information in a particular way.

Police reports are also in form format. Mostly, there are fill-in-the-blank types with standard fillers given in the legend. You choose the filler based on the type of report you are writing. Traffic tickets, accident reports, property inventory sheets, and vehicle tow are all types of forms. When an offender is arrested and charged with a crime, the charging sheet is also a form with fill-in-the-blank slots where pertinent information to the arrest will be supplied.

Police reports and other departmental forms are used in a variety of ways during a police investigation, and you will examine several of the more important forms in the coming paragraphs. Let's take a look at police reports, evidence inventory and analysis forms, and charging information forms in more depth to increase your understanding of the makeup and importance of these items to police work.

# Police Reports

Police reports are almost always used in court as evidence. These reports are also used by a variety of people within and outside the police department. Detectives use the report to conduct follow-up investigations, whereas criminal analysts use the same report to develop criminal trends. Insurance agencies and investigators also use the same reports to process insurance claims.

We will not dive into examples of how police reports are used within and outside the police departments in this book. This is simple because there are too many to mention here.

# Evidence Inventory and Analysis Forms

Evidence inventory forms are very critical for any type of investigation. Detectives rely on these forms to ensure that everything collected as evidence is processed by the crime lab. Agencies might name the form differently, but the form's purpose is uniform across the organizations. Evidence inventory forms are crucial in case trials and are commonly used by prosecutors, defense attorneys, judges, and juries alike. A single piece of evidence can make or break a case for the police department.

# Charging Information Forms

A charging information form is filled out for every person who is arrested for a crime. This form includes all the elements of crime. For example, if a person is arrested for stealing, a standard charging information form is filled out for the theft charge. The charging information sheet might include information such as date and time of the occurrence, victim, and value of the property taken. Again, just like other areas, this form might differ from organization to organization, but similar forms are used in all law enforcement agencies. Charging information forms are also used in courts across the country by prosecutors, defense attorneys, judges, and juries alike. If the charging information form is not filled out correctly (for example, if the actual charge or the right criminal code is not used), a case might not be tried or upheld in court. For criminal cases, charging information is very important for both the law enforcement agency and the suspect. You don't want to charge a person wrongfully. There could be civil and criminal liabilities in doing so.

If you present the wrong charging information, the district attorney or prosecutor would not file the charges. If you have worked long and hard on a case, all your hard work would go to waste. If the judge found a defendant not guilty of a murder based on an evidence form on which someone checked a wrong check box, it would be devastating. The chances of something like that happening are fairly slim, but the possibility does exist.

> **NOTE**
>
> Correctly filling out forms becomes very important in court because the defense will often try to highlight mistakes to the jury in an attempt to throw doubt on the credibility of officers and witnesses.

> **EXAM ALERT**
>
> The exam instructions, given in the beginning of the form portion of the test, are very important. These instructions are general in nature and apply to questions in the current portion.

# What's on the Police Test?

Now that you have been introduced to some of the more important forms police officers must use correctly, let's examine what you will face on the forms and reports section of the police exam. This portion of the police test will examine your ability to follow simple instructions. This test is not very hard. There is nothing to memorize or understand; it is a matter of following the instructions. All the answers to the questions are right in front of you. It all comes down to your ability to pay attention to the details being presented.

Because the police officer's ability to handle information is critical for job performance, this portion of the test is designed to test that. To evaluate this ability, the test is divided into two types of questions:

**Question type 1**—In this type of question, you will be given a scenario, that includes a variety of information about an incident, in a short story format. You will then need to fill out a blank form utilizing the information given in the scenario and written instruction given before the exam. For example, instructions might say that you are the responding officer for all the following questions. Based on this instruction and the information given in the scenario, you will have to fill out a blank form.

**Question type 2**—In this type of question, you will be given a form with the data already in it. You are to extract the data from the form and answer a series of questions based on the scenario.

Let's look at some scenarios to practice with and get a better understanding of what you will face on exam day.

> **EXAM ALERT**
>
> Always use military time when filling in a police report.

# Question Type 1

The following two scenarios will give you a practice run at question type 1 from the forms and reports section of the police exam. Be sure to read and follow all instructions carefully.

## Officer Arrest Report

The officer enforcing an arrest on a suspect initially completes an arrest form. It is necessary to complete this form to record who made the arrest and who transported the suspect to the jail or hospital. Read the scenario and then follow the instructions provided to complete the form accordingly.

Based on the information given in the scenario and instruction for the form, fill the form given in Figure 5.1. You can use the form as it is in the book or a make a copy for your convenience.

### Scenario 1

On March 15, 2009, at 5:30 P.M., you are dispatched to 3423 W. Lake Street to investigate suspected narcotics activity. As you arrive on the scene, you see a white male standing in the street. You observe the subject from a distance, and see him approach a passing vehicle and exchange something. From your training and experience, you believe this is an indication of a narcotics transaction taking place. Based on some additional evidence, you arrest the subject and transport him to jail.

The following is the personal information and identifiers of the person you stopped and arrested:

Michael D. Smith

White, Male, Date of Birth: 12-29-74

Social Security Number: 311-93-9987

Address: 2348 W. 24th Street, Logansport, IN 46325

Home Phone: 219-345-3487

Work Phone: 229-748-4867

Height: 5 feet, 11 inches

Weight: 185 pounds

Hair: Blond

For officer information, fill in your name, your ID number as 23057, badge number 844.

**Instructions for Officer Arrest Report**

**Arrest Form**

| 1. Arresting Officer | | 2. ID Number | | 3. Badge Number | |
|---|---|---|---|---|---|
| 4. Transporting Officer | | 5. ID Number | | 6. Badge Number | |
| 7. Arrestee | | 8. DOB | 9. Age | | |
| 10. Address | | 11. City | 12. Zip Code | | |
| 17. S.S.N. | | 14. H. Phone | 15. W. Phone | | |
| 16. Height | 17. Weight | 18. Hair | 19. Race | 20. Sex | |

**FIGURE 5.1**   Officer arrest report form.

**Form instructions**

**Space 1.** Fill in the arresting officer's last name, first name, and middle initial.

**Space 2.** Fill in the arresting officer's identification number.

**Space 3.** Fill in arresting officer's badge number.

**Space 4.** Fill in the transporting officer's last name, first name, and middle initial.

**Space 5.** Fill in the transporting officer's identification number.

**Space 6.** Fill in the transporting officer's badge number.

**Space 7.** Fill in the arrested person's last name, first name, and middle initial.

**Space 8.** Fill in the arrested person's date of birth, using the mm/dd/yyyy format.

**Space 9.** Fill in the arrested person's age.

**Space 10.** Fill in the arrested person's address.

**Space 11.** Fill in the arrested person's city.

**Space 12.** Fill in the arrested person's ZIP code.

**Space 13.** Fill in the arrested person's Social Security number, using the XXX-XX-XXXX format.

**Space 14.** Fill in the arrested person's home phone number, area code first using the following format:

(Area Code)-number

**Space 15.** Fill in the arrested person's work phone number, area code first using the following format:

(Area Code)-number

**Space 16.** Fill in the arrested person's height using following format:

Number only. (For example, 5 feet, 10 inches; use 5'10".)

**Space 17.** Fill in the arrested person's weight using the following format:

Numbers only. (For example, 180 pounds; use 180 lbs.)

**Space 18.** Fill in the arrested person's hair type.

**Space 19.** Fill in the arrested person's race using following values:

W for White, B for Black, I for Indian, H for Latino, O for other races.

**Space 20.** Fill in the arrested person's sex using following values:

M for male, F for female.

## Questions

1. Which one of the following dates of birth is correctly listed?

   ○ A. 12/29/74
   ○ B. 29/12/1974
   ○ C. 12/29/1974
   ○ D. 29/12/74

   **Answer C is correct.** Answers A, B, and D are incorrect because dates should be written as xx/xx/xxxx; two numbers for the month, two numbers for the day, and four numbers for the year.

2. Which of the following names is listed correctly?

   ○ A. Smith, Michael D.
   ○ B. Michael D. Smith
   ○ C. D. Smith Michael
   ○ D. Michael, Smith D.

   **Answer A is correct.** Answers B, C, and D are incorrect because the last name should precede the first name and the middle initial.

3. Which of the following heights is listed correctly?

   ○ A. 11 inches, 5 feet
   ○ B. 11" 5'
   ○ C. 5'11"
   ○ D. 5 feet, 11 inches

   **Answer C is correct.** Answers A, B, and D are incorrect because feet are written with numbers, followed by an apostrophe; inches are written with number followed by quotation marks.

4. Which of the times is correctly listed?

   ○ A. 1730 hrs
   ○ B. 5:30 PM
   ○ C. 0530 hrs
   ○ D. 1730 PM

   **Answer A is correct.** Answers B and C are not shown in military time, and answer D indicates PM, which is redundant when using military time.

## Uniform Traffic Ticket

As a police officer, you are required to issue traffic citations for traffic offenses. The citation is written on a standard form provided by the police department to its police officers.

Based on the information given in the scenario and instruction for the form, fill the form given in Figure 5.2. You can use the form as it is the book or a make a copy for your convenience.

## Scenario 2

On May 12, 2009, at 1:30 PM, while on patrol assignment, you observe a 2003 Chevy Tahoe disregard the automatic control signal located at the intersection of 11th Street and N. Keystone. You stop the driver at the intersection of 12th and N. Keystone for this traffic violation. You decide to write a citation for disregard of the traffic signal.

The following is the information and identifiers of the driver you stopped:

David J. Jones

White, Male, Date of Birth: 9-23-80

Social Security Number: 312-66-2241

Address: 1176 W. Main Street, Indianapolis, IN 46222

Home Phone: 317-455-5684

Work Phone: 317-455-5684

Height: 5 feet, 9 inches

Weight: 170 pounds

Hair: Blond

Charge: Failure to stop

Charge type: Infraction

Code: 32-34-6-28

For officer information fill in your name, your ID number is 23068, badge number 488.

### Instructions Uniform Traffic Ticket

**Traffic Ticket**

| | | |
|---|---|---|
| 1. Date | 2. Time | 3. Location |
| 4. Officer | 5. ID Number | 6. Badge Number |
| 7. Assisting Officer | 8. ID Number | 9. Badge Number |
| 10. Driver | 11. DOB | 12. Age |
| 13. Address | 14. City | 15. Zip Code |
| 16. S.S.N. | 17. H. Phone | 18. W. Phone |
| 19. Vehicle Make | 20. Model | 21. Lic. |
| 22. Charge | 23. Traffic Code | |
| 24. Fine | 25. Due Date | |

**FIGURE 5.2**  Uniform traffic ticket form.

**Form Instructions**

**Space 1.** Fill the date of the offense, using the following format: mm/dd/yyyy.

**Space 2.** Fill in time of the offense, in military time format: 1:00 PM = 1300 hrs.

**Space 3.** Fill in the location of the offense. The city is required information. State information is not required.

**Space 4.** Fill in the officer's last name, first name, and middle initial.

**Space 5.** Fill in the officer's identification number.

**Space 6.** Fill in the officer's badge number.

**Space 7.** Fill in the assisting officer's last name, first name, and middle initial.

**Space 8.** Fill in the assisting officer's identification number.

**Space 9.** Fill in the assisting officer's badge number.

**Space 10.** Fill in the driver's last name, first name, and middle initial.

**Space 11.** Fill in the driver's person's date of birth, using the following format: mm/dd/yyyy.

**Space 12.** Fill in the driver's age.

**Space 13.** Fill in the driver's address.

**Space 14.** Fill in the driver's city.

**Space 15.** Fill in the driver's ZIP code.

**Space 16.** Fill in the driver's Social Security number, using following format: XXX-XX-XXXX

**Space 17.** Fill in the driver's home phone number, area code first, using the following format:
(Area Code)-number.

**Space 18.** Fill in the driver's work phone number, area code first, using the following format:
(Area Code)-number.

**Space 19.** Fill in the vehicle make.

**Space 20.** Fill in the vehicle model.

**Space 21.** Fill in the vehicle license number.

**Space 22.** Fill in the charge information.

**Space 23.** Fill in the traffic code including charge type.

Format:

XX-XX-XX-XX NC (NC for infraction)

XX-XX-XX-XX MC (MC for misdemeanor)

**Space 24.** Fill in the fine information.

**Space 25.** Fill in the due date. The due date is 15th day from the offense date.

## Questions

1. Which one of the following social security numbers is properly listed?
   - ○ A. 312-662241
   - ○ B. 31266-2241
   - ○ C. 312-66-2241
   - ○ D. 312662241

   **Answer C is correct.** Answers A, B, and D are incorrect because they either do not have the dashes in the proper place or they are missing the dashes.

2. Which of the following times is correctly listed?
   - ○ A. 1:30 PM
   - ○ B. 1330 hrs.
   - ○ C. 0130 hrs.
   - ○ D. 1330 PM

   **Answer B is correct.** Answers A and C are incorrect because they do not show accurate military time. Answer D is incorrect because it is redundant to say PM with military time.

3. Which one of the following dates of birth is correctly listed?
   - ○ A. 05122009
   - ○ B. 05/12/2009
   - ○ C. 12/2009/05
   - ○ D. 12/05/2009

   **Answer B is correct.** Answers A, C, and D are incorrect. Answer A does not have dashes, answer C is not in the proper order of month/day/year, and answer D has the month and day reversed.

4. Which one of the following is the proper way to fill in the offense code?

- ○ A. 32.34.6.28 NC
- ○ B. 32-34-6-28 MC
- ○ C. 32-34-6-28 NC
- ○ D. 28-6-34-32 NC

**Answer C is correct.** Answer A is incorrect because it uses a period (.) instead of dashes between the numbers. Answer B is incorrect because it has the wrong letter code, and answer D is incorrect because the numbers are in the wrong order.

**EXAM ALERT**

There is no shortcut to these types of questions. You have to look at each blank and the corresponding instructions and then fill in the information. Never ignore the format, and always look and verify. For example, let's say that you just filled in someone's date of birth. On the next blank, you get another date of birth. Look at the instructions again. More than likely, the instructions will be the same as the previous date of birth, but don't take a chance: always verify. It is better to spend that little extra time to look at the instruction again than to answer the question incorrectly.

**NOTE**

Always read the instructions carefully. If need be, reread the instruction and highlight the main points.

# Question Type 2—Extracting Information

Another type of question you might see in the form and report section of the exam tests your ability to extract information from a report form. The following is a sample accident report form that an officer might be required to fill out. Another officer might use this form to extract necessary information about the incident. For instruction purposes, this form is fairly simple. The form in the exam will be fairly complicated.

## Accident Report Scenario 1

You are assigned to investigate a traffic accident by your sergeant. The sergeant gives you a copy of the accident report. Evaluate the accident report form in Figure 5.3 and answer the following questions.

**Accident Report**

| | | |
|---|---|---|
| 1. Investigating Officer *King, R* | 2. ID Number *K-0221* | 3. Badge Number *844* |
| 4. Assisting Officer *Jones, B* | 5. ID Number *J-2231* | 6. Badge Number *932* |

| | | |
|---|---|---|
| Location *1512 E. Lawrence Street* | Date *4-3-04* | Time *4:15 PM* |

| | | |
|---|---|---|
| 7. Driver 1 *Smith, Michael* | 8. DOB *9-22-80* | 9. Age *24* |
| 10. Address *1152 E. 16th Street* | 11. City *Indianapolis* | 12. Zip Code *46256* |
| 13. S.S.N. *314-06-9932* | 14. H. Phone *317-598-2241* | 15. W. Phone *317-632-1991* |
| 15. Vehicle 1 *Green* Striking Vehicle | 17. Make *Toyota* | 18. Model *Corolla* | 19. Lic. *34F7890* |
| 20. Driver 2 *Kennedy, David* | 21. D.O.B. *11-11-79* | 22. Age *25* |
| 23. Address *6332 W. Horseshoe Ln* | 24. City *Indianapolis* | 25. Zip Code *46232* |
| 27. S.S.N. *312-86-2219* | 28. H. Phone *317-635-7381* | 29. W. Phone *317-925-6619* |
| 10 Vehicle *Red* | 17. Make *Jeep* | 18. Model *Wrangler* | 19. Lic. *63A5253* |

**FIGURE 5.3**   Accident report scenario form.

## Questions

1. What is the location where this accident occurred?
   - ○  A.  1512 E. Lawrence Street
   - ○  B.  1215 E. Lawrence Street
   - ○  C.  1512 W. Lawrence Street
   - ○  D.  1512 S. Lawrence Street

   **Answer A is correct.** Answers A, B, and D are incorrect because the numbers are in the wrong order and/or the direction of the street is wrong (W or S instead of E).

2. What time did this accident occur?
   - ○  A.  4:15 AM
   - ○  B.  1615 PM
   - ○  C.  4:15 PM
   - ○  D.  2:15 AM

   **Answer C is correct.** Answers A, B, and D are incorrect because they simply do not match the time noted in the description.

3. Who was the assisting officer?
   - ○  A.  Officer Smith
   - ○  B.  Officer Jones
   - ○  C.  Officer Sickels
   - ○  D.  Officer George

   **Answer B is correct.** Answers A, C, and D are incorrect. The assisting officer is Officer Jones; check the report again carefully.

4. What is the make, model and license number of the striking vehicle?

- ○ A. Buick, Skylark, 48Y3423
- ○ B. Honda, Accord, 68T2957
- ○ C. Olds, Delta 88, 49Y3478
- ○ D. Toyota, Corolla, 34F7890

**Answer D is correct.** Answers A, B, and C are incorrect. The striking vehicle is the Toyota Corolla, 34F7890. Check the report again carefully.

## Accident Report Scenario 2

Just as you did in scenario 1 and Figure 5.3, use Figure 5.4 to answer the following questions.

**Accident Report**

| | | |
|---|---|---|
| 1. Investigating Officer *Smith, D* | 2. ID Number *5-2241* | 3. Badge Number *2367* |
| 4. Assisting Officer *Gannon, D* | 5. ID Number *6-3546* | 6. Badge Number *914* |

| | | |
|---|---|---|
| Location *5600 N. Washington Blvd.* | Date *9-1-2003* | Time *7:00 PM* |

| | | |
|---|---|---|
| 7. Driver 1 *Major, John* | 8. DOB *4-4-62* | 9. Age *42* |
| 10. Address *2345 W. Michigan Street* | 11. City *Indianapolis* | 12. Zip Code *46222* |
| 13. S.S.N. *216-09-2114* | 14. H. Phone *317-623-7741* | 15. W. Phone *317-925-1732* |
| 15. Vehicle 1 *Black*     17. Make *Olds*   Striking Vehicle | 18. Model *Delta 88* | 19. Lic. *32J6623* |
| 20. Driver 2   *Rogers, Anthony* | 21. D.O.B. *6-3-70* | 22. Age *34* |
| 23. Address *9935 Six Point Road* | 24. City *Plainfield* | 25. Zip Code *46237* |
| 27. S.S.N. *346-28-9876* | 28. H. Phone *317-839-9913* | 29. W. Phone *317-235-1125* |
| 10 Vehicle *Blue*     17. Make *Honda* | 18. Model *Accord* | 19. Lic. *68T2957* |

**FIGURE 5.4**   Accident report scenario form.

### Questions

1. What is address of driver number 1?

- ○ A. 2345 W. Michigan Street
- ○ B. 2345 E. Michigan Street
- ○ C. 1983 W. Oliver Street
- ○ D. 3567 W. Lawrence

**Answer A is correct.** Answers B, C, and D are incorrect. Be sure you carefully read addresses denoting street direction and number order. It can make a big difference if you misread the direction and go to E. Michigan when you should be on W. Michigan.

2. What is the make, model and license number of vehicle number 2?

   ○ A. Toyota, Corolla, 34F7890
   ○ B. Olds, Delta 88, 49Y3478
   ○ C. Buick, Skylark, 48Y3423
   ○ D. Honda, Accord, 68T2957

   **Answer D is correct.** Answers A, B, and C are incorrect. Be sure to read the report carefully for the correct automobile information. License numbers are very easy to misread.

3. What is the Social Security number of driver number 2?

   ○ A. 346-28-9876
   ○ B. 236-86-2563
   ○ C. 436-28-9872
   ○ D. 347-98-0023

   **Answer A is correct.** Answers B, C, and D are incorrect. The other answers do not have the numbers in the correct order.

4. What is the badge number of the investigating officer?

   ○ A. 844
   ○ B. 2367
   ○ C. 4378
   ○ D. 3467

   **Answer B is correct.** Answers A, C, and D are incorrect. Read the report carefully; again, it is important to examine numbers on reports to avoid mistakes.

**EXAM ALERT**

Again, as in the previous section, there is no shortcut to answering these types of questions. But one test-taking approach that has been found to be successful is to read the question first before looking at the form. By looking at the questions first, you will have some idea of the type of information you are looking for when you do look at the form or report provided. If the examiner allows it, you should also highlight the key pieces of information based on what you read in the questions.

# Exam Prep Questions

1. Choose the correct answer from the following choices:
   - ○ A. Detectives use the report to conduct follow-up investigation, and criminal analysts use the same report to develop criminal trends.
   - ○ B. Police reports are almost always used in court as evidence.
   - ○ C. Both of the above.
   - ○ D. None of the above.

2. Evidence inventory forms are used by which of the following:
   - ○ A. Detectives
   - ○ B. Prosecutors in case trials
   - ○ C. Defense attorney(s) in case trials
   - ○ D. All of the above

3. Charging information is filled in on a police report to record specific information. Which of the following items is most likely to appear on a police report?
   - ○ A. The officer or officers who placed the suspect under arrest
   - ○ B. The name of the offense or the criminal code for the crime for which the suspect is being charged
   - ○ C. The date and time when the crime took place
   - ○ D. The date and time when the crime was reported

4. Police forms are an important part of police work for a number of reasons. Based on the information given in this chapter, choose all of the reasons that are correct.
   - ○ A. They standardize information
   - ○ B. They provide a way to record specific information in a particular way
   - ○ C. They are used in a variety of ways during a police investigation
   - ○ D. All of the above

5. Which of the statements that follow is incorrect regarding who makes use of police forms?
   - ○ A. Only police department personnel
   - ○ B. Insurance agencies and insurance claims investigators
   - ○ C. Courts
   - ○ D. Criminal analysts

6. Which is the correct way to record time on a police report?
   - ○ A. 2:30 p.m.
   - ○ B. 02:30 p.m.
   - ○ C. 1400
   - ○ D. 1400 hours

7. According to the chapter narrative, the arrested party's name is recorded in a specific format. Choose the correct one from the choices that follow.

   ○ A. First name, middle initial, and last name

   ○ B. Last name, first name, and middle initial

   ○ C. Last name, first name, and Social Security number

   ○ D. Last name, first name, and prisoner number

# Exam Prep Answers

Question 1: **Answer C is correct.** Reports are used for both follow-up investigations and as evidence in court, which makes it very important to complete the reports accurately and clearly.

Question 2: **Answer D is correct.** Evidence forms are used by all of these people during court trials; therefore, it is very important to complete the forms accurately and clearly.

Question 3: **Answer B is correct.** According to the narrative, the charging form is used to record *the actual charge or the right criminal code*.

Question 4: **Answer D is correct.** According to the narrative, answers A, B, and C are all reasons why police departments use forms to record information.

Question 5: **Answer A is incorrect and therefore the correct choice**. According to the narrative, police forms are used by all those listed in B, C, and D.

Question 6: **Answer C is correct.** Time is always recorded as military time. Answer D is incorrect because it isn't necessary to add *hours* because that is already shown or assumed on the form.

Question 7: **Answer B is correct.** Name information should be recorded in "last name, first name, and middle initial" format. Social Security number, prisoner number, or other identifying information is recorded in sections provided for such information, not in the Name section of the form.

CHAPTER SIX

# Writing Skills

---

## Terms You'll Need to Understand:

✓ Subject

✓ Verb

✓ Proper spelling

✓ Punctuation

✓ Vocabulary

---

## Concepts You'll Need to Master:

✓ Subject-verb agreement

✓ Tense consistency

✓ Sentence structure

✓ Using writing in police work

In this chapter, you will become familiar with some important aspects of the type of writing that is required in police work. That will be followed by the skills required in the written exam.

# Importance of Writing Skills in Police Work

Not everyone is born a writer. Writing is a skill mostly learned and developed over a period of time. As a police officer, you won't be expected to create a piece of literature, but you will definitely need to be able to write effectively.

The aim of your writing should not be to influence others, but to record and report. The required written communication will mainly be reports, inter-departmental memos, emails, and field investigation reports. These might sound easy to write, but composing even the simplest two-line memo can sometimes take some thinking if you're not used to writing. Most people prefer to give verbal reports rather than to sit and begin the mundane task of writing. Unfortunately for those who don't care for writing, it is a must-do in police work. Later, I list some factors that affect the quality of report writing and other general forms of writing used in police work.

You have seen some examples of incident reports in previous chapters. These are mainly factual accounts of an event and give very little personal style or flair options to the writer. While writing descriptive accounts of an incident or writing your field investigation notes, there are some important factors to keep in mind. Here are some helpful tips:

- ▶ Stick to facts
- ▶ Express yourself clearly
- ▶ Keep it simple
- ▶ Always proofread

You will investigate each of these factors in more detail in the following sections.

**CAUTION**

When you're new to police work, people do not know you or your name. Therefore, the only thing that sergeants, detectives, district attorneys, judges, and others have to judge you by is your writing ability. You can be the greatest police officer in the world, but if you can't write well, your usefulness to the department and any ongoing investigations that you are involved with is severely limited. Your ability to write clearly and effectively will help you immensely.

# Stick to Facts

While giving an account, try to keep it focused and objective. If you begin giving your personal opinion, you might stray from your focus and record an inaccurate report. You must write what happened in the correct sequence. Doing so will make recall easier for your reference at a later time. The easiest way to do this is to jot down the main facts and some information that might be crucial to the situation. Use your judgment to recognize even the most minor details as important for recording. At a later time, write the report based on those notes. Do not attempt to write the final report while taking notes. Much depends on the incident description by the police officer before it is handed over to other authorities for action, because your ability to keep the report factual and clear is imperative.

# Express Yourself Clearly

Clarity plays a key role in report writing, as in all forms of written communication. If sentences are vague and shrouded with irrelevant words, readers are unable to understand what is actually being said.

Decide what to include in the report and construct sentences that are simple and coherent. It is better not to write long, winding sentences. By the time the reader reaches the end, he might forget what was said in the beginning!

Jumbled-up sentences could also confuse the reader. It is always useful to reread your report after some time, as if you were reading it for the first time. Often, you will immediately be able to recognize the sections that lack clarity. It is usually better to restructure the complete sentence rather than to add a word or two to make it sound better.

# Keep It Simple!

Don't make your reports too wordy or use complex words. The effectiveness of your description largely depends on your choice of words. If you initially write a three- to four-syllable word, immediately consider whether a simpler word could substitute for it. Sometimes a single word explains a two-line phrase or sentence.

**TIP**

Add variety to your work by not using the same words frequently.

Keeping the language simple does not mean that you will use only simple words in your writing. Certain technical words, such as *dispatched*, *run*, *backup*, and *apprehension*, are a basic requirement of any police incident or investigative report. It will hardly serve your purpose if you write *catch* for *apprehend* or *get* for *recovered*. Use the technical words well, so that they match the flow and do not stick out.

## Always Proofread

Whether you're writing a report, a memo, or an email, it is always important that you proofread what you have written. Incorrectly spelled words and careless errors are signs of hasty work, and in police work you have to remain careful about what you write.

A piece of advice: No matter what you write, keep your goal in mind so that you know why you began writing in the first place. In other words, do not steer away from the topic.

**NOTE**

As you proofread, make sure that everything you've written is in chronological order. Remember, it is critical to list events in the order they happened from beginning to end.

# Grammar Basics

The basic rules of grammar are wide and varied and can be learned only with years of academic study and application. It would be misleading to give you a simple picture and say, "Here are the rules and examples. Learn them and you'll get all answers correct in the exam!"

In this context, I can only attempt to guide you in the simplest way on the types of questions and grammatical concepts you might encounter on the exam. Be sure to consult a grammar guide if you are unsure of your grammar abilities. You will, of course, see the sample questions in this book and they will give you an idea about the grammatical principles you might see on the exam.

The police officer exam assesses grammar proficiency. Understanding the following topics will help you with your grammar task on the exam:

- Subject-verb agreement
- Tense consistency
- Sentence structure

- ▶ Apostrophes
- ▶ Sentence fragments
- ▶ Double negatives
- ▶ Punctuation
- ▶ Vocabulary and spelling

Let's investigate these areas in more depth. The following sections will give you an idea of what you need to know for the exam.

# Subject-Verb Agreement

Your subjects and verbs should agree in number. Plural subjects require plural verbs and singular subjects require singular verbs. That is the simple principle behind subject-verb agreement. The following sentences give you examples of subject-verb agreement.

> Singular subject: "The man running down the road was being followed by a blue van."

> Plural subject: "The men running down the road were being followed by a blue van."

For the singular subject *man*, the singular verb *was* is used. For the plural subject *men*, the plural verb *were* is used.

Certain words, such as *everyone, everybody, someone, somebody, no one,* and *nobody,* sound plural but they are always singular and take a singular verb. The same is true for *either* and *neither*. The following is an example using the word everyone:

> Everyone included in the volunteer force is determined to be an active part of the effort.

Although the word "everyone" may sound plural here, it is used as singular and will need a singular verb "is."

# Tense Consistency

Maintaining the correct tense is often a difficult exercise. If you're writing in the present tense, don't shift to the past tense unless there is a reason to do so. There should be consistency of tenses, not only in a single sentence, but also in the body of work being presented. The following two sentences demonstrate this concept:

(Inconsistent) I took a deep breath and opened the door; there stands a tired, old man.

(Consistent) I took a deep breath and opened the door; there stood a tired, old man.

Notice the verb *took* is in past tense and *stands* is in the present tense in the first sentence. This is why it is inconsistent. In the second sentence, both verbs used are in the past tense, which makes it consistent.

# Sentence Structure

While writing a sentence, make sure that the structure is strong. Understand that the length of a sentence has nothing to do with correct structure. Be able to understand the varieties of sentence structures. You can begin your sentence with an adverb clause followed by a simple sentence. You also can use compound sentences with semicolons, but do not use commas to join two independent clauses. Either add a semicolon or use words like *but* and *and* with a comma to offset the independent clauses. It is always better to separate the clauses into two different sentences. The following sentences are examples:

(Incorrect) Some parents think it is important for them to stay up all night with an infant, they are probably wrong.

(Correct) Some parents think it is important for them to stay up all night with an infant. They are probably wrong.

The two independent clauses in the first sentence cannot be joined by using a comma. They should either be separated by a semicolon or made into independent sentences, as in the second example.

# Apostrophes

Apostrophes are mainly used to indicate possession for nouns and contracted verbs. In general, they are not used to indicate plurals.

Apostrophe errors are made when an apostrophe is added to a plural; for example, "The car's collided as one skidded on the icy road." It is incorrect to place an apostrophe on the plural *cars* because the way it is written in the example shows possession. The cars that are colliding do not possess anything in this example.

Indicating possession for singular nouns is simple enough when used as *Pat's belt* or *the cat's whiskers*. It becomes confusing when indicating possession for plural nouns. For this, remember a simple rule: Place the apostrophe before the "s" when indicating possession for a singular noun and place the apostrophe after the "s" when indicating possession for a plural noun. Note the following examples:

> One student: "The student's plans for a hike were ruined because of bad weather."

> More than one student: "The students' plans for a hike were ruined because of bad weather."

Notice the apostrophe placed for a single student is before the "s" and the one placed for more than one student is placed after the "s."

Apostrophes are often misused for personal pronouns such as *its*, *your*, *their*, and *whose*. They are mistaken for contractions such as *it's* (it is), *who's* (who is), *you're* (you are) and *they're* (they are). The following two sentences give you examples of incorrect and correct apostrophe usage:

> Incorrect "In this situation, its difficult to conclude who's rights their violating."

> Correct "In this situation, it's difficult to conclude whose rights they're violating."

Note in the incorrect example that *its* is without an apostrophe although it's a contraction of *it is*. The contracted word *who's* is used incorrectly. The word *their* is used incorrectly instead of the contraction *they're* or the words *they are*.

Using apostrophes is tricky at most times. Remember not to use them for indicating plurals. Remember the rules for indicating possession for singular and plural nouns. Most importantly, remember that when you're using an apostrophe in a contraction, you're putting in two words, not one.

# Sentence Fragments

Sentence fragments generally occur when an incomplete sentence is written. To avoid making this error, make sure that each word group you write is grammatically complete and makes sense as an independent thought. For example: "Frequent robberies have been reported in the last one week in that area." "Although it is considered a low crime district." Here the second group of words is a fragment because it can't stand alone as an independent sentence. You can easily correct it by joining it to the first sentence by adding a comma as in the following example: "Frequent robberies have been reported for the last one week in that area, although it is considered a low crime district."

Sentence fragments often occur when a subject or a verb is missing. For example, "Came home from work" does not have a subject. By adding I or any other subject, the fragment becomes a complete sentence. Similarly, "I looked out the window. A car on the road," does not have a verb in the second group of words. It can be made into a sentence from a fragment by adding a verb such as "A car was on the road."

Another type of sentence fragment occurs in sentences that have a verb and a subject, but use a prepositional phrase as a sentence. For example, "When I came home from work," is a sentence fragment. To correct it, add another group of words that make sense if read independently; for example, "When I came home from work, I parked the car in the garage."

When writing a sentence, make sure that it has the necessary elements to make it complete and conveys the meaning as an independent thought.

# Double Negatives

It is not always wrong to use double negatives, but if you want to be clear about what you're writing, stick to one negative per sentence. Using a sentence such as "It was not an unclear account of the incident" is grammatically correct. It is simpler to write "It was a clear account of the incident."

When you use double negatives in a simple sentence such as "He doesn't know nothing about the robbery," you are probably easily understood but grammatically incorrect.

# Punctuation

Even while writing in simple language, the effectiveness of your work could be determined by the type of punctuation you use. Even a well-written piece of work seems absurd with faulty or no punctuation at all.

A few of the most important parts of punctuation are the use of commas, semicolons, dashes, exclamation marks, and question marks. The following list gives you some more information on these punctuation elements:

- ▶ You may use a comma for sentences that have two different meanings and by adding a comma, convey the intended meaning.

- ▶ The dash has a number of meanings. It shows the word that needs to stand out in the sentence or can be used when the sentence shifts abruptly.

- ▶ It is advisable to use exclamation marks sparingly as they generally portray emotion in the form of surprise, fear, or other similar emotions.

- Semicolons are used when there are two clauses in a sentence and the writer does not want to make it formal by dividing the single sentence into two sentences.

- Be careful about the use of question marks; although they seem the easiest punctuation to use, many people mistake statements for questions.

- When you place a question mark make sure that the sentence is actually interrogative. Sometimes, a question mark is mistakenly placed at the end of a sentence that sounds interrogative.

**NOTE**

Too many punctuation marks distract the reader and change the meaning of a sentence.

# Vocabulary and Spelling

There is no easy rule to follow to improve your vocabulary and spelling. But these are two of the most important areas that will be part of your exam. Here are some useful tips:

- Write down new words carefully

- Repeat proper pronunciation

- Visualize syllable division

- Clarify commonly confused words

The following sections provide more detail concerning these vocabulary and spelling tips.

## Write Down New Words Carefully

One of the ways in which you can improve your spelling and vocabulary is to write down any new word you encounter and repeat it a few times. Review the word at a later stage and make sure that you understand its meaning.

## Repeat Proper Pronunciation

When using a new word, make sure that you know the correct pronunciation and repeat it out loud. When it is time for you to recall this word, the correct pronunciation will immediately lead you toward the correct spelling.

## Visualize Syllable Division

It is always wise to recognize a word's syllable division. Children use this strategy, but that does not mean you cannot use it too! It is a very simple and effective method of learning to spell correctly.

When you improve your spelling, your vocabulary will automatically improve and vice versa. The trick is to learn the meaning of the new words. Of course, the best way to improve your spelling and vocabulary is to read extensively.

## Commonly Confused Words

Many words have similar meanings that can cause confusion. As part of your exam, you will be also be given questions that test your knowledge of similar-sounding words in the form of multiple-choice or fill-in-the-blank questions.

Example:

Sex offenders need to be <u>superviced</u> closely. How should the underlined word be spelled?

**A.** Supervised

**B.** Supervized

**C.** Suppervizzed

**D.** No change is required

Another type of question regarding commonly confused words might involve filling in the blanks. The following are examples of this type of question:

Sex offenders need to be _____ closely. How should the underlined word be spelled?

**A.** Supervised

**B.** Supervized

**C.** Suppervizzed

**D.** No change is required

It was my duty to _____ my boss of the day's happenings.

Choose the correct word:

**A.** Appraise

**B.** Apprise

The correct word is *apprise* because it means to inform. *Appraise* is incorrect because it means to assess.

Under those _____ circumstances, he had no option but to surrender.

Choose the correct word:

**A.** Adverse

**B.** Averse

*Adverse* is the correct answer here as it means *unfavorable* or *bad*. *Averse* is the incorrect answer because it means to have a *strong dislike to something*.

Some words sound similar but have different meanings. These are most commonly confused. Here are some examples.

The _____ is a suitable place to construct a building.

Choose the correct word:

**A.** Cite

**B.** Site

*Site* is correct because it means a *place or location*. *Cite* is incorrect because it means *to mention or call attention to*.

All bones of his extremities were fractured _____ the left femur.

Choose the correct word:

**A.** Except

**B.** Accept

*Except* is correct because it means *to exclude*. *Accept* is incorrect because it means *to take willingly*.

The following are some examples of words that are commonly confused due to similar pronunciations, definitions, or both:

▶ Accede/exceed

▶ Accept/except

▶ Advice/advise

▶ Actual fact/actually

▶ Alternate/alternative

▶ Appraise/apprise

- ▸ Cite/site
- ▸ Core/corps
- ▸ Dilemma/difficulty
- ▸ Incidences/incident
- ▸ Impertinent/irrelevant
- ▸ Interment/internment
- ▸ Ravaging/ravishing

**EXAM ALERT**

It is not necessary to spend hours cramming for the written exam, but you should practice and refine the skills mentioned in this chapter. Go through the sample questions provided. You'll develop confidence in your abilities when you are able to give the correct answers.

## Spelling Guide

For your convenience, a reference list of words common on various police officer exams is provided in Table 6.1. This does not preclude the possibility of seeing other words or variations of the same word. You can use this table to learn how to spell many of the words you'll use everyday as a police officer. Learn to understand the meaning and use them in context. Writing the words down with their meaning would be helpful. Test yourself by spelling the words out loud accurately.

**Table 6.1    A List of More Than 200 Words That Relate to Law Enforcement**

| | | |
|---|---|---|
| Abandoned | Banishment | Jurisdiction |
| Abandonment | Battery | Jury trial |
| Abate | Bench warrant | Justice model |
| Abatement | Bindle | Kidnap |
| Abduct | Biohazard | Larceny |
| Absconder | Biological | License |
| Abstract of trust | Boundaries | Looting |
| Abut | Burglary | Memorandum |
| Accessory | Business | Minor |
| Accomplice | Capital punishment | Miranda |
| Accord | Case file | Misdemeanor |
| Accordance | Case identifiers | Mitigating circumstances |
| Accurate | Chain of custody | Monitor |

(continued)

**Table 6.1    A List of More Than 200 Words That Relate to Law Enforcement *(continued)***

| | | |
|---|---|---|
| Acknowledgment | Change of venue | Multiple scenes |
| Acquittal | Charge | Narc |
| Action | Circumstances | Notified |
| Actual damages | Circumstantial evidence | Notify |
| Addendum | Citation | Nuisance |
| Adjudication | Citizen's arrest | Occurrence |
| Administration | Civil law | Origin |
| Administrator | Claims | Original |
| Admissible evidence | Classify | Outnumbered |
| Admission | Collision | Paraphernalia |
| Adopt | Community policing | Parole |
| Adoption | Comparison samples | Perpetrators |
| Adult | Competitive | Personnel |
| Adultery | Complaint | Physical force |
| Advance | Concurrent sentence | Pleonasm |
| Adverse | Consistent | Possessed |
| Advocate | Constitute | Possession |
| Affiant | Contamination | Preliminary |
| Affirmative | Controlled | Premise |
| Agent | Conviction | Presumptive test |
| Aggravated | Copyright | Prevention |
| Aggravating | Counter-violence | Probable cause |
| Agreement | Criminal | Probation |
| Alcohol | Criteria | Procedure |
| Alias | Death penalty | Processed |
| Alien | Deferred adjudication | Profiling |
| Alimony | Designated | Progress |
| Allegation | Determination | Projectile trajectory analysis |
| Alter ego | Direct evidence | Property |
| Alternate | Directive | Prosecution |
| Alternative | Disability | Protection |
| Ambiguity | Dispatcher | Racial |
| Amendment | Dispute | Reasonable |
| Analyze | Domestic violence | Reasonable force |
| Annual | Double jeopardy | Recidivism |

*(continued)*

**Table 6.1    A List of More Than 200 Words That Relate to Law Enforcement *(continued)***

| | | |
|---|---|---|
| Annuity | Dying declaration | Recovered |
| Annulment | Elements | Recurring |
| Answer | Employment | Redundancy |
| Anticipation | Enforcement | Referral |
| Antiques | Escalating | Regulations |
| Appeal | Espionage | Reportable |
| Appellant | Ethnicity | Resolution |
| Appellate | Executive clemency | Responds |
| Appraisal | Exigent circumstances | Retrieve |
| Appreciation | Felony | Review |
| Apprehend | Firearm | Search warrant |
| Apprised | Forensic | Shoplifting |
| Appropriate | Forgery | Stabilize |
| Arbitration | Good faith exception | Stalling |
| Arbitrator | Grand larceny | Status |
| Argument | Grievance | Submit |
| Arraignment | Harassment | Substances |
| Arrearages | Harmony | Substituted |
| Arrest | Hate crime | Supervisor |
| Arrest warrant | Hate-motivated | Terminate |
| Assault | Hazardous | Threaten |
| Asset | Hearing | Trace evidence |
| Assignee | Hostile | Trauma |
| Assignment | Identify | Uniform Crime Reports |
| Assist | Index offenses | Unlawful |
| Association | Initial appearance | Vandalism |
| Asylum | Initiate | Vehicle |
| Attestation | Injunction | Victim |
| Attractive | Injured | Violation |
| Authenticate | Institution | Violence |
| Autopsy | Insurance | Warrant |
| Avails | Intermediate | Weapon |
| Avowal | Intervene | Witness |
| Award | Intimidation | Workplace |
| Bail | Investigator | Wreck |
| Ballistics | Judgment | Writ |

# Exam Prep Questions

1. Which of the following is the purpose of police writing?
   - O   A.   Influence others
   - O   B.   Record and report
   - O   C.   Both of the above
   - O   D.   None of the above

2. A police report should
   - O   A.   Not include the reporting officer's opinions
   - O   B.   Remain focused and objective
   - O   C.   Record the information in its proper sequence
   - O   D.   All of the above

3. When writing a police report, you should
   - O   A.   Choose simple, yet appropriate, words
   - O   B.   Avoid technical terms
   - O   C.   Elaborate and go into as much detail as possible
   - O   D.   Include your supervisor's opinions about what occurred

4. Choose the sentence with the incorrect subject-verb agreement.
   - O   A.   The leaders of several unions are all planning to attend arbitration.
   - O   B.   The president of several local service organizations are interested in helping with the FOP's latest fundraiser.
   - O   C.   Each of the suspects has been convicted of at least one previous crime.
   - O   D.   The members of the police union were happy they'd reached an agreement with the city.

5. Choose the sentence with the correct consistent tense.
   - O   A.   Officer Miller arrested the suspect and reads him his Miranda Warning.
   - O   B.   Officer Miller observes a male subject steal a purse and arrested him on the spot.
   - O   C.   Officer Miller called the vehicle license plate number into dispatch and then proceeded to stop the vehicle.
   - O   D.   Officer Miller attended roll call and then goes to work his shift.

6. Choose the sentence with the best structure.
- ○ A. Officer Maxwell checked the report; all appeared to be okay.
- ○ B. Officer Maxwell pursued the suspect and he used red lights and siren.
- ○ C. Officer Maxwell wrote his report about the event and then he turned it into his supervisor and then he went back out on patrol.
- ○ D. Officer Maxwell stopped the speeding vehicle and then gave the driver a field sobriety test; he then arrested the driver for driving while under the influence and he called a tow truck to impound the driver's vehicle and took the driver to take a field sobriety test.

7. Choose the sentence with the proper punctuation.
- ○ A. What was the suspect wearing.
- ○ B. How; he wondered, did that guy ever think he could pull that off?
- ○ C. The robber got away with cash; cigarettes, and dental floss.
- ○ D. How many were arrested?

For questions 8–10, choose the correct word that should be inserted into the sentence.

8. Officer Meyers lost _____ of the vehicle.
- ○ A. site
- ○ B. cite
- ○ C. sight
- ○ D. ceit

9. Because of the driver's erratic driving, Officer Blair decided to _____ him for reckless operation.
- ○ A. site
- ○ B. cite
- ○ C. sight
- ○ D. ceit

10. Officer Crawford responded to the _____ of the accident.
- ○ A. site
- ○ B. cite
- ○ C. sight
- ○ D. ceit

# Exam Prep Answers

1. **Answer B is correct.** According to information in this chapter, the aim of your writing should be to record and report. Your required written communication will mainly be writing reports, interdepartmental memos, emails, and field investigation reports. Therefore, answers A, C, and D are incorrect.

2. **Answer D is correct.** Rather than focusing on the reporting officer's opinions about an event, a police report should be a record of the information. The report should be written in such a way that it maintains the chronological and proper sequence of events. Therefore, answers A, B, and C are correct, which makes answer D the correct answer for this question.

3. **Answer A is correct.** Answer A is correct because your police report should be an accurate, concise portrayal of what occurred. This type of report often requires that you use technical terms or police jargon, which makes answer B incorrect. Answer C is incorrect because a concise report is better than a wordy one. Answer D is incorrect because a police report is simply a record of the facts surrounding an event as you experienced them, and not your opinions or anyone else's opinions.

4. **Answer B is correct.** The question says to choose the incorrect sentence. Because in the singular subject (*president*) and plural verb (*are*) do not agree, answer B is incorrect. In answer A, the plural subject (*leaders*) and verb (*are*) agree. In answer C, the singular subject (*each*) agrees with the singular verb (has). In answer D, the plural subject (*members*) agrees with the verb (were).

5. **Answer C is correct.** The tenses of the verbs don't agree in answer A (*arrested, reads*), answer B (*observes, arrested*), and answer D (*attended, goes*).

6. **Answer A is correct.** Answers B, C, and D are run-on sentences.

7. **Answer D is correct.** Answer D ends with the proper punctuation: a question mark. Answer A incorrectly ends with a period. Answers B and C should have been punctuated with commas instead of semicolons.

8. **Answer C is correct.** *Sight* is the act of seeing (something) and is the proper word for the sentence.

9. **Answer B is correct.** To *cite* in this context means to issue a summons to court, and is the correct word for the sentence.

10. **Answer A is correct.** *Site* in this context means the setting or location for something, and is the correct word for the sentence.

# PART II
## Oral Interview

CHAPTER SEVEN

# Oral Interview

## Terms You'll Need to Understand:

✓ Structured oral interview

✓ Individual interview

✓ Thank you letter

## Concepts You'll Need to Master:

✓ Inventory of personal and professional accomplishments

✓ Resume

✓ Two-minute introduction

✓ Five-minute introduction

The oral interview is one of the most important sections you will face in your journey to becoming a police officer. An oral interview provides you a chance to show your would-be supervisors and peer officers that you have what it takes to become a police officer. As with other exam sections we have covered, the oral interview might vary between agencies.

An oral interview can take different approaches, but before we get into the details of these approaches, let's take a quick overview. While in the oral interview phase, you could face a structured interview in which you face a panel of supervisors and fellow officers and respond to a battery of questions. Or, if you apply to a smaller agency, you might be talking to the chief of police one-on-one. Either way, this is your opportunity to present yourself as the person the agency would want to hire as a police officer.

In this chapter, you will be introduced to each of these interview types. Later in the chapter, you will learn how to score the maximum amount of points on your interview(s).

# Preparation Before the Oral Interview

Before we get into the details of an oral interview, let's look at some of the things that you should do before you go. These activities will help you organize the critical information that you are likely to discuss during the oral interview.

## Create an Inventory of Personal and Professional Accomplishments

The first thing to do before you sit for an oral interview is to take a personal inventory. This inventory should list the things that you have accomplished in your life, and include when you accomplished them. This only needs to be a simple list and is for your benefit during the interview. This list will serve two purposes. First, it will help you prepare your resume. Second, it will arm you with material to answer questions about your accomplishments during your oral interview. All your accomplishments are important, but concentrate your efforts in gathering points for the following categories:

- ▶ Goal setting
- ▶ Problem solving
- ▶ Leadership

- ▶ Counseling

- ▶ Working well with others

- ▶ Imagination

- ▶ Innovation

- ▶ Communication skills

When gathering this information, be sure to include the dates and examples of your experience

Prepare a list of special skills you possess or languages you speak. Computer skills are most in demand. Even though you are seeking a position as a police officer, remember that computer-literate police officers are in high demand. Furthermore, almost all police departments have advanced technology. All criminal and driving records are kept in some type of computer system. All calls for help and police dispatches are logged in big data warehouses for analysis and criminal trends.

# Resume

A *resume* is basically a document that lists your significant accomplishments in a neat and orderly fashion. It is important to note that when an interview board member or human resource manager is reading your resume, you will have a very limited time to get his attention. That is why your resume should be strong and able to get the reader's attention.

A strong resume needs a solid foundation. If you lie in your resume, sooner or later the truth will be discovered. When preparing your resume, customize it according to the job you are applying for. That means your resume for a smaller agency would be a little different than if you were applying for a large metropolitan police department. Even though the form of the resume can be different, certain information is standard regardless of where you are applying. The following list describes the standard information that all resumes require:

- ▶ **Contact information**—Provide your contact information at the top of the resume. Include your full name, mailing address, phone number, and email address. Use a large, easy-to-read font.

- ▶ **Goal**—The goal section gives the human resources department or the interviewer immediate information of who you are and what you're looking for without reading through the entire resume.

► **Employment experience**—List your experience chronologically with your most recent job first. Always provide complete information, including company name, location, and dates of employment. While listing your important responsibilities, add a brief description of your accomplishments.

► **Educational accomplishments**—List your most recent degree first and work backward. Even if you did not finish an advanced degree, list the course work you completed as additional courses taken toward the degree you are seeking. Include your major, minor, location of school, and date of attendance.

► **Technical education and experience**—In this category, add any law–enforcement-related experience or other skills of interest. More and more, smaller police agencies are seeking candidates who are technically advanced because police departments, themselves, have advanced with technology. If you hold computer or technical skills or certifications, this is a good place to add them.

► **References**—You can list some references here or write *Available upon request*. Human resources departments assume that you will provide references upon completion of the employment application or during background investigation.

**NOTE**

If you are applying for a position at smaller agencies, it might be of interest to them if you have already completed your law enforcement training. Be sure to provide this information, including dates and location of attendance.

## Finishing Touches

Now that you have uncovered some of the more critical items you should include on your resume, let's cover some final items that are important to remember with your resume:

► Create several versions of your resume, each tailored to a specific police agency.

► Research the position and the police department that you are applying to, and highlight your qualifications according to the needs of that agency.

► Be concise. Stick to one page, if possible. Make sure that every word is meaningful.

► Choose fonts that are easy-to-read, clean, and consistent. Don't use nontraditional or overly creative fonts.

▶ Read, edit, and reread your resume to make sure that it's well written and free of typos. Ask a family member or friend who is knowledgeable in grammar and syntax to look over your resume.

▶ With some careful self-evaluation, thoughtful organization, and smart choice of words, your resume will rise to the top of the human resources department's files.

# Preparing a Two-Minute and Five-Minute Introduction

It is common practice during an interview for a candidate to be asked to tell the board a little about himself. You might say, "That's not hard at all." But it is harder than you think. Often, when you do not expect a question like this, you can be caught off-guard. To prevent such a situation, prepare a two-minute introduction about yourself. Talk about your goals, accomplishments, work experience, and educational background. Just as when preparing answers for any other questions, you should practice delivering this short introduction about yourself to perfect your delivery. Note that a confident delivery of any information will be a plus for you.

In addition to a two-minute introduction, also prepare a five-minute introduction. The approach is the same as the two-minute introduction, but this one provides a little more detail. Having a five-minute introduction prepared is a good idea in case some extra time is given and you need to provide more details about yourself.

> **TIP**
>
> Remember, oral interviews are your opportunity to market yourself to the interview board. This is one time in life you should not be shy about "tooting your own horn."

# Discovering the Oral Interview

Now that you are familiar with some of the critical preparation steps for the oral interview, let's jump into what is involved in the actual interview. You will start by learning about three different types of interview environments you are likely to face. Then you will learn about the details of how to handle each environment, and what it takes to score highly in these interview environments.

# Structured Oral Interview

The structured oral interview is nothing more than what it sounds like. You will face a panel of potential fellow officers and supervisors. They will ask you a series of questions prepared in advance and you will respond to them. All the candidates are asked the same questions. The questions can be on a variety of issues, numbering anywhere from 6 to 12 questions. Out of the 6 to 12 questions, some departments give half of the questions to interviewees before the actual interview and allow them to prepare notes for the answers. You are allowed to take these notes with you during the interview and refer to them. The other questions are a complete surprise. On the other hand, some departments do not give any time in advance to prepare for the questions, and you are asked the questions as you progress through the interview.

## Interview Board

Structured interviews are conducted in the physical presence of the board. There is usually a panel of four to six members. Although most of the members would be from the agency to which you are applying, from time to time the department might invite officers from outside agencies to sit on the interview board for opinion.

## Scoring the Structured Interview

To score the interview, board members are given standard scoring sheets. These sheets list guidelines for the answers received called *anchors*. By providing a standard scoring sheet to the board members, the human resources group of the hiring agency provides a standard scale against which the interviewees are scored. This standard sheet also makes the scoring easy because it provides expected answers and their weight in the overall score of the interview. For the most part, all the candidates start out in the middle and build their way to a higher or lower score. So for example, on a scale from 1 through 10, a candidate would start with a score of 5 and be given points for hitting all the anchors in her response(s), or points would be taken away if the candidate did not mention any anchors in her response.

# Videotaped Interviews

With growing technology, police departments are employing newer cost-effective methods when hiring police officers. One of these methods is videotaping the candidate's oral interview. One officer, most likely a sergeant or a lieutenant, asks you a series of questions just like an interview board and makes a video recording of your responses. At a later time, the recording is viewed by different evaluators. Recording the interview has both pros and cons. Some agencies prefer to do this style of interview because it gives them the opportunity to review the candidate again, if need be. The interview also can be shown to different members of the interview board at different times to gather the results of their impressions. Having board members watch the interview separately at different times decreases the chance that one board member will be influenced by another board member's opinion or scoring.

Some departments view recorded interviews as cost effective. It reduces the overtime for the officers or time away from the streets while they serve on the interview board. Additionally, if department policy requires having outside agency members on the board, video interviews eliminate the need for travel costs for outside agency members.

Along the same lines of videotaping an interview, some agencies like to make an audio tape of the interview and have the interview board evaluate the intervie-wee's responses and not the way the candidate looks. The idea is that having only the audio will prevent any hidden ethnic or racial biases, if any exist.

The scoring process for videotaped interviews is similar to that used in the board interview. The members are given similar scoring sheets, and with the video interview, the members have the option of looking at the video over and over again before giving their final score.

# Oral Interviews with Smaller Police Departments

Unlike large police departments, where the final decision to hire the candidate is made by a neutral merit board, in many smaller agencies the chief of police makes the final decision to hire the candidate. In these smaller agencies, the final interview is done by the chief of police or his designated representative. Again, a series of 6 to 12 questions will be asked. In small agencies, you may or may not have the opportunity to look at the questions in advance. The scoring of responses is also done individually, based on the impressions the chief of police or his representative has of your answers—unlike the police depart-ments' structured interview, where members of a board are provided with stan-dard scoring sheets.

# Prepare Questions

Regardless of the type of interview you are in, the bottom line remains the same. You must prepare for the interview and prepare for it well. One basic preparation that you can perform is to think of the sort of questions that might be on the interview. You might not be able to come up with the exact questions that you will face during the interview, but you will come quite close. Think of it this way: Those who prepare interview questions are people just like you and me. All you have to do is think like them. If you were working for a consulting firm and were asked to prepare questions for a police oral interview, what types of things would you like to know about the person being interviewed? If you were going to interview a person for a police officer position, what would you want to know about them? Learn as much as possible about the job of a police officer. When you have a full understanding of the job, preparing interview questions will be much easier. Make a list of as many questions about the job of a police officer as you can. Try to write as many possible interview questions and answers when preparing your questions. Try to cover as many avenues of police work as possible, and this will help you prepare for the oral interview effectively.

# Prepare Answers

Along with the potential questions, you should also prepare appropriate answers to these questions. Again, place yourself in the position of the interviewer. As an interviewer, what would you like to hear from the interviewee? When preparing your answers to the questions, do so in the form of an essay and go into as much detail as possible. After you have written the essay, create a list of the important points from the essay. At a later time, you should try to write your answers again from memory as a way of reviewing for the interview. This will help not only in recalling the answer, but will also help you correct yourself if there are any missing pieces of information. When preparing your answers, use power statements. By *power statements* I mean sentences that portray a positive image. For example:

- Demonstrated a high level of expertise
- Effectively handled high-stress situations
- Performed well in high-pressure situations
- Made a substantial contribution to the growth of the organization

**EXAM ALERT**

When preparing your answers, give plenty of examples of your real-life experiences. Interviewers are going to like hearing about real experience you have.

For example, you could say, "I handled high pressure situations well. I remember one time my current supervisor gave me a project to work on. Even though the deadline was very close, I took that challenge and had to work long hours, but I was able to make all the deliverables. In fact, I received a commendation from the company vice president for meeting all the deadlines."

**CAUTION**

> If you have already worked in some type of law enforcement capacity and are looking
> to change to another area of law enforcement, be sure to let the interview board know.
> Don't assume that they know what you do. Candidates often assume that the interview
> board members know what they do, but that might not be the case. If what you do is
> important for the interview board to know, always mention it in your answers.

When preparing power statements, try to use as many powerful words as
possible. Create your own sentences using power words and use them frequently. Refer to the following sample list of power words:

| | | |
|---|---|---|
| Achieved | Ensured | Introduced |
| Contributed | Excellence | Managed |
| Coordinated | Influenced | Negotiated |
| Designed | Initiated | Represented |
| Developed | Instrumental | Successfully |

## Sample Practice Interview Questions

Use the following questions as a guideline to prepare your own practice
interview questions:

▶ Why do you want to be a police officer?

If you have always wanted to be a police officer—because a relative is an officer,
for example—it's okay to say so. However, the interview board will also want to
know what specific factors influenced your desire to go into law enforcement.
If you believe that investigative work would be a challenge you would enjoy, say
so. Likewise, if you like the idea of protecting your community, point that out.
Make a list of the things that attract you to a law enforcement career so that you
can better recall them during the interview.

If you are asked why you want a job with that specific agency or department,
say it's because they are the best agency only if you have specific examples of
how you reached that conclusion. Flattery isn't your objective. If you know a
member of that agency or department, it is okay to mention that person if
you are confident that he or she knows you well enough to provide a recom-
mendation. If you do not have specific knowledge of the department itself,
mention reasons why you want to work in the community.

▶ What skills do you have that you think will make a good police officer?

When preparing answers for a question like this, talk about the skills needed to be a good police officer. For example, "I possess good communication skills," "I have strong observation skills and I pay attention to detail," and so on.

> ▶ Being a police officer can be a physically demanding job. What have you done to prepare for this type of challenge?

When faced with this type of question, talk about your workout regimen or a special diet you might have started to shed any extra poundage. For example, "I work out three times a week with weights and run on the three other days. I am trying to lose weight and have started a high-protein / low-carb diet."

> ▶ Rules and regulations are important for any organization. How do you think they are important for a police department?

For a question like this, talk about the positive sides of the topic. For example, you could say, "Rules and regulations are very important. They are there to provide guidance to employees with regard to what is expected of them. Rules and regulations also protect the employee. If you do a job according to rules and regulations of the company you work for, no one can say you did not do your job well."

> ▶ As a police officer, at times you are required to work as a team. How do you work as a team member?

Tell the interviewer that you are a team player. Give examples if you have worked in teams before or if you currently work on a team. If someone has given you an accolade for being a good team player, mention that.

> ▶ If we talk to your peers, how would they describe you?

Always use positive statements. For example, you could say, "I have been known to be a 'go-to' person in the department," or "I have been known to be a positive role model for new employees," and so forth.

> ▶ If we talk to your supervisors, how would they describe you?

Again, use positive statements. For example, "My supervisor will say I take my work very seriously," or "I am not afraid of long hours," or "I am very reliable."

> ▶ As a police officer, you might be required to work with people belonging to different cultures. How do you work with cultural diversity?

Tell the interviewer that you are very open to other cultures. If you have any friends from other cultures, this is a good place to mention that. If you know any foreign languages, that's a good point to bring out here. More and more police agencies are looking for bilingual officers.

▶ Verbal and written communication is very essential in police work. Describe your skills in this area and give examples.

If you have taken any writing or public speaking courses, or have done something that has helped you polish your written or verbal skills, make a list. Even if this type of question doesn't arise in the interview, you should mention these skills in some of your other answers.

▶ Being a police officer gives you a lot of authority and discretion. Tell us in your own words how you would not abuse this authority.

Tell the interviewers that you are not a person who would do that. Assure them that you believe in treating people as you want to be treated. Tell them that you are fair in all your dealings and you always treat people with respect. If you remember something that shows an application of such behavior, give an example.

▶ Being a police officer can often be stressful. How do you deal with stress?

The worst thing you can do in answering a question like this is to say that you don't get stressed. Everybody feels stress. The key is to communicate how well you handle stress and what you do to handle it. Everyone has a different way of handling stress. Some people like to work out, whereas others like to go for a walk. It seems it always helps if you talk to someone.

Tell the interviewer that you are not shy about talking to someone when something bothers you to the point that it starts to interfere with your work. Let the person asking the question know that you like to work out to relieve stress. The point of this question is to see if you are aware of what stress is and whether you are willing to do something about it.

▶ Being a police officer you face conflict in your job. How do you deal with conflict?

Here, you could emphasize that everyone has his own way of handling conflict. That's part of human nature. Having open communication always helps. Tell the interviewer that you like to hear other people's story completely before you come to any type of conclusion. Also note that you don't like to impose your beliefs on other people, nor are you judgmental when dealing with conflict. If you have an example of how you handled a conflict successfully, this is the best time to mention it.

# Practice, Practice, Practice

Preparing written questions and answers will not help you in the oral interview unless you practice repeating your answers verbally. The more you practice, the better you will become. You are selling yourself. By practicing your answers, you will build confidence. That confidence will show when you are answering your questions. You can effectively practice answering your questions in front of the mirror. Also, you can practice with family members in a role-playing session. They can be interviewers and you can be the interviewee.

# Dressing and Appearance for the Oral Interview

It is imperative that you look your best, for two reasons. First, the board members will look at you and you want to look sharp. Second, if you think you look good, you will be confident and this confidence will show. When I say that board members will look at you, I really mean that they will form opinions of you based on their first impression; your hair, clothes, shoes, and even your socks and fingernails. It is a true statement that you get only one chance to make a first impression, and you absolutely want that impression to be a good one. I have seen board members notice and discuss both small and big details, including the candidate's appearance, after the interview.

# Sending a Thank You Letter

Immediately after your interview, always send a thank you letter to each of your interviewers by fax, mail, or email. Don't underestimate the power of a thank you letter. It might be the deciding factor in your favor, especially when there are other candidates with the same qualifications as yours. With the advancements in information technology, email is the quickest way to send thank you letters to interviewers, and is perfectly acceptable these days. When sending your thank you letter via email, maintain a professional style in your format. Avoid using colorful backgrounds, caricatures, or emoticons.

**EXAM ALERT**

At the completion of your interview, ask each board member for his or her contact information and correct name spelling. There is nothing worse than spelling your interviewer's name wrong.

Most interview board members expect you to send a thank you letter. It shows the member that you are courteous, knowledgeable about etiquette, and a professional. In addition, a thank you letter enables the board members to evaluate your writing skills and makes you stand out in their minds. It puts you ahead of the other candidates who appeared in the interview but did not take time to write a letter.

**NOTE**

A thank you letter is also an excellent opportunity to reinforce your positive points and add some information that you did not have time to cover during your oral interview.

# Exam Prep Questions

During your police agency or department employment interview, you might be asked some hypothetical questions. This is done to gauge your logic and personal philosophies or ethics, or how you would respond in a given situation.

For each of the questions that follow, choose the answer that you believe would be the appropriate course of action.

1. You and your partner are transporting a known violent gang member whom you've placed under arrest. While en route to the station, you come across what appears to be a motor vehicle accident. The damage to the vehicles involved leads you to believe there are probably injuries to the drivers and passengers. What should you do?

   ❑ A. Stop to assess the damage so that you can provide any needed assistance while waiting for department and emergency units to arrive.

   ❑ B. Stop and determine whether there are any life-threatening injuries; if the injuries appear to be minor, report the accident to dispatch and then proceed to the station.

   ❑ C. Report the accident to dispatch and proceed to the station.

   ❑ D. Stop your police unit, shackle the gang member, have your partner guard him at gunpoint, and then assess the situation for any life-threatening injuries. If the injuries appear to be minor, notify dispatch, remove the restraints from the arrested subject, and secure him in the back seat of your patrol unit. Have your partner holster his weapon, and then proceed to the station.

2. While investigating an incident at a local bar, the proprietor offers you a free cup of coffee. What should you do?

   ❑ A. Accept the coffee or preferred other choice of nonalcoholic beverage, and thank the proprietor.

   ❑ B. Accept the coffee or preferred other choice of nonalcoholic beverage, but insist on paying for it.

   ❑ C. Immediately place the proprietor under arrest for bribery.

   ❑ D. Immediately place the proprietor under arrest for hindering a police investigation.

3. You are assigned to a supervisor of the opposite sex. You suspect that this new supervisor doesn't like you, and in your opinion that assumption is confirmed when you are given a low performance rating. What should you do?

   ❑ A. Talk with the supervisor to determine whether you can resolve the reasons why he or she is not pleased with your work performance.

   ❑ B. File a grievance.

   ❑ C. Be diligent in how you perform your duties and wait until your next performance review to see whether his or her opinion of you changes.

   ❑ D. Schedule a meeting with the chief of police to discuss a possible sexual harassment lawsuit.

4. You are working your current shift without a partner. Upon your arrival to investigate what was reported as a neighborhood loud music complaint, you exit your patrol unit to begin walking toward the front door of the residence. As you round your patrol unit, a male subject throws open the front door of the residence. The subject is armed with a handgun and immediately begins to fire at you. What is the first thing you should do?

❑   A.  Yell "This is the police. Drop your weapon. You are under arrest."

❑   B.  Radio for backup.

❑   C.  Draw your gun and return fire.

❑   D.  Take cover.

# Exam Prep Answers

1. **Answer C is correct.** Your priority is to maintain control of your prisoner. At this point, you have no way of knowing whether the accident was staged to act as a diversion so that other gang members can free your prisoner. Therefore, it is not practical to leave it to your partner to guard the prisoner, regardless of how well you are able to restrain him. Your best option for providing help in this situation is to immediately report the accident to dispatch so that police and emergency units can be dispatched to the scene; during the time that it would take you to secure the prisoner, those units can already be en route.

2. **Answer B is correct.** Without contributing evidence to the contrary, you have no way of knowing for certain that you were offered a free service as a form of graft or a bribe; the proprietor might just be hospitable. However, at this point, you do not know that it isn't a bribe either. (His liquor license might be expired or he might know that he's facing suspension of that liquor license because of serial offenses occurring at the bar, for example.) So, although you lack probable cause to place the proprietor under arrest, you still need to keep all business on an ethical level. Your integrity as an officer depends on maintaining that trust. Therefore, if it is convenient to drink a beverage while you conduct your business at the bar, you should pay for your choice of acceptable beverage.

3. **Answer A is correct.** It is possible that your supervisor is not one who micromanages and simply isn't one who will tell you at the time when something you are doing doesn't meet with his or her satisfaction. You can argue that this makes him or her a poor supervisor, but in reality, it is also imperative that you are able to work within the rules of your department. (This is especially important during the time you are in your probationary period with that department; however, it is also important throughout your career.) Answer C is incorrect because you shouldn't just ignore what is obviously a problem—either with the supervisor or your performance. Requesting an immediate chance to discuss the matter with this supervisor shows good faith on your part, and helps establish that you do not have issues with following orders or direction from a member of the opposite sex. If, and only if, your supervisor refuses to discuss the matter with you in a timely matter should you appeal to the next person in the chain of command.

4. **Answer D is correct.** The subject is firing a weapon at you and it is not cowardly behavior that your immediate concern is your personal safety. When it is safe for you to do so, you should radio for assistance.

# PART III
# Physical Agility

8 Physical Agility

CHAPTER EIGHT

# Physical Agility

---

## Terms You'll Need to Know:

- ✓ Push-ups
- ✓ Sit-ups
- ✓ Flexibility
- ✓ Running
- ✓ Sprinting

---

## Concepts You'll Need to Understand:

- ✓ Importance of physical fitness in police work
- ✓ What to expect during the physical agility test
- ✓ Physical agility standards
- ✓ Improving your scores

# Importance of Physical Fitness in Police Work

Being a police officer can be a physically demanding and challenging position. Even though plenty of time is spent in the patrol car traveling from call to call, there are times when you are required to stand for a long period of time directing traffic or guarding crime scenes. There are also times when you have to chase a suspect on foot or physically subdue a subject when he resists arrest. For times like these, a police officer must be in good physical shape.

The physical agility portion of the police officer selection process is designed to test your general fitness. The hiring agency wants to make sure that you will be able to handle the daily rigors of being a police officer. Another reason for the physical agility test is to ensure that a police candidate will be able to successfully complete the required police officer academy. The period at the training academy is very physically challenging. There will be a lot of running, push-ups, sit-ups, defensive tactics, and other physically demanding exercises.

The state law enforcement training board sets the standards for the academy. These standards are based on validated research and analysis of the tasks that a police officer performs or must be prepared to perform.

# What to Expect During the Physical Agility Test

On the day of the test, you will probably be asked to come dressed in physical training (PT) clothes. By PT clothes, I mean clothes in which you can work out. These clothes should be comfortable and allow freedom of movement. When dressing for this portion of the process, always wear clothes in layers. If you dress in layers, you can easily take layers off if it gets too warm or add a layer or two if it gets too cold. The test is usually conducted in groups of 8 to 12 people. This is just to ease the grading process. After you've been grouped together, you will be given an introduction of what is going to happen. Some agencies like to do a quick blood pressure screening, even though you will go through an extensive medical screening before you are hired. This screening is just to make sure that you do not have high blood pressure just before the agility test.

Events in the physical agility portion might be different for each agency, just like the written exam or oral interview, but the basics will still be there. The three basics for physical agility are as follows:

▶ **Push-ups**—This event tests your upper body strength.

▶ **Sit-ups**—This event tests the strength of your stomach muscles and back.

▶ **Run**—This event tests your endurance and speed at short distances.

Even though the run event is common all across the agencies, the distances might be different. The common distance for a run is 1 1/2 miles. Some agencies have 2-mile standards just like the military. After the run portion, there might be a quarter-mile sprint portion.

Some agencies add other events to the physical agility portion. The following are some of the additional events that have been included by different agencies:

▶ **Wall**—Some agencies have added a six-foot wall to the agility portion. It is basically a six-foot-tall chain-link fence with padding on top. Some departments build a six-foot wooden wall to make things fancier. You are required to scale this wall and jump to the other side.

▶ **Flexibility test**—Another variation is a flexibility test. This is done to ensure that you have certain levels of flexibility. The test is done while you sit down and reach on scale.

▶ **Vertical Jump**—Vertical jump measures explosive leg strength. This test measures the candidate's ability to sprint, jump an obstacle using lower body strength, and demonstrate other uses of lower body strength during the performance of daily duties.

▶ **Trigger squeeze**—This is when you are given two police service pistols or revolvers. You are to squeeze the trigger a certain number of times, with a strong and weak hand.

▶ **Drag a dummy**—Another event that you might experience is dragging a 150-pound dummy. At the end of the quarter-mile run, there is a 150-pound dummy waiting for you. You will be expected to drag this dummy 20 to 30 feet. The idea is that your partner needs help and you are trying to save his life after sprinting a quarter-mile.

▶ **Obstacle course**—Some agencies also add an obstacle course. This obstacle course could be a combination of events already covered. For example, one agency I know had a quarter-mile run around the track. The whole quarter-mile was set as an obstacle course. You start with the run; the first obstacle was a set of clothes lines strung across four poles. After another short distance was a six-foot wall, followed by a set of eight tires. You were to run through these tires. After another short distance was a six-inch wide, 20-foot beam and finally 30 steps on the bleachers and a dummy drag.

# Physical Agility Standards

Standards for the physical agility portion are very similar to the ones for the United States military. Again, just like any other tests, these standards might differ among agencies. The standards to be hired by a police agency sometimes are different from the passing standards of the law enforcement training academy. The reason is that human resource departments are aware of the fact that not everyone will be able to pass high standards of the law enforcement academy initially. But you are expected to improve as you progress though the academy.

As a guide, a chart of United States Army physical training standards and scoring information has been added to give you an idea what the standards are to pass the law enforcement training academy.

Use Figure 8.1 as a guide to set score goals.

**NOTE**

Be prepared to take several diagnostic physical training tests during your time at the law enforcement training.

The reason for these diagnostic physical training tests is to chart your progress and improvement during the training.

## PUSH-UP STANDARDS

| Repetitions | 17-21 M | 17-21 F | 22-25 M | 22-25 F | 27-31 M | 27-31 F | 32-36 M | 32-36 F | 37-41 M | 37-41 F | Repetitions | 42-46 M | 42-46 F | 47-56 M | 47-56 F | 52-58 M | 52-58 F | 57-61 M | 57-61 F | 62+ M | 62+ F | Repetitions |
|---|---|---|---|---|---|---|---|---|---|---|---|---|---|---|---|---|---|---|---|---|---|---|
| 77 | | | | | 100 | | | | | | 77 | | | | | | | | | | | 77 |
| 76 | | | | | 99 | | | | | | 76 | | | | | | | | | | | 76 |
| 75 | | | 100 | | 98 | | 100 | | | | 75 | | | | | | | | | | | 75 |
| 74 | | | 99 | | 97 | | 99 | | | | 74 | | | | | | | | | | | 74 |
| 73 | | | 97 | | 96 | | 98 | | 100 | | 73 | | | | | | | | | | | 73 |
| 72 | | | 96 | | 95 | | 97 | | 99 | | 72 | | | | | | | | | | | 72 |
| 71 | 100 | | 95 | | 94 | | 96 | | 98 | | 71 | | | | | | | | | | | 71 |
| 70 | 99 | | 94 | | 93 | | 95 | | 97 | | 70 | | | | | | | | | | | 70 |
| 69 | 97 | | 93 | | 92 | | 94 | | 96 | | 69 | | | | | | | | | | | 69 |
| 68 | 96 | | 92 | | 91 | | 93 | | 95 | | 68 | | | | | | | | | | | 68 |
| 67 | 94 | | 91 | | 89 | | 92 | | 94 | | 67 | | | | | | | | | | | 67 |
| 66 | 93 | | 90 | | 88 | | 91 | | 93 | | 66 | 100 | | | | | | | | | | 66 |
| 65 | 92 | | 89 | | 87 | | 90 | | 92 | | 65 | 99 | | | | | | | | | | 65 |
| 64 | 90 | | 87 | | 86 | | 89 | | 91 | | 64 | 98 | | | | | | | | | | 64 |
| 63 | 89 | | 86 | | 85 | | 88 | | 90 | | 63 | 97 | | | | | | | | | | 63 |
| 62 | 88 | | 85 | | 84 | | 87 | | 89 | | 62 | 96 | | | | | | | | | | 62 |
| 61 | 86 | | 84 | | 83 | | 86 | | 88 | | 61 | 94 | | | | | | | | | | 61 |
| 60 | 85 | | 83 | | 82 | | 85 | | 87 | | 60 | 93 | | | | | | | | | | 60 |
| 59 | 83 | | 82 | | 81 | | 84 | | 86 | | 59 | 92 | | 100 | | | | | | | | 59 |
| 58 | 82 | | 81 | | 80 | | 83 | | 85 | | 58 | 91 | | 99 | | | | | | | | 58 |
| 57 | 81 | | 79 | | 79 | | 82 | | 84 | | 57 | 90 | | 98 | | | | | | | | 57 |
| 56 | 79 | | 78 | | 78 | | 81 | | 83 | | 56 | 89 | | 96 | | 100 | | | | | | 56 |
| 55 | 78 | | 77 | | 77 | | 79 | | 82 | | 55 | 88 | | 95 | | 99 | | | | | | 55 |
| 54 | 77 | | 76 | | 76 | | 78 | | 81 | | 54 | 87 | | 94 | | 98 | | | | | | 54 |
| 53 | 75 | | 75 | | 75 | | 77 | | 79 | | 53 | 86 | | 93 | | 97 | | 100 | | | | 53 |
| 52 | 74 | | 74 | | 74 | | 76 | | 78 | | 52 | 84 | | 92 | | 96 | | 99 | | | | 52 |
| 51 | 72 | | 73 | | 73 | | 75 | | 77 | | 51 | 83 | | 91 | | 94 | | 98 | | | | 51 |
| 50 | 71 | | 71 | | 72 | | 74 | | 76 | | 50 | 82 | | 89 | | 93 | | 97 | | 100 | | 50 |
| 49 | 70 | | 70 | | 71 | 99 | 73 | | 75 | | 49 | 81 | | 88 | | 92 | | 95 | | 99 | | 49 |
| 48 | 68 | | 69 | | 69 | 98 | 72 | | 74 | | 48 | 80 | | 87 | | 91 | | 94 | | 98 | | 48 |
| 47 | 67 | | 68 | | 68 | 96 | 71 | | 73 | | 47 | 79 | | 86 | | 90 | | 93 | | 96 | | 47 |
| 46 | 66 | | 67 | 100 | 67 | 95 | 70 | | 72 | | 46 | 78 | | 85 | | 89 | | 92 | | 95 | | 46 |
| 45 | 64 | | 66 | 99 | 66 | 94 | 69 | 100 | 71 | | 45 | 77 | | 84 | | 88 | | 91 | | 94 | | 45 |
| 44 | 63 | | 65 | 97 | 65 | 93 | 68 | 99 | 70 | | 44 | 76 | | 82 | | 87 | | 90 | | 93 | | 44 |
| 43 | 61 | | 63 | 96 | 64 | 92 | 67 | 97 | 69 | | 43 | 75 | | 81 | | 86 | | 89 | | 92 | | 43 |
| 42 | 60 | 100 | 62 | 94 | 63 | 90 | 66 | 96 | 68 | | 42 | 73 | | 80 | | 85 | | 87 | | 91 | | 42 |
| 41 | 59 | 98 | 61 | 93 | 62 | 89 | 65 | 95 | 67 | | 41 | 72 | | 79 | | 83 | | 86 | | 89 | | 41 |
| 40 | 57 | 97 | 60 | 92 | 61 | 88 | 64 | 93 | 66 | 100 | 40 | 71 | | 78 | | 82 | | 85 | | 88 | | 40 |
| 39 | 56 | 95 | 59 | 90 | 60 | 87 | 63 | 92 | 65 | 99 | 39 | 70 | | 76 | | 81 | | 84 | | 87 | | 39 |
| 38 | 54 | 93 | 58 | 89 | 59 | 85 | 61 | 89 | 64 | 97 | 38 | 69 | | 75 | | 80 | | 83 | | 86 | | 38 |
| 37 | 53 | 91 | 57 | 88 | 58 | 84 | 60 | 88 | 63 | 95 | 37 | 68 | 100 | 74 | | 79 | | 82 | | 85 | | 37 |
| 36 | 52 | 90 | 55 | 86 | 56 | 83 | 60 | 88 | 62 | 94 | 36 | 67 | 98 | 73 | | 78 | | 81 | | 84 | | 36 |
| 35 | 50 | 88 | 54 | 85 | 56 | 82 | 58 | 87 | 61 | 93 | 35 | 66 | 97 | 72 | | 77 | | 79 | | 82 | | 35 |
| 34 | 49 | 86 | 53 | 83 | 55 | 81 | 58 | 85 | 60 | 91 | 34 | 64 | 95 | 71 | 100 | 76 | | 78 | | 81 | | 34 |
| 33 | 48 | 84 | 52 | 82 | 54 | 79 | 57 | 84 | 59 | 89 | 33 | 63 | 94 | 69 | 98 | 74 | | 77 | | 80 | | 33 |
| 32 | 46 | 83 | 51 | 81 | 53 | 78 | 56 | 83 | 58 | 88 | 32 | 62 | 92 | 68 | 97 | 73 | | 76 | | 79 | | 32 |
| 31 | 45 | 81 | 50 | 79 | 52 | 77 | 55 | 81 | 57 | 87 | 31 | 61 | 90 | 67 | 95 | 72 | 100 | 75 | | 78 | | 31 |
| 30 | 43 | 79 | 49 | 78 | 50 | 76 | 54 | 80 | 56 | 85 | 30 | 60 | 89 | 66 | 93 | 71 | 98 | 74 | | 76 | | 30 |
| 29 | 42 | 77 | 47 | 77 | 49 | 75 | 53 | 79 | 55 | 84 | 29 | 59 | 87 | 65 | 92 | 70 | 96 | 73 | | 75 | | 29 |
| 28 | 41 | 76 | 46 | 75 | 48 | 73 | 52 | 77 | 54 | 82 | 28 | 58 | 86 | 64 | 90 | 69 | 95 | 71 | 100 | 73 | | 28 |
| 27 | 39 | 74 | 45 | 74 | 47 | 72 | 51 | 76 | 53 | 81 | 27 | 57 | 84 | 62 | 88 | 68 | 93 | 70 | 98 | 73 | | 27 |
| 26 | 38 | 72 | 44 | 72 | 46 | 71 | 50 | 75 | 52 | 79 | 26 | 56 | 82 | 61 | 87 | 67 | 91 | 69 | 96 | 72 | | 26 |
| 25 | 37 | 70 | 43 | 71 | 45 | 70 | 49 | 73 | 51 | 78 | 25 | 54 | 81 | 60 | 85 | 66 | 89 | 68 | 94 | 71 | 100 | 25 |
| 24 | 35 | 69 | 42 | 70 | 44 | 68 | 48 | 72 | 50 | 76 | 24 | 53 | 79 | 59 | 83 | 64 | 87 | 67 | 92 | 69 | 98 | 24 |
| 23 | 34 | 67 | 41 | 68 | 43 | 67 | 47 | 71 | 49 | 75 | 23 | 52 | 78 | 58 | 81 | 63 | 85 | 66 | 90 | 68 | 96 | 23 |
| 22 | 32 | 65 | 39 | 67 | 42 | 66 | 46 | 69 | 48 | 73 | 22 | 51 | 76 | 56 | 80 | 62 | 84 | 65 | 88 | 67 | 93 | 22 |
| 21 | 31 | 63 | 38 | 66 | 41 | 65 | 45 | 68 | 47 | 72 | 21 | 50 | 74 | 55 | 78 | 60 | 82 | 64 | 86 | 65 | 91 | 21 |
| 20 | 30 | 62 | 37 | 64 | 40 | 64 | 44 | 67 | 46 | 70 | 20 | 49 | 73 | 54 | 77 | 60 | 80 | 62 | 84 | 65 | 89 | 20 |
| 19 | 28 | 60 | 36 | 62 | 39 | 63 | 43 | 65 | 45 | 69 | 19 | 48 | 71 | 53 | 75 | 59 | 78 | 61 | 82 | 64 | 87 | 19 |
| 18 | 27 | 58 | 35 | 61 | 38 | 61 | 42 | 64 | 44 | 66 | 18 | 47 | 70 | 52 | 73 | 58 | 76 | 60 | 80 | 62 | 84 | 18 |
| 17 | 26 | 57 | 34 | 60 | 37 | 60 | 41 | 63 | 43 | 66 | 17 | 46 | 68 | 51 | 72 | 57 | 75 | 59 | 78 | 61 | 82 | 17 |
| 16 | 24 | 55 | 33 | 59 | 35 | 58 | 38 | 60 | 41 | 63 | 16 | 44 | 66 | 48 | 70 | 55 | 73 | 58 | 76 | 60 | 80 | 16 |
| 15 | 23 | 53 | 31 | 57 | 35 | 58 | 38 | 60 | 41 | 63 | 15 | 43 | 65 | 48 | 68 | 54 | 71 | 57 | 74 | 59 | 78 | 15 |
| 14 | 21 | 51 | 30 | 56 | 34 | 56 | 36 | 59 | 39 | 61 | 14 | 41 | 62 | 46 | 67 | 53 | 69 | 55 | 72 | 58 | 76 | 14 |
| 13 | 20 | 50 | 29 | 54 | 33 | 55 | 36 | 58 | 38 | 60 | 13 | 40 | 62 | 46 | 65 | 52 | 67 | 54 | 70 | 56 | 73 | 13 |
| 12 | 19 | 48 | 28 | 52 | 32 | 54 | 35 | 56 | 37 | 59 | 12 | 40 | 60 | 45 | 63 | 51 | 65 | 53 | 68 | 55 | 71 | 12 |
| 11 | 17 | 46 | 27 | 50 | 31 | 52 | 34 | 54 | 36 | 57 | 11 | 39 | 58 | 44 | 61 | 50 | 64 | 52 | 66 | 54 | 69 | 11 |
| 10 | 16 | 44 | 26 | 49 | 29 | 50 | 33 | 52 | 35 | 56 | 10 | 38 | 57 | 42 | 60 | 49 | 62 | 51 | 64 | 53 | 67 | 10 |
| 9 | 14 | 43 | 25 | 49 | 28 | 49 | 31 | 49 | 33 | 53 | 9 | 37 | 55 | 42 | 59 | 47 | 60 | 50 | 62 | 52 | 65 | 9 |
| 8 | 13 | 41 | 23 | 48 | 27 | 49 | 31 | 49 | 33 | 53 | 8 | 36 | 54 | 40 | 57 | 47 | 58 | 49 | 60 | 51 | 62 | 8 |
| 7 | 12 | 38 | 22 | 46 | 26 | 48 | 30 | 49 | 32 | 51 | 7 | 34 | 52 | 39 | 55 | 46 | 56 | 47 | 58 | 49 | 60 | 7 |
| 6 | 10 | 37 | 21 | 45 | 25 | 47 | 29 | 48 | 31 | 50 | 6 | 33 | 50 | 38 | 53 | 44 | 55 | 46 | 56 | 48 | 58 | 6 |
| 5 | 9 | 36 | 20 | 43 | 24 | 45 | 28 | 47 | 30 | 48 | 5 | 32 | 49 | 36 | 52 | 43 | 53 | 45 | 54 | 47 | 56 | 5 |
| 4 | 8 | 34 | 19 | 42 | 23 | 44 | 27 | 45 | 29 | 47 | | | | | | | | | | | | 4 |
| 3 | 6 | 32 | 18 | 41 | 22 | 43 | 26 | 44 | 28 | 45 | | | | | | | | | | | | 3 |
| 2 | 5 | 30 | 17 | 39 | 21 | 42 | 25 | 43 | 27 | 44 | | | | | | | | | | | | 2 |
| 1 | 3 | 29 | 15 | 38 | 20 | 41 | 24 | 41 | 26 | 42 | | | | | | | | | | | | 1 |
| Repetitions | M | F | M | F | M | F | M | F | M | F | Repetitions | M | F | M | F | M | F | M | F | M | F | Repetitions |
| Age Group | 17-21 | | 22-25 | | 27-31 | | 32-36 | | 37-41 | | Age Group | 42-46 | | 47-51 | | 52-56 | | 57-61 | | 62+ | | Age Group |

Scoring standards are used to convert raw scores to point scores after test events are completed. Male point scores are indicated by the M at the top and bottom of the shaded column. Female point scores are indicated by the F at the top and bottom of the unshaded column. To convert raw scores to point scores, find the number of repetitions performed in the left-hand column. Next, move right along that row and locate the intersection of the soldier's appropriate age column. Record that number in the Push-Up points block on the front of the scorecard.

## SIT-UP STANDARDS

| Repetitions | 17-21 MF | 22-25 MF | 27-31 MF | 32-36 MF | 37-41 MF | Repetitions | 42-46 MF | 47-51 MF | 52-56 MF | 57-61 MF | 62+ MF | Repetitions |
|---|---|---|---|---|---|---|---|---|---|---|---|---|
| 82 |  |  | 100 |  |  | 82 |  |  |  |  |  | 82 |
| 81 |  |  | 99 |  |  | 81 |  |  |  |  |  | 81 |
| 80 |  | 100 | 98 |  |  | 80 |  |  |  |  |  | 80 |
| 79 |  | 99 | 97 |  |  | 79 |  |  |  |  |  | 79 |
| 78 | 100 | 97 | 96 |  |  | 78 |  |  |  |  |  | 78 |
| 77 | 98 | 96 | 95 |  |  | 77 |  |  |  |  |  | 77 |
| 76 | 97 | 95 | 94 | 100 | 100 | 76 |  |  |  |  |  | 76 |
| 75 | 95 | 93 | 92 | 99 | 99 | 75 |  |  |  |  |  | 75 |
| 74 | 94 | 92 | 91 | 98 | 98 | 74 |  |  |  |  |  | 74 |
| 73 | 92 | 91 | 90 | 96 | 97 | 73 |  |  |  |  |  | 73 |
| 72 | 90 | 89 | 89 | 95 | 96 | 72 | 100 |  |  |  |  | 72 |
| 71 | 89 | 88 | 88 | 94 | 95 | 71 | 99 |  |  |  |  | 71 |
| 70 | 87 | 87 | 87 | 93 | 94 | 70 | 98 |  |  |  |  | 70 |
| 69 | 86 | 85 | 86 | 92 | 93 | 69 | 97 |  |  |  |  | 69 |
| 68 | 84 | 84 | 85 | 91 | 92 | 68 | 96 |  |  |  |  | 68 |
| 67 | 82 | 83 | 84 | 89 | 91 | 67 | 95 |  |  |  |  | 67 |
| 66 | 81 | 81 | 83 | 88 | 89 | 66 | 94 | 100 | 100 |  |  | 66 |
| 65 | 79 | 80 | 82 | 87 | 88 | 65 | 93 | 99 | 99 |  |  | 65 |
| 64 | 78 | 79 | 81 | 86 | 87 | 64 | 92 | 98 | 98 | 100 |  | 64 |
| 63 | 76 | 77 | 79 | 85 | 86 | 63 | 91 | 97 | 97 | 99 | 100 | 63 |
| 62 | 74 | 76 | 78 | 84 | 85 | 62 | 90 | 96 | 96 | 98 | 99 | 62 |
| 61 | 73 | 75 | 77 | 82 | 84 | 61 | 89 | 94 | 95 | 97 | 98 | 61 |
| 60 | 71 | 73 | 76 | 81 | 83 | 60 | 88 | 93 | 94 | 96 | 97 | 60 |
| 59 | 70 | 72 | 75 | 80 | 82 | 59 | 87 | 92 | 93 | 95 | 96 | 59 |
| 58 | 68 | 71 | 74 | 79 | 81 | 58 | 86 | 91 | 92 | 94 | 95 | 58 |
| 57 | 66 | 69 | 73 | 78 | 80 | 57 | 85 | 90 | 91 | 92 | 94 | 57 |
| 56 | 65 | 68 | 72 | 76 | 79 | 56 | 84 | 89 | 89 | 91 | 92 | 56 |
| 55 | 63 | 67 | 71 | 75 | 78 | 55 | 83 | 88 | 88 | 90 | 91 | 55 |
| 54 | 62 | 65 | 70 | 74 | 77 | 54 | 82 | 87 | 87 | 89 | 90 | 54 |
| 53 | 60 | 64 | 69 | 73 | 76 | 53 | 81 | 86 | 86 | 88 | 89 | 53 |
| 52 | 58 | 63 | 68 | 72 | 75 | 52 | 80 | 84 | 85 | 87 | 88 | 52 |
| 51 | 57 | 61 | 66 | 71 | 74 | 51 | 79 | 83 | 84 | 86 | 87 | 51 |
| 50 | 55 | 60 | 65 | 69 | 73 | 50 | 78 | 82 | 83 | 85 | 86 | 50 |
| 49 | 54 | 59 | 64 | 68 | 72 | 49 | 77 | 81 | 82 | 84 | 85 | 49 |
| 48 | 52 | 57 | 63 | 67 | 71 | 48 | 76 | 80 | 81 | 83 | 84 | 48 |
| 47 | 50 | 56 | 62 | 66 | 69 | 47 | 75 | 79 | 80 | 82 | 83 | 47 |
| 46 | 49 | 55 | 61 | 65 | 68 | 46 | 74 | 78 | 79 | 81 | 82 | 46 |
| 45 | 47 | 53 | 60 | 64 | 67 | 45 | 73 | 77 | 78 | 79 | 81 | 45 |
| 44 | 46 | 52 | 59 | 63 | 66 | 44 | 72 | 76 | 77 | 78 | 79 | 44 |
| 43 | 44 | 50 | 58 | 61 | 65 | 43 | 71 | 74 | 76 | 77 | 78 | 43 |
| 42 | 42 | 49 | 57 | 60 | 64 | 42 | 70 | 73 | 75 | 76 | 77 | 42 |
| 41 | 41 | 48 | 56 | 59 | 63 | 41 | 69 | 72 | 74 | 75 | 76 | 41 |
| 40 | 39 | 47 | 55 | 58 | 62 | 40 | 68 | 71 | 73 | 74 | 75 | 40 |
| 39 | 38 | 45 | 54 | 56 | 61 | 39 | 67 | 70 | 72 | 73 | 74 | 39 |
| 38 | 36 | 44 | 52 | 55 | 60 | 38 | 66 | 69 | 71 | 72 | 73 | 38 |
| 37 | 34 | 43 | 51 | 54 | 59 | 37 | 65 | 68 | 69 | 71 | 72 | 37 |
| 36 | 33 | 41 | 50 | 53 | 58 | 36 | 64 | 67 | 68 | 70 | 71 | 36 |
| 35 | 31 | 40 | 49 | 52 | 57 | 35 | 63 | 66 | 67 | 69 | 70 | 35 |
| 34 | 30 | 39 | 48 | 50 | 56 | 34 | 62 | 64 | 66 | 68 | 69 | 34 |
| 33 | 28 | 37 | 47 | 49 | 55 | 33 | 61 | 63 | 65 | 66 | 68 | 33 |
| 32 | 26 | 36 | 46 | 48 | 54 | 32 | 60 | 62 | 64 | 65 | 66 | 32 |
| 31 | 25 | 35 | 45 | 47 | 53 | 31 | 59 | 61 | 63 | 64 | 65 | 31 |
| 30 | 23 | 33 | 44 | 46 | 52 | 30 | 58 | 60 | 62 | 63 | 64 | 30 |
| 29 | 22 | 32 | 43 | 45 | 50 | 29 | 57 | 59 | 61 | 62 | 63 | 29 |
| 28 | 20 | 31 | 42 | 44 | 49 | 28 | 56 | 58 | 60 | 61 | 62 | 28 |
| 27 | 18 | 29 | 41 | 42 | 48 | 27 | 55 | 57 | 59 | 60 | 61 | 27 |
| 26 | 17 | 28 | 39 | 41 | 47 | 26 | 54 | 56 | 58 | 59 | 60 | 26 |
| 25 | 16 | 27 | 38 | 40 | 46 | 25 | 53 | 54 | 57 | 58 | 59 | 25 |
| 24 | 14 | 25 | 37 | 39 | 45 | 24 | 52 | 53 | 56 | 57 | 58 | 24 |
| 23 | 12 | 24 | 36 | 38 | 44 | 23 | 51 | 52 | 55 | 56 | 57 | 23 |
| 22 | 10 | 23 | 35 | 36 | 43 | 22 | 50 | 51 | 54 | 55 | 56 | 22 |
| 21 | 9 | 21 | 34 | 35 | 42 | 21 | 49 | 50 | 53 | 54 | 55 | 21 |
| Repetitions | MF | MF | MF | MF | MF | Repetitions | MF | MF | MF | MF | MF | Repetitions |
| Age Group | 17-21 | 22-25 | 27-31 | 32-36 | 37-41 | Age Group | 42-46 | 47-51 | 52-56 | 57-61 | 62+ | Age Group |

Scoring standards are used to convert raw scores to point scores after test events are completed. To convert raw scores to point scores, find the number of repetitions performed in the left-hand column. Next, move right along that row and locate the intersection of the soldier's appropriate age column. Record that number in the Sit-Up points block on the front of the scorecard.

## 2-MILE RUN STANDARDS

| Age Group Time | 17-21 M | 17-21 F | 22-25 M | 22-25 F | 27-31 M | 27-31 F | 32-36 M | 32-36 F | 37-41 M | 37-41 F | Age Group Time | 42-46 M | 42-46 F | 47-51 M | 47-51 F | 52-56 M | 52-56 F | 57-61 M | 57-61 F | 62+ M | 62+ F | Age Group Time |
|---|---|---|---|---|---|---|---|---|---|---|---|---|---|---|---|---|---|---|---|---|---|---|
| 12:54 | | | | | | | | | | | 12:54 | | | | | | | | | | | 12:54 |
| 13:00 | 100 | | 100 | | | | | | | | 13:00 | | | | | | | | | | | 13:00 |
| 13:06 | 99 | | 99 | | | | | | | | 13:06 | | | | | | | | | | | 13:06 |
| 13:12 | 97 | | 98 | | | | | | | | 13:12 | | | | | | | | | | | 13:12 |
| 13:18 | 96 | | 97 | | 100 | | 100 | | | | 13:18 | | | | | | | | | | | 13:18 |
| 13:24 | 94 | | 96 | | 99 | | 99 | | | | 13:24 | | | | | | | | | | | 13:24 |
| 13:30 | 93 | | 94 | | 98 | | 98 | | | | 13:30 | | | | | | | | | | | 13:30 |
| 13:36 | 92 | | 93 | | 97 | | 97 | | 100 | | 13:36 | | | | | | | | | | | 13:36 |
| 13:42 | 90 | | 92 | | 96 | | 96 | | 99 | | 13:42 | | | | | | | | | | | 13:42 |
| 13:48 | 89 | | 91 | | 95 | | 95 | | 98 | | 13:48 | | | | | | | | | | | 13:48 |
| 13:54 | 88 | | 90 | | 94 | | 95 | | 97 | | 13:54 | | | | | | | | | | | 13:54 |
| 14:00 | 86 | | 89 | | 92 | | 94 | | 97 | | 14:00 | | | | | | | | | | | 14:00 |
| 14:06 | 85 | | 88 | | 91 | | 93 | | 96 | | 14:06 | 100 | | | | | | | | | | 14:06 |
| 14:12 | 83 | | 87 | | 90 | | 92 | | 95 | | 14:12 | 99 | | | | | | | | | | 14:12 |
| 14:18 | 82 | | 86 | | 89 | | 91 | | 94 | | 14:18 | 98 | | | | | | | | | | 14:18 |
| 14:24 | 81 | | 84 | | 88 | | 90 | | 93 | | 14:24 | 97 | | 100 | | | | | | | | 14:24 |
| 14:30 | 79 | | 83 | | 87 | | 89 | | 92 | | 14:30 | 97 | | 99 | | | | | | | | 14:30 |
| 14:36 | 78 | | 82 | | 86 | | 88 | | 91 | | 14:36 | 96 | | 99 | | | | | | | | 14:36 |
| 14:42 | 77 | | 81 | | 85 | | 87 | | 90 | | 14:42 | 95 | | 98 | | | | | | | | 14:42 |
| 14:48 | 75 | | 80 | | 84 | | 86 | | 90 | | 14:48 | 94 | | 97 | | 99 | | | | | | 14:48 |
| 14:54 | 74 | | 79 | | 83 | | 85 | | 89 | | 14:54 | 93 | | 96 | | 98 | | | | | | 14:54 |
| 15:00 | 72 | | 78 | | 82 | | 85 | | 88 | | 15:00 | 92 | | 95 | | 98 | | | | | | 15:00 |
| 15:06 | 71 | | 77 | | 81 | | 84 | | 87 | | 15:06 | 91 | | 95 | | 97 | | | | | | 15:06 |
| 15:12 | 70 | | 76 | | 79 | | 83 | | 86 | | 15:12 | 90 | | 94 | | 96 | | | | | | 15:12 |
| 15:18 | 68 | | 74 | | 78 | | 82 | | 86 | | 15:18 | 90 | | 93 | | 95 | | 100 | | | | 15:18 |
| 15:24 | 67 | | 73 | | 77 | | 81 | | 85 | | 15:24 | 89 | | 92 | | 95 | | 99 | | | | 15:24 |
| 15:30 | 66 | | 72 | | 76 | | 80 | | 84 | | 15:30 | 88 | | 91 | | 94 | | 98 | | | | 15:30 |
| 15:36 | 64 | 100 | 71 | 100 | 75 | | 79 | | 83 | | 15:36 | 87 | | 91 | | 93 | | 97 | | | | 15:36 |
| 15:42 | 63 | 99 | 70 | 99 | 74 | | 78 | | 82 | | 15:42 | 86 | | 90 | | 92 | | 97 | | 100 | | 15:42 |
| 15:48 | 61 | 98 | 69 | 98 | 73 | 100 | 76 | | 81 | | 15:48 | 85 | | 89 | | 91 | | 96 | | 99 | | 15:48 |
| 15:54 | 60 | 96 | 68 | 97 | 72 | 99 | 76 | 100 | 80 | | 15:54 | 84 | | 88 | | 91 | | 95 | | 98 | | 15:54 |
| 16:00 | 59 | 95 | 67 | 96 | 71 | 98 | 75 | 99 | 80 | | 16:00 | 83 | | 87 | | 90 | | 94 | | 97 | | 16:00 |
| 16:06 | 57 | 94 | 66 | 95 | 70 | 97 | 75 | 99 | 79 | | 16:06 | | | 87 | | 89 | | 93 | | 96 | | 16:06 |
| 16:12 | 56 | 93 | 64 | 94 | 69 | 97 | 74 | 98 | 78 | | 16:12 | 82 | | 86 | | 86 | | 92 | | 95 | | 16:12 |
| 16:18 | 54 | 92 | 63 | 93 | 68 | 96 | 73 | 97 | 77 | | 16:18 | 81 | | 85 | | 87 | | 91 | | 94 | | 16:18 |
| 16:24 | 53 | 90 | 62 | 92 | 66 | 95 | 72 | 97 | 76 | | 16:24 | 80 | | 84 | | 87 | | 90 | | 93 | | 16:24 |
| 16:30 | 52 | 89 | 61 | 91 | 65 | 94 | 71 | 96 | 75 | | 16:30 | 79 | | 84 | | 86 | | 90 | | 93 | | 16:30 |
| 16:36 | 50 | 88 | 60 | 90 | 64 | 93 | 70 | 95 | 74 | | 16:36 | 78 | | 83 | | 85 | | 89 | | 92 | | 16:36 |
| 16:42 | 49 | 87 | 59 | 89 | 63 | 92 | 69 | 94 | 74 | | 16:42 | 77 | | 82 | | 84 | | 88 | | 91 | | 16:42 |
| 16:48 | 48 | 85 | 58 | 88 | 62 | 91 | 68 | 94 | 73 | | 16:48 | 77 | | 81 | | 84 | | 87 | | 90 | | 16:48 |
| 16:54 | 46 | 84 | 57 | 87 | 61 | 91 | 67 | 93 | 72 | | 16:54 | 76 | | 80 | | 83 | | 86 | | 89 | | 16:54 |
| 17:00 | 45 | 83 | 56 | 86 | 60 | 90 | 66 | 92 | 71 | 100 | 17:00 | 75 | | 80 | | 82 | | 85 | | 88 | | 17:00 |
| 17:06 | 43 | 82 | 54 | 85 | 59 | 89 | 65 | 92 | 70 | 99 | 17:06 | 74 | | 79 | | 81 | | 84 | | 87 | | 17:06 |
| 17:12 | 42 | 81 | 53 | 84 | 58 | 88 | 65 | 91 | 69 | 98 | 17:12 | 73 | | 78 | | 80 | | 83 | | 86 | | 17:12 |
| 17:18 | 41 | 79 | 52 | 83 | 57 | 87 | 64 | 90 | 68 | 98 | 17:18 | 72 | | 78 | | 80 | | 83 | | 85 | | 17:18 |
| 17:24 | 39 | 78 | 51 | 82 | 56 | | 63 | 90 | 68 | 97 | 17:24 | 71 | | 77 | | 79 | | 82 | | 84 | | 17:24 |
| 17:30 | 38 | 77 | 50 | 81 | 55 | 86 | 62 | 89 | 67 | 96 | 17:30 | 70 | | 76 | | 78 | | 81 | | 83 | | 17:30 |
| 17:36 | 37 | 76 | 49 | 80 | 54 | 85 | 61 | 88 | 66 | 96 | 17:36 | 70 | | 75 | | 78 | | 80 | | 82 | | 17:36 |
| 17:42 | 35 | 75 | 48 | 79 | 52 | 84 | 60 | 88 | 65 | 95 | 17:42 | 69 | | 74 | 99 | 76 | | 79 | | 81 | | 17:42 |
| 17:48 | 34 | 73 | 47 | 78 | 51 | 83 | 59 | 87 | 64 | 94 | 17:48 | 68 | | 73 | 98 | 75 | | 78 | | 80 | | 17:48 |
| 17:54 | 32 | 72 | 46 | 77 | 50 | 82 | 58 | 86 | 63 | 94 | 17:54 | 67 | | 73 | | 75 | | 77 | | 80 | | 17:54 |
| 18:00 | 31 | 71 | 44 | 76 | 49 | 81 | 57 | 86 | 63 | 93 | 18:00 | 66 | 96 | 72 | 97 | 74 | | 77 | | 79 | | 18:00 |
| 18:06 | 30 | 70 | 43 | 75 | 48 | 80 | 56 | 85 | 62 | 92 | 18:06 | 65 | 96 | 71 | 97 | 73 | | 76 | | 78 | | 18:06 |
| 18:12 | 28 | 68 | 42 | 74 | 47 | 80 | 55 | 84 | 61 | 92 | 18:12 | 64 | 95 | 70 | 96 | 73 | | 75 | | 77 | | 18:12 |
| 18:18 | 27 | 67 | 41 | 73 | 46 | 79 | 55 | 83 | 60 | 91 | 18:18 | 63 | 94 | 69 | 96 | 72 | | 74 | | 76 | | 18:18 |
| 18:24 | 26 | 66 | 40 | 72 | 45 | 78 | 54 | 83 | 59 | 90 | 18:24 | 63 | 94 | 69 | 95 | 71 | | 73 | | 75 | | 18:24 |
| 18:30 | 24 | 65 | 39 | 71 | 44 | 77 | 53 | 82 | 58 | 89 | 18:30 | 62 | 93 | 68 | 94 | 70 | | 72 | | 74 | | 18:30 |
| 18:36 | 23 | 64 | 38 | 70 | 43 | 76 | 52 | 81 | 57 | 89 | 18:36 | 61 | 92 | 67 | 94 | 69 | | 71 | | 73 | | 18:36 |
| 18:42 | 21 | 62 | 37 | 69 | 42 | 76 | 51 | 81 | 57 | 88 | 18:42 | 60 | | 65 | 87 | 61 | | 70 | | 72 | | 18:42 |
| 18:48 | 20 | 61 | 36 | 68 | 41 | 74 | 50 | 80 | 56 | 87 | 18:48 | 59 | 91 | 65 | 92 | 68 | | 70 | | 71 | | 18:48 |
| 18:54 | 19 | 60 | 34 | 67 | 39 | 74 | 49 | 79 | 55 | 87 | 18:54 | 58 | 90 | 65 | 92 | 67 | | 69 | | 70 | | 18:54 |
| 19:00 | 17 | 59 | 33 | 66 | 38 | 73 | 48 | 79 | 54 | 86 | 19:00 | 57 | 90 | 64 | 91 | 66 | 100 | 68 | | 69 | | 19:00 |
| 19:06 | 16 | 58 | 32 | 65 | 37 | 72 | 47 | 78 | 53 | 85 | 19:06 | 57 | 89 | 63 | 91 | 65 | 99 | 67 | | 68 | | 19:06 |
| 19:12 | 14 | 56 | 31 | 64 | 36 | 71 | 46 | 77 | 52 | 85 | 19:12 | 56 | 89 | 62 | 90 | 65 | 99 | 66 | | 67 | | 19:12 |
| 19:18 | 13 | 55 | 30 | 63 | 35 | 70 | 45 | 77 | 51 | 84 | 19:18 | 55 | 88 | 62 | 89 | 64 | 98 | 65 | | 67 | | 19:18 |
| 19:24 | 12 | 54 | 29 | 62 | 34 | 69 | 45 | 76 | 51 | 83 | 19:24 | 54 | 87 | 61 | 89 | 63 | 97 | 64 | | 66 | | 19:24 |
| 19:30 | 10 | 53 | 28 | 61 | 33 | 69 | 44 | 75 | 50 | 82 | 19:30 | 53 | 87 | 60 | 88 | 62 | 96 | 63 | | 65 | | 19:30 |
| 19:36 | 9 | 52 | 27 | 60 | 32 | 68 | 43 | 74 | 49 | 82 | 19:36 | 52 | 86 | 59 | 87 | 62 | 96 | 63 | | 64 | | 19:36 |
| 19:42 | 8 | 50 | 26 | 59 | 31 | 67 | 42 | 74 | 48 | 81 | 19:42 | 51 | 85 | 58 | 87 | 61 | 95 | 62 | 100 | 63 | | 19:42 |
| 19:48 | 6 | 49 | 24 | 58 | 30 | 66 | 41 | 73 | 47 | 80 | 19:48 | 50 | 85 | 58 | 86 | 60 | 94 | 61 | 99 | 62 | | 19:48 |
| 19:54 | 5 | 48 | 23 | 57 | 29 | 65 | 40 | 72 | 46 | 78 | 19:54 | 50 | 84 | 57 | 85 | 59 | 93 | 60 | 98 | 61 | | 19:54 |
| 20:00 | 3 | 47 | 22 | 56 | 28 | 64 | 39 | 72 | 46 | 79 | 20:00 | 49 | 83 | 56 | 85 | 58 | 93 | 59 | 98 | 60 | 100 | 20:00 |
| 20:06 | | 45 | 21 | 55 | | 63 | 38 | 71 | | 78 | 20:06 | 48 | | 55 | 84 | 58 | | 58 | 97 | 59 | 99 | 20:06 |

*(continued)*

| Time | 17-21 M | 17-21 F | 22-25 M | 22-25 F | 27-31 M | 27-31 F | 32-36 M | 32-36 F | 37-41 M | 37-41 F | Time | 42-46 M | 42-46 F | 47-51 M | 47-51 F | 52-56 M | 52-56 F | 57-61 M | 57-61 F | 62+ M | 62+ F | Time |
|---|---|---|---|---|---|---|---|---|---|---|---|---|---|---|---|---|---|---|---|---|---|---|
| 20:00 | 3 | 47 | | 56 | | | | 72 | 46 | 79 | 20:00 | 49 | 83 | | | 59 | 93 | | | | | 20:00 |
| 20:06 | 2 | 45 | 21 | 55 | 28 | 63 | 38 | 71 | 45 | 78 | 20:06 | 48 | 83 | 55 | 84 | 58 | 92 | 58 | 97 | 59 | 99 | 20:06 |
| 20:12 | 1 | 44 | 20 | 54 | 25 | 63 | 37 | 70 | 44 | 78 | 20:12 | 47 | 82 | 55 | 84 | 57 | 91 | 57 | 96 | 58 | 98 | 20:12 |
| 20:18 | 0 | 43 | 19 | 53 | 24 | 62 | 36 | 70 | 43 | 77 | 20:18 | 46 | 82 | 54 | 83 | 56 | 90 | 57 | 95 | 57 | 98 | 20:18 |
| 20:24 | | 42 | 18 | 52 | 23 | 61 | 35 | 69 | 42 | 76 | 20:24 | 45 | 81 | 53 | 82 | 55 | 90 | 56 | 95 | 56 | 97 | 20:24 |
| 20:30 | | 41 | 17 | 51 | 22 | 60 | 35 | 68 | 41 | 75 | 20:30 | 44 | 80 | 52 | 82 | 55 | 89 | 55 | 94 | 55 | 96 | 20:30 |
| 20:36 | | 39 | 16 | 50 | 21 | 59 | 34 | 68 | 40 | 75 | 20:36 | 43 | 80 | 51 | 81 | 54 | 88 | 54 | 93 | 54 | 95 | 20:36 |
| 20:42 | | 38 | 14 | 49 | 20 | 58 | 33 | 67 | 40 | 74 | 20:42 | 43 | 79 | 51 | 81 | 53 | 87 | 53 | 92 | 53 | 94 | 20:42 |
| 20:48 | | 37 | 13 | 48 | 19 | 57 | 32 | 66 | 39 | 73 | 20:48 | 42 | 78 | 50 | 80 | 52 | 87 | 52 | 91 | 53 | 94 | 20:48 |
| 20:54 | | 36 | 12 | 47 | 18 | 57 | 31 | 66 | 38 | 73 | 20:54 | 41 | 78 | 49 | 79 | 51 | 86 | 51 | 91 | 52 | 93 | 20:54 |
| 21:00 | | 35 | 11 | 46 | 17 | 56 | 30 | 65 | 37 | 72 | 21:00 | 40 | 77 | 48 | 79 | 51 | 85 | 50 | 90 | 51 | 92 | 21:00 |
| 21:06 | | 33 | 10 | 45 | 16 | 55 | 29 | 64 | 36 | 71 | 21:06 | 39 | 77 | 47 | 78 | 50 | 84 | 50 | 89 | 50 | 91 | 21:06 |
| 21:12 | | 32 | 9 | 44 | 15 | 54 | 28 | 63 | 35 | 71 | 21:12 | 38 | 76 | 47 | 77 | 49 | 84 | 49 | 88 | 49 | 90 | 21:12 |
| 21:18 | | 31 | 8 | 43 | 14 | 53 | 27 | 63 | 34 | 70 | 21:18 | 37 | 75 | 46 | 77 | 48 | 83 | 48 | 87 | 48 | 90 | 21:18 |
| 21:24 | | 30 | 7 | 42 | 12 | 52 | 26 | 62 | 34 | 69 | 21:24 | 37 | 75 | 45 | 76 | 47 | 82 | 47 | 87 | 47 | 89 | 21:24 |
| 21:30 | | 28 | 6 | 41 | 11 | 51 | 25 | 61 | 33 | 68 | 21:30 | 36 | 74 | 44 | 76 | 47 | 81 | 46 | 86 | 46 | 88 | 21:30 |
| 21:36 | | 27 | 4 | 40 | 10 | 51 | 25 | 61 | 32 | 68 | 21:36 | 35 | 73 | 44 | 75 | 46 | 81 | 45 | 85 | 45 | 87 | 21:36 |
| 21:42 | | 26 | 3 | 39 | 9 | 50 | 24 | 60 | 31 | 67 | 21:42 | 34 | 73 | 43 | 74 | 45 | 80 | 44 | 84 | 44 | 86 | 21:42 |
| 21:48 | | 25 | 2 | 38 | 8 | 49 | 23 | 59 | 30 | 66 | 21:48 | 33 | 72 | 42 | 74 | 44 | 79 | 43 | 84 | 43 | 86 | 21:48 |
| 21:54 | | 24 | 1 | 37 | 7 | 48 | 22 | 59 | 29 | 66 | 21:54 | 32 | 71 | 41 | 73 | 44 | 79 | 43 | 83 | 42 | 85 | 21:54 |
| 22:00 | | 22 | 0 | 36 | 6 | 47 | 21 | 58 | 29 | 65 | 22:00 | 31 | 71 | 40 | 72 | 43 | 78 | 42 | 82 | 41 | 84 | 22:00 |
| 22:06 | | 21 | | 35 | 5 | 46 | 20 | 57 | 28 | 64 | 22:06 | 30 | 70 | 40 | 72 | 42 | 77 | 41 | 81 | 40 | 83 | 22:06 |
| 22:12 | | 20 | | 34 | 4 | 46 | 19 | 57 | 27 | 64 | 22:12 | 30 | 70 | 39 | 71 | 41 | 76 | 40 | 80 | 40 | 82 | 22:12 |
| 22:18 | | 19 | | 33 | 3 | 45 | 18 | 56 | 26 | 63 | 22:18 | 29 | 69 | 38 | 71 | 40 | 76 | 39 | 80 | 39 | 82 | 22:18 |
| 22:24 | | 18 | | 32 | 2 | 44 | 17 | 55 | 25 | 62 | 22:24 | 28 | 68 | 37 | 70 | 40 | 75 | 38 | 79 | 38 | 81 | 22:24 |
| 22:30 | | 16 | | 31 | 1 | 43 | 16 | 54 | 24 | 61 | 22:30 | 27 | 68 | 36 | 69 | 39 | 74 | 37 | 78 | 37 | 80 | 22:30 |
| 22:38 | | 15 | | 30 | 0 | 42 | 15 | 54 | 23 | 61 | 22:38 | 26 | 67 | 36 | 69 | 38 | 73 | 37 | 77 | 36 | 79 | 22:38 |
| 22:42 | | 14 | | 29 | | 41 | 15 | 53 | 23 | 60 | 22:42 | 25 | 66 | 35 | 68 | 37 | 73 | 36 | 76 | 35 | 78 | 22:42 |
| 22:48 | | 13 | | 28 | | 40 | 14 | 52 | 22 | 59 | 22:48 | 24 | 66 | 34 | 67 | 38 | 72 | 35 | 76 | 34 | 78 | 22:48 |
| 22:54 | | 12 | | 27 | | 40 | 13 | 52 | 21 | 59 | 22:54 | 23 | 65 | 33 | 67 | 36 | 71 | 34 | 75 | 33 | 77 | 22:54 |
| 23:00 | | 10 | | 26 | | 39 | 12 | 51 | 20 | 58 | 23:00 | 23 | 64 | 33 | 66 | 35 | 70 | 33 | 74 | 32 | 76 | 23:00 |
| 23:06 | | 9 | | 25 | | 38 | 11 | 50 | 19 | 57 | 23:06 | 22 | 64 | 32 | 66 | 34 | 70 | 32 | 73 | 31 | 75 | 23:06 |
| 23:12 | | 8 | | 24 | | 37 | 10 | 49 | 18 | 56 | 23:12 | 21 | 63 | 31 | 65 | 33 | 69 | 31 | 73 | 30 | 74 | 23:12 |
| 23:18 | | 7 | | 23 | | 36 | 9 | 49 | 17 | 56 | 23:18 | 20 | 63 | 30 | 64 | 33 | 68 | 30 | 72 | 29 | 74 | 23:18 |
| 23:24 | | 5 | | 22 | | 35 | 8 | 48 | 17 | 55 | 23:24 | 19 | 62 | 29 | 64 | 32 | 67 | 30 | 71 | 28 | 73 | 23:24 |
| 23:30 | | 4 | | 21 | | 34 | 7 | 48 | 16 | 54 | 23:30 | 18 | 61 | 29 | 63 | 31 | 67 | 29 | 70 | 27 | 72 | 23:30 |
| 23:38 | | 3 | | 20 | | 34 | 7 | 47 | 15 | 54 | 23:38 | 17 | 61 | 28 | 62 | 30 | 66 | 28 | 69 | 27 | 71 | 23:38 |
| 23:42 | | 2 | | 19 | | 33 | 5 | 46 | 14 | 53 | 23:42 | 17 | 60 | 27 | 62 | 29 | 65 | 27 | 69 | 26 | 70 | 23:42 |
| 23:48 | | 1 | | 18 | | 32 | 5 | 46 | 13 | 52 | 23:48 | 16 | 59 | 26 | 61 | 28 | 65 | 26 | 68 | 25 | 70 | 23:48 |
| 23:54 | | 0 | | 17 | | 31 | 4 | 45 | 12 | 52 | 23:54 | 15 | 59 | 25 | 61 | 28 | 64 | 25 | 67 | 24 | 69 | 23:54 |
| 24:00 | | | | 16 | | 30 | 3 | 44 | 11 | 51 | 24:00 | 14 | 58 | 25 | 60 | 27 | 63 | 24 | 66 | 23 | 68 | 24:00 |
| 24:06 | | | | 15 | | 29 | 2 | 43 | 11 | 50 | 24:06 | 13 | 57 | 24 | 59 | 26 | 62 | 23 | 65 | 22 | 67 | 24:06 |
| 24:12 | | | | 14 | | 29 | 1 | 43 | 10 | 49 | 24:12 | 12 | 57 | 23 | 59 | 25 | 61 | 23 | 65 | 21 | 66 | 24:12 |
| 24:18 | | | | 13 | | 28 | 0 | 42 | 9 | 49 | 24:18 | 11 | 56 | 22 | 58 | 25 | 61 | 22 | 64 | 20 | 66 | 24:18 |
| 24:24 | | | | 12 | | 27 | | 41 | 8 | 48 | 24:24 | 10 | 56 | 22 | 57 | 24 | 60 | 21 | 63 | 19 | 65 | 24:24 |
| 24:30 | | | | 11 | | 26 | | 41 | 7 | 47 | 24:30 | 10 | 55 | 21 | 57 | 23 | 59 | 20 | 62 | 18 | 64 | 24:30 |
| 24:38 | | | | 10 | | 25 | | 40 | 8 | 47 | 24:38 | 9 | 54 | 20 | 56 | 22 | 59 | 19 | 62 | 17 | 63 | 24:38 |
| 24:42 | | | | 9 | | 24 | | 39 | 6 | 46 | 24:42 | 8 | 54 | 19 | 56 | 22 | 58 | 18 | 61 | 16 | 62 | 24:42 |
| 24:48 | | | | 8 | | 23 | | 39 | 5 | 45 | 24:48 | 7 | 53 | 18 | 55 | 21 | 57 | 17 | 60 | 15 | 62 | 24:48 |
| 24:54 | | | | 7 | | 23 | | 38 | 4 | 45 | 24:54 | 6 | 52 | 18 | 54 | 20 | 56 | 17 | 59 | 14 | 61 | 24:54 |
| 25:00 | | | | 6 | | 22 | | 37 | 3 | 44 | 25:00 | 5 | 52 | 17 | 54 | 19 | 56 | 16 | 58 | 13 | 60 | 25:00 |
| 25:06 | | | | 5 | | 21 | | 37 | 2 | 43 | 25:06 | 4 | 51 | 16 | 53 | 18 | 55 | 15 | 58 | 13 | 59 | 25:06 |
| 25:12 | | | | 4 | | 20 | | 36 | 1 | 42 | 25:12 | 3 | 50 | 15 | 52 | 18 | 54 | 14 | 57 | 12 | 58 | 25:12 |
| 25:18 | | | | 3 | | 19 | | 35 | 0 | 42 | 25:18 | 3 | 50 | 15 | 52 | 17 | 53 | 13 | 56 | 11 | 58 | 25:18 |
| 25:24 | | | | 2 | | 18 | | 34 | | 41 | 25:24 | 2 | 49 | 14 | 51 | 16 | 53 | 12 | 55 | 10 | 57 | 25:24 |
| 25:30 | | | | 1 | | 17 | | 34 | | 40 | 25:30 | 1 | 49 | 13 | 51 | 15 | 52 | 11 | 55 | 9 | 56 | 25:30 |
| 25:36 | | | | 0 | | 17 | | 33 | | 40 | 25:36 | 0 | 48 | 12 | 50 | 15 | 51 | 10 | 54 | 8 | 55 | 25:36 |
| 25:42 | | | | | | 16 | | 32 | | 39 | 25:42 | | 47 | 11 | 49 | 14 | 50 | 10 | 53 | 7 | 54 | 25:42 |
| 25:48 | | | | | | 15 | | 32 | | 38 | 25:48 | | 47 | 11 | 49 | 13 | 50 | 9 | 52 | 6 | 54 | 25:48 |
| 25:54 | | | | | | 14 | | 31 | | 38 | 25:54 | | 46 | 10 | 48 | 12 | 49 | 8 | 51 | 5 | 53 | 25:54 |
| 26:00 | | | | | | 13 | | 30 | | 37 | 26:00 | | 45 | 9 | 47 | 11 | 48 | 7 | 51 | 4 | 52 | 26:00 |
| 26:06 | | | | | | 12 | | 30 | | 36 | 26:06 | | 45 | 8 | 47 | 11 | 47 | 6 | 50 | 3 | 51 | 26:06 |
| 26:12 | | | | | | 11 | | 29 | | 35 | 26:12 | | 44 | 7 | 46 | 10 | 47 | 5 | 49 | 2 | 51 | 26:12 |
| 26:16 | | | | | | 11 | | 28 | | 35 | 26:16 | | 43 | 6 | 46 | 9 | 46 | 4 | 48 | 1 | 50 | 26:16 |
| 26:24 | | | | | | 10 | | 28 | | 34 | 26:24 | | 43 | 6 | 45 | 9 | 46 | 3 | 47 | 0 | 49 | 26:24 |
| 26:30 | | | | | | 9 | | 27 | | 33 | 26:30 | | 42 | 5 | 44 | 7 | 44 | 3 | 47 | 0 | 48 | 26:30 |
| Time | M | F | M | F | M | F | M | F | M | F | Time | M | F | M | F | M | F | M | F | M | F | Time |
| Age Group | 17-21 | | 22-25 | | 27-31 | | 32-36 | | 37-41 | | Age Group | 42-46 | | 47-51 | | 52-56 | | 57-61 | | 62+ | | Age Group |

Scoring standards are used to convert raw scores to point scores after test events are completed. Male point scores are indicated by the M at the top and bottom of the shaded column. Female point scores are indicated by the F at the top and bottom of the unshaded column. To convert raw scores to point scores, find the number of repetitions performed in the left-hand column. Next, move right along that row and locate the intersection of the soldier's appropriate age column. In all cases, when a time falls between two point values, the lower point value is used. Record that number in the 2MR points block on the front of the scorecard.

# Demonstration

Before the actual test, you will be given an introduction on all the events. An officer, who will be in good shape, will give a demonstration of all the events. This demonstration will be for push-ups and sit-ups that have to be performed according to strict standards. No sagging of the back while doing push-ups will be tolerated. These standards are covered in more detail later in the chapter.

A trainee should enter the police academy at a fitness level that will provide him the most potential for successful completion of all phases of training. This will help him to attain passing standards by the final testing phase of the training academy. Failure to meet the passing standards might result in a retest; failing to pass the retest could result in dismissal from the academy.

# The Test

The following sections will give you the information you need to know for the exam. You will find guidelines that will help you for the different types of exercises you will be expected to do for the exam.

## Guidelines for Push-ups

The following are instructions on how to perform a proper push-up. Follow the instructions accurately. If you fail to perform the proper push-up, it will not be counted toward your score.

Purpose: Push-ups measure the endurance of the chest, shoulder, and triceps muscles.

1. Lie chest down with your hands at shoulder level, palms flat on the floor and a little more than shoulder width apart, feet together.

2. Make your chin touch the floor.

3. Straighten your arms as you push your body up off the floor. Keep your back straight.

4. Breathe out as the arms begin to get straight.

5. Lower your body to the floor, bending your arms and keeping your body straight.

6. Lower your body until your chest touches the floor.

7. Pause and start again to do a second, third, and so on.

**EXAM ALERT**

During the test, the instructor will place his hand on your back (in the form of a fist) to ensure that you are going all the way down to the floor for a complete push-up.

**EXAM ALERT**

You may rest during the exercise. The only acceptable resting position that does not result in disqualification during the test is an upright position. If your knee touches the floor, you will be disqualified.

See Figure 8.2 for a better understanding of the exercise.

PUSH-UPS

**FIGURE 8.2**   Proper push-up form.

# Guidelines for Sit-ups

Purpose: Sit-ups test the strength of your stomach muscles.

1. Lie down on your back with knees bent.

2. Keep your feet flat on the floor, close to your buttocks.

3. Interlace your fingers behind the back of your head.

4. No jerking or twisting movements.

5. Commence curl with your shoulders, followed by your upper back, and finally your lower back.

6. Bring your torso up and beyond the 60 degrees position.

7. Hold momentarily.

8. Lower your torso to the ground.

9. Your head and shoulders should not touch the ground after the set has started.

10. Repeat sit-up.

See Figure 8.3 for a better understanding of the exercise.

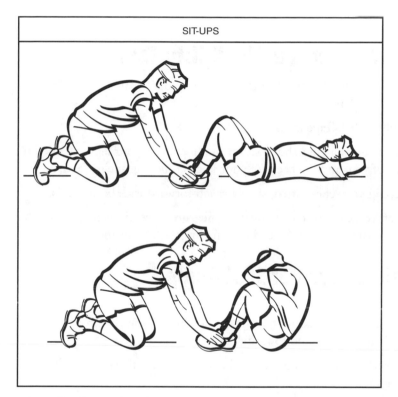

**FIGURE 8.3**   Proper sit-up form.

**EXAM ALERT**

You may rest during the exercise. The only acceptable resting position that does not result in disqualification during the test is an upright position. If your hands come apart from behind your neck, you are considered disqualified for the test.

# Guidelines for the Running Test

There are no particular instructions or guidelines for the running event. You basically have to finish the distance in the required time. If you are really a fast walker, you can even walk the course. While running, you will be allowed to stop and walk the distance as long as you finish the course in the required time. If you fail this event, most of the agencies offer a re-test. But the re-test will be for the whole physical agility section and not just the failed event. So, if you are borderline in another event besides running, it is best to pass the running test in the first attempt; or otherwise, you will have to go and be re-tested on the entire physical agility portion.

# Guidelines for the Flexibility Test

Purpose: The purpose of this test is to measure your flexibility in your torso and upper shoulders.

Equipment needed: Tape measure

1. After removing your shoes, sit on the floor with your legs extended in front of you, and the backs of your knees touching the ground.

2. Keeping your chest lifted, slowly reach forward with both hands.

3. When you can't reach any further, measure in centimeters (you might need a partner) from the end of your fingers to your toes.

# Guidelines for Vertical Jump

The following are instructions on how to perform a proper vertical jump. Follow the instructions accurately. If you fail to perform the proper vertical jump, it will not be counted toward your score.

Purpose: Vertical jump measures explosive leg strength and overall lower body strength.

Equipment: Measuring tape on smooth wall and a piece of chalk or a commercially designed vertical jump measuring device.

1. Candidates must jump from a stationary, standing position with both feet on the ground.

2. Jump vertically.

3. While jumping in the air, extend arms above your head to reach maximum height.

4. While in the air, mark the maximum height reached with a chalk mark on the wall.

Although acceptable scores might differ with individual agencies, as a general guideline, a minimum score of between 12 and 16 inches is required.

# How to Improve Your Score

As you train and prepare, persistence is one of the biggest factors for your success. However, there are some things you can do that might possibly improve your scores. The following sections highlight some of the things you can do in an attempt to improve your scores.

## Push-ups

The following steps will give you tools that can help you improve your chances for success with the push-ups test:

▶ Determine the number of correct push-ups you can do in one minute. Multiply the number by 0.75. This is the number of push-ups that you need to do in each set. For example, 52 push-ups in one minute. Number for the individual set: 52 × 0.75 = 39.

▶ Perform three to five one-minute sets of push-ups, while maintaining proper form.

▶ Do not rest for more than one minute between the sets.

▶ If the last set becomes too difficult to finish, rest just enough to finish the set.

▶ Perform this routine three times a week.

▶ Increase the number of repetition by one or two repetitions each week.

## Sit-ups

The following steps will give you tools that can help you improve your chances for success with the sit-ups test:

▶ Determine the number of correct sit-ups you can do in one minute. Multiply the number by 0.75. This is the number of sit-ups you need to do in each set. For example, 40 sit-ups in one minute. Number for the individual set: 40 × 0.75 = 30.

▶ Perform three to five one-minute sets of sit-ups, maintaining proper form.

▶ Do not rest for more than one minute between sets.

▸ If the last set becomes too difficult to finish, rest just enough to finish the set.

▸ Perform this routine three times per week.

▸ Increase the number of repetitions by one or two each week.

# Running Test

To prepare for the test, gradually increase your running endurance. Start with a level you feel comfortable with. Use Table 8.1 as a guideline for building your endurance.

| Table 8.1 | Schedule for Building Running Endurance | | | |
|---|---|---|---|---|
| Week | Activity | Distance in Miles | Duration in Minutes | Times Per Week |
| 1 | Walk | 1 | 17–20 | 5 |
| 2 | Walk | 1.5 | 25–29 | 5 |
| 3 | Walk | 2 | 32–35 | 5 |
| 4 | Walk/Jog | 2 | 28–30 | 5 |
| 5 | Walk/Jog | 2 | 27 | 5 |
| 6 | Walk/Jog | 2 | 26 | 5 |
| 7 | Walk/Jog | 2 | 25 | 5 |
| 8 | Walk/Jog | 2 | 24 | 5 |
| 9 | Jog | 2 | 23 | 4 |
| 10 | Jog | 2 | 22 | 4 |
| 11 | Jog | 2 | 21 | 4 |
| 12 | Jog | 2 | 20 | 4 |

# Sprints Workout

To prepare for this event, interval training seems to be the best choice. Preparation for this event has been divided in three phases.

1. Measure the time for your all-out effort for 110 yards.

2. Multiply your all out-time by .80 to determine your training time.

   For example: $40 \times 0.80 = 32$ seconds.

3. Follow Table 8.2 and gradually increase your speed and short distance endurance.

| Table 8.2 | Schedule for Building Sprinting Abilities | | | | |
|-----------|-------------------|------|----------------------------|-----------|-------------------|
| Weeks | Distance in Yards | Reps | Training Time in Seconds | Rest Time | Times Per Week |
| 1–2 | 110 | 10 | 32 | | |
| 3–4 | 110 | 10 | 32 – 2 to 3 sec. | | |
| 5–6 | 110 | 10 | 32 – 5 to 6 sec. | | |
| 7–8 | 220 | 8 | 64 | | |
| 9–10 | 220 | 8 | 64 – 4 sec. | | |

**EXAM ALERT**

Always warm up before any physical exercise and cool down after the exercise.

# Flexibility

The best way to improve flexibility is by proper stretching. Stretching is useful in preventing injury and treatment of any injury. Add a variety of exercises to your stretching regimen before your workout as a warm-up phase and after workout as a cool-down process. The best time to increase flexibility is after you have worked out and your body has been warmed up. To improve flexibility, think of flexibility training and not just brief stretching periods before workout.

# Exam Prep Questions

Because there are no true questions for the physical ability part of the exam, we are not offering this section in its usual form. However, you should do your own exam preparation at this point by assessing your abilities with all of the physical aspects that you covered in this chapter. Take this time to figure out what you do well, and what you need to work on. Set baselines right now and use them to begin improving your physical fitness in order to be successful on the exam. Remember to refer to the military standards you covered earlier as a measuring stick for your improvement.

# PART IV
# Maximizing Test Scores

CHAPTER NINE

# Time Management

## Terms You'll Need to Understand:

✓ Prioritize your study tasks

✓ Develop self-discipline

✓ Designate a study area

✓ Practice, practice, and more practice

✓ Review your performance

## Concepts You'll Need to Master:

✓ Time management before test

✓ Time management during test

✓ Time management during the oral interview

✓ Time management during the physical agility test

Time management is very critical when preparing for any test. All the hard work of learning the subject material will not help you score high on the test if you don't have time to answer the question. For the written test, it is very important to utilize your time well so that you can complete all the questions. Time management is also critical during the oral interview. You have a limited amount of time in which to answer a number of questions. You want to manage time in such a manner that you have enough time to answer all the questions and, at the same time, have enough time to properly give answers to the questions. There will be a time limit to answer a series of questions. In the following section, you will uncover some important information about how to manage your time before and during the test.

# Time Management Before the Test

Be sure to schedule your time according to test dates and tasks you need to accomplish before the test. Simply put: plan ahead. Most of the time you will know the test date well ahead of time. Do some backward planning. By *backward planning*, I mean—working backward from the date of the test—list some of the tasks you want to accomplish and the deadlines for those tasks. Make sure that your deadlines are realistic. Don't be too aggressive with the deadline, but at the same time make it challenging.

For example, if the test is November 1, 2004, Table 9.1 shows you a simple backward planning scheme that sets tasks and deadlines.

| Table 9.1 Time Management Before the Police Exam | |
| --- | --- |
| **Task** | **Date** |
| Final review should be completed by | October 15 |
| Review 2 | October 10 |
| Review 1 | October 5 |
| Final outline prepared | October 1 |
| Question prepared | September 15 |
| Initial outline prepared | September 1 |
| Initial Review | August 30 |
| Test material received | August 15 |

## Prioritize Your Study Tasks and Time

Prioritizing your study tasks will allow you ample time for reviewing exam content. For difficult tasks, study when you are the most productive. For example, some people are productive in the morning when their mind is fresh and absorbs the study material quickly. Other people are more productive at night, when it's quiet and there are fewer distractions. Whatever your habits, schedule your study time accordingly. It is better for you to handle tough tasks when you feel most productive, and save simple, interesting tasks that require minimal effort for the times you are likely to be tired or unproductive.

> **NOTE**
>
> Know and plan exactly how much time you'll need for the full exam preparation. Also be able to identify your weak areas while you study. Knowing where you need more practice and reinforcement is a solid way to prepare fully for the exam.

# Keep Time for Your Personal Commitments and Routines

Balance is the key. Don't overlook your other personal commitments. You might have to juggle a few things to fit in some study time. There is nothing more frustrating than falling behind in personal tasks. Remember that after you have been selected and are in the police training academy, there will be even less time to catch up on personal commitment, so stay current on everything.

Generally it is beneficial to make a list of all the tasks you need to do in a day. For example, make a rough list of all the things you do in a day and how many hours do you need for them, such as

- ▶ Sleep—7 hours

- ▶ Personal grooming—2 hours

- ▶ Meals—2 hours

- ▶ Work—8 hours

- ▶ Entertainment—2 hours

When you have done that, calculate the number of hours that you will have for study each day as you approach the test. If you have three hours per day, you have a substantial amount of time that you can use for a well-defined plan of study. This list will also help you note how many hours are wasted on less important things.

# Develop Self-Discipline

Self-discipline is required for a well managed study plan. Time management essentially deals with how much discipline you have in your life; how well do you deal with deadlines in general and how do you cope with all the tasks you have to do on a regular basis? Try to develop this discipline by making your hours productive. Having regular times for waking up, for sleeping, and for other things can do this. You don't need to have a strict regimen, but organizing yourself requires some patterns of habits and you need to follow them to study effectively.

> **NOTE**
>
> Start preparing for the test on the day you receive the test material. You can do this by reading the introduction material, determining the test date, and doing some backward planning of how you are going to approach the test.

# Maintain Healthy Eating and Sleeping Habits

You need energy for the test, and for energy, you need a well-balanced diet and ample amounts of sleep. You know your body. For some people, six hours sleep is plenty. Others are dysfunctional unless they sleep a full eight hours. Know yourself and listen to your body. All the hard work will go to waste if you cannot stay awake during the test. In addition to good eating and sleeping habits, you will feel a lot healthier and fit by doing regular exercise. Exercise will keep you alert and relieve the stress and tiredness of long hours of study.

# Take Short Breaks While Studying

Don't get burned out with studying. I have seen many people start at a very aggressive pace in the beginning of their study period, but when the test gets closer, they are burned out and don't want to study anymore. Crucial time is being wasted when the test is near and you can't motivate yourself to open a book. Pace yourself and take plenty of breaks during preparation. Most people can concentrate on a task for an hour and lose interest after that. So, don't put yourself through the ordeal of trying to study for more than an hour at a time. Take a break as soon as you feel distracted. Set a personal timetable of study time and play time.

> **TIP**
>
> If it is possible, find a study partner. A partner can make studying a lot more fun and more productive.

# Designate a Study Area

A study area should be an area free of distractions, such as telephones, television, children, and so on. You don't need to have a special room. Just about any corner of the house will do, as long as it is free and clear of any distractions. You might also want to look at the schedules of others around you, and schedule your studying for a time when you can have peace and quiet and the fewest disturbances.

> **TIP**
>
> Making flashcards might be a helpful way to review test material or understand unfamiliar terms. Study the cards in random order, and then review only those terms that you have difficulty remembering.

# Practice, Practice, and More Practice

As part of your studies, you should complete many practice tests so that you will gain confidence in your abilities. Look at the test questions and try to determine how they are structured, patterned, and styled. Learn the pattern and predict what type of question requires what type of response. This will be a very powerful time-saver for you during the actual test because you will not have to waste time trying to understand the demands of the question.

# Review Your Study Performance

It is important for you to review your work regularly as you study. Evaluate what goals you set for yourself at the beginning of your study period and take note of what you have achieved in comparison to what you still need to accomplish before test day. Reflect on what you have accomplished regularly so that you can speed up or slow down studying, as required. This review will give you a good opportunity to sit back and see your progress from an objective point of view. You also can identify whether you need to change your study hours or your study habits.

Try to recognize your maximum output time and reschedule your plans accordingly. Unless you review your study hours, your motivation levels, and your achievements, it will be difficult for you to follow a successful study plan.

## Relax

It is critical to relax a little before the exam. You should worry about scoring high, but not to the point where you cannot think or function anymore. Do something you enjoy a night or two before the exam to help you unwind and get your mind off the exam. Also, do not try to cram at the last moment. Getting a good night's sleep and having a good breakfast on exam morning is also critical. Finally, if possible, find a minute or two to chat with a friend to laugh and relax before the test.

# Time Management During the Police Test

As you go through the different procedures of the police officer selection process, you will need to apply different sets of time management skills for each type of test. In this section, I have given some important details related to how you can manage your time during the written test by applying some time-saving techniques. You will also see what strategies you need to apply to manage time effectively for the oral interview and the physical agility test.

## Time Management During the Written Test

In this section, you will encounter some time management strategies that will be helpful during the written test. You will uncover ideas on how to time yourself, how to tackle test questions without wasting time, and what type of expectations you should keep to make sure that you complete your test within the given time limit.

### Time Yourself

Scan through the full test first to know how many questions are on the test and how much time you have to finish them. A quick calculation will tell you how much time you have to answer each question. To help yourself practice having a limited amount of time to answer a question, use a stopwatch while practicing for the test. Realize that some questions will take longer than others. But that's all right because some questions will take less time and it will even out.

## Answer the Most Difficult Questions First, When You Are Most Motivated and Least Tired

Do a quick scan of the test. Plan an approach of attack. In your test strategy, you need to mark the easy questions first so that you can differentiate between the hard and easy questions and focus more on the hard questions. Depending on your test style and habits, it might be wiser to do the tough questions first, but if that means wasting too much time, skip the tough questions and go to the easy ones. You might be able to handle the difficult questions better before your mind gets cluttered with the easy test questions.

## Take Notes Carefully During the Pre-Test Period

It's best to make notes in simple bulleted form. They are much easier to remember. You will be given several sheets of scratch paper. Take full advantage of that. Be aware that while taking the actual police test, you will not be allowed to look at the notes you took during the study session. But your notes will not be written in vain, either. When you first sit for the test, you will be allowed to write down information from your notes on scratch paper. This is essentially performing a brain dump of all the items you noted in the pre-test period. Write down all the main points as soon as you are allowed to do so. Your bulleted outline will certainly come in handy when answering some of the questions.

## Don't Spend Too Much Time Reviewing Answers to Exam Questions

When you have decided what the answer is, do not waste too much time thinking about it. Do not brood over or be unsure of the answer. Many people waste valuable time by constantly thinking of answers that they have given rather than focusing on the next question. Remember that you can always review your test at the end, if there is time. Even during a review session at the end of the test, it is advisable not to mull over test answers too much. It is commonly known that your first response to a question will generally be correct, so don't talk yourself out of a correct answer just because you are dwelling on whether your answer is correct.

To ensure that you have enough time to finish the test, and if you want to review your work, keep time during the test. Bring a watch and do some self-monitoring during the test to make certain that you have time to complete everything and have some time to review after all questions are answered.

## Maintain Your Concentration Levels During the Exam

It is important to keep in mind that the test takes some time to complete and, therefore, keeping a full concentration level throughout the exam might be a challenge. So, try not to be distracted either by people around you or your own thoughts as the exam period moves forward. Sometimes when people are tired or in uncomfortable clothes, or other physical discomfort, they tend to get distracted. Be aware of all the things that could disturb your concentration and make sure that you have planned for them before the test.

## Keep Realistic and Practical Expectations

During the test, it is useful for you to keep practical and realistic expectations for yourself. If you remain worried about perfection and scoring very high during the test, you might lose valuable time. During this time, it is also important for you to keep a positive view of your capabilities and not let any negative thoughts of failure bother you. Dwelling on these thoughts may seriously affect your efficiency in coping with the task at hand. So, use your time wisely.

## A Last-Minute Time Management Checklist

Here's a checklist for you to follow for better time management before and during the written test:

- ▶ Start your preparation early.
- ▶ Avoid sudden surprises by making sure that you know all details.
- ▶ Make sure to visit the location and know the timing and schedule.
- ▶ Know how long the test lasts.
- ▶ Prepare the materials you need to take with you a night before.
- ▶ Do not reach the venue too early or too late. Both can cause stress.
- ▶ Make sure you take a watch along.
- ▶ Make brief notes during the study period.
- ▶ Jot down notes as soon as you enter the test hall.
- ▶ Read the exam through.
- ▶ Identify the difficult and easy questions and allocate time accordingly.
- ▶ Begin work on the answers.
- ▶ Do not spend too much time if you don't know the answer. Skip to the next question.
- ▶ Maintain speed, but remember to understand each question and give answers accordingly.

▶ Keep an eye on the watch and review how you're doing in terms of time management.

▶ Speed up or slow down as required.

▶ Try to complete all questions.

▶ Leave a little time cushion for the unexpected.

▶ Leave time to review your answers.

▶ Submit the test.

# Time Management During the Oral Interview

The oral interview is one of the most important phases of the entire police officer selection process. This is one time where you get to talk about yourself and you should not be shy about it. It is very critical to manage your time properly during this phase to score high. Use the following tips as guidelines to take advantage of the time allocated during the interview.

## Start Early

Start preparing for the oral interview early in your preparation time. Don't wait to pass the written test to start preparing for the oral interview. After the written exam, you might not have much time to prepare for the oral interview. If you cram too much at the end, you will get flustered during the interview and will not answer your questions properly.

## Know How Many Questions You Have to Answer Versus How Much Time Is Given to Answer the Questions

During the oral interview, it is very important to know your time limit. You want to be able to give an appropriate answer in the given time. While watching your time, it is also very important for your answer to be detailed enough to cover all points being asked. A quick calculation of the number of questions divided by time allowed will tell you how much time that you have to answer your questions. Practicing your replies to questions will help you know exactly how much time you will need to sufficiently answer specific questions.

**EXAM ALERT**

Talk out loud to yourself while you practice answers to oral questions. This will help build confidence and it also lets you know if you're stumbling on a question.

## Answer All Questions

Most of the time, there will be a clock facing you as you sit in the chair. Keep an eye on the clock as you answer the questions. If you are not finished with your answer and see that you are running out of time, it is better to find a stopping point and move on to the next question. It's better to move on than to run out of time at the end and not answer all the questions.

## Listen to the Question the First Time

Time is of the essence. Every second counts. Pay attention when the interviewer is asking the question. If you wander away from what is being asked, you will end up asking for the question to be repeated. If the interviewer has to repeat the question, even though there is no penalty, the time it takes for the interviewer to repeat the question comes out of your allocated time for the whole interview.

## Save Your Own Questions for Later

If, during the interview, a question about something pops up in your mind, it is best to save it for a later time. If you ask the question during the interview, you might be wasting valuable time that would be better served answering the interviewer's questions.

# Time Management During the Physical Agility Test

Just as any other phase of the police selection process, time management in the physical agility test is also very important. You will be graded not solely on your ability to do strenuous activity—the test will also be timed and you must meet certain expectations within that time period.

## Start Preparing Early

Assess your physical condition and start preparing for the physical agility test early. Pace yourself during training. If you wait until the last minute and try to do too much in very little time, you could end up injuring yourself and miss the test date or fail completely.

## Know Your Limitations

Knowing your limitations simply means you should know before you go to the test how many push-ups or sit-ups you can do and how long it will take you to do it. The time keeper will be calling time as you do your activity. Pace your repetitions according to the time limit.

## Pace Yourself During the Test

If a rest period is allowed, take full advantage of the time allotted. Do not be too enthusiastic about the upcoming activity and be the first one in line, ignoring your rest period. There is nothing worse than jumping between activities and burning all your energy. If there are no rest periods, be aware of your body and pace yourself throughout the activities well enough to not run out of energy too soon.

## Carry Your Own Stopwatch

This is very important for the running portion of the test. Even though the timekeeper will be calling the time, it is nice to have your own watch. You will be able to keep better time during the run if you keep an eye on yourself.

## Be Well Rehearsed for the Physical Activities

You should know your scoring standards well ahead of time. You should know what it will take for you to pass the test. All activities should be well rehearsed. Basically, you should have each repetition and each running lap down to seconds. These activities should be practiced well enough to be executed automatically.

# Avoid Stress—The Key to Better Time Management

During the testing phases of the police officer selection process, you will realize that preparation and undergoing testing can place you in stressful situations. Remember that stress is one of the most significant things that might affect the way in which you maintain your time throughout the process of preparing and during the testing process. Stress can make you forget information you have previously spent hours studying.

If you have given yourself plenty of time to prepare for the exam, you will face less stress. Perfectionism causes undue stress and time delays. Know what signal your body gives when you are under stress. If stress is being conveyed, control it by self-counseling and deep breathing. Try to know your limitations and do not stretch yourself beyond them.

When you manage your time effectively, you see a bigger picture and have the option to look at what you are doing. If you do not plan ahead and are always rushed for time, you never get to look at some of the most important things you are heading for nor review how you have achieved most of your targets. You can either achieve these in an organized manner or you can work on a day-to-day basis as you come face to face with tasks. You might achieve your targets in both ways, but one approach will definitely be more relaxed and the other will be done definitely under stress. Only you can decide how you want to work. If you feel you are motivated and want to prepare well before the exam, make sure that you follow these time management strategies.

# Exam Prep Questions

As you can imagine, there are not too many actual questions that I can give you for a chapter on time management. Time management isn't a topic area on the exam; rather, it is a set of techniques and ideas you should follow to maximize study time and time allotted during the exam itself. The following text provides time management exercises that will help you build time management skills that are sure to help you with your police exam preparations and the exam itself.

## Finding Extra Time for Study

Your personal learning style should dictate how you go about learning the material you'll need to know for the exam. In other words, you need ways to find extra time for study, but you also need to make that extra study time as productive as possible—for you. Finding out the best way you learn will help you in your study. If you learn best in a certain way, your study time will be more efficient and productive. There are eight learning styles, which are

▶ **Active Learners**: Learn by doing something active with the information

▶ **Global Learners**: Learn in fits and starts, by studying the overall picture; often confused at first until after absorbing the information when they finally "get it."

▶ **Intuitive Learners**: Learn by exploring relationships and discerning and contemplating possibilities.

▶ **Reflective Learners**: Learn by thinking about and quietly pondering information alone (as opposed to a group, brainstorming session).

▶ **Sensing Learners**: Learn by studying the facts.

▶ **Sequential Learners**: Learn by studying the information in linear steps.

▶ **Verbal Learners**: Learn by studying and absorbing words, both by reading and by listening.

▶ **Visual Learners**: Learn better what they can see, such as diagrams, films, pictures, and so forth.

There are a number of tests online to help you determine your best learning styles. One such test is the Index of Learning Styles Questionnaire created by Dr. Richard M. Felder, Department of Chemical Engineering, North Carolina State University at www.engr.ncsu.edu/learningstyles/ilsweb.html. When you've determined your optimal learning styles, you can create ways to work additional study into your day in a way that will help you best. For example, if you are a visual learner, carry your flashcards with you at all times, pull them out, and read over them whenever you find spare minutes during the day, such as when you're waiting in line somewhere or tied up in traffic. On the other hand, if you're a verbal learner, you'd benefit by recording the information on your flashcards and then listening to your tapes or CDs while you jog or drive.

When you put your mind to it, you'll be amazed at the creative ways you can come up with to work in small study segments during what would ordinarily be unproductive time. Every little (study) bit helps, so take advantage of every little bit of time that you can find.

# Take Time to Time Yourself

As you know, your replies during your oral interview need to be direct and to the point. In order to help yourself determine how to convey information about yourself in effective *sound bite* segments, as described below, you'll need to practice your responses and time them as you practice. You'll need to have answers to typical interview questions written out, and then you can time yourself as you read these answers out loud to make sure you are adequately stating what needs to be said while keeping the time you take to answer to a minimum.

Set the timer for 30 seconds. Read a passage aloud and stop when the timer goes off. Count how many words you've read during that time. Next, increase the amount of time to 60 seconds. Again, stop reading aloud when the timer goes off and count the number of words.

You now know how many words you'll need for your oral interview sound bites. (A *sound bite* is a brief statement that a politician, for example, hopes will be picked up by the media and repeated later during a broadcast. In that case, it's the meat of the speech.) Later, after you've taken the exam and are preparing for your oral interview, go over the answers you've prepared for that interview and edit them so that they fit within those sound bite time limits. In your case, your sound bites are what you want those conducting your oral interview to remember about you. By doing so, you'll figure out which of your answers warrant longer explanation and which ones should be limited to a short response.

The last thing you want to occur during your oral interview is for your responses to sound like canned answers. Varying the length and emphasis of those answers will help you avoid a potential canned answer problem, and provide you with the confidence of knowing you have replies ready. Such preparation also helps you avoid stammering and searching for words, or worse—such as inserting "ahs" or "you know" into your speech patterns while you pause to think of what you want to say.

# 10

## CHAPTER TEN

# Test Taking Strategies

## Terms You'll Need to Understand:

✓ Keywords

✓ Negatives

✓ Qualifiers

## Concepts You'll Need to Master:

✓ Review the test

✓ Predict the correct answer

✓ Highlight key words

✓ Ignore nothing

✓ Understand the question

✓ Look for clues

The standard assessment method for the police officer test is the multiple-choice questionnaire. Multiple-choice questions are an objective test of knowledge and considered more reliable than other traditional methods of assessment. The grader will not rely on personal judgment to mark the answers, but will do so against a standard format. This will make it a valid test of your knowledge and recall.

To score high on this type of test, you need to master a few test techniques or strategies. This book focuses on these techniques and you have read about them in several other chapters. In this chapter, you will discover the strategies you will employ when you are in the test hall and begin your written test. But remember that no test strategy can be effective unless you have studied, revised, and practiced before the test. I say this because if your preparation is weak, you might freeze at the sight of the test and forget all that you've learned. Here are some important areas that you need to focus on as part of effective test strategies so that you are well prepared.

**TIP**

Go to the test facility early and get checked in. Also, be sure to get a good night of sleep and eat a good breakfast. You don't want to be hungry or tired before the test begins.

**NOTE**

Have some type of photo identification. It will be checked prior to the test.

# Review the Test

Before you start your work on the test, read it once all the way through before you write anything down. You will want to give yourself only ten minutes to do this as part of your time management plan. It is important for you to read the entire test so that you can develop a fairly good idea how the test is set up, how the test is styled, the types of questions being asked, and how the test is graded. By doing this, you will have a fair idea of the level of difficulty of the questions.

It might be useful to mark the questions you know the answer to as you skim through the test; that is, differentiate between the easy and hard questions so that you know what questions you can focus more time on later.

Also, it is important to read the test fully in the beginning to make sure that there are no surprises at a later stage. When you know which questions will pose the most difficulty, you can organize your time accordingly and feel more relaxed that you have seen the worst.

# Know the Grading Scheme

It is important for you to determine at the earliest stage possible how the test as a whole will be graded and also how each section of the test will be graded. The first thing to do is to read the instructions carefully, and look for signs of how the section will be graded.

You need to be able to recognize the different types of grading schemes. One possible grading scheme is when grading is done for all correct answers and nothing is deducted for wrong answers. This scheme is not commonly used because it encourages guesswork and you are not penalized for giving wrong answers. A type of grading that is commonly used is negative grading, in which wrong answers are deducted.

Your test could use either one of these schemes and you need to be aware of them because the grading scheme will affect how you approach questions. For example, if you know that wrong answers are not deducted from your overall score, it is worth guessing at each question because you might be lucky and answer a question correctly and have it count for you. However, those sections that do count wrong answers against you are ones in which you do not want to guess at questions you don't know because all wrong answers will negatively affect your overall score.

Most questions on the police exam are scored with the same weight and level. Yet there might be times when some questions are scored differently; therefore, you should be sure to focus on questions with higher weighting when at all possible. Try to answer all questions, but if you have to leave out some questions, try not to miss ones that have higher scoring potential.

# Understand the Question

Your score can depend on how well you understand the questions in the test. It will not be possible for you to get correct answers if you misinterpret the meaning of the question, which consequently leads you to a wrong answer. The sections that follow discuss some important points that will be helpful for you in understanding questions. The concepts discussed include highlighting key words in the questions, paying attention to detail, looking for twists and clues in the questions, being able to predict the correct answer, and identifying qualifiers and negatives.

## Highlight Key Words in the Questions

One of the most important things for you to do as you read the test questions is to highlight key words. These might be instructional words such as *compare*, *contrast*, *characterize*, *indicate*, and so on. Understand the meaning of these words and what the question demands you to do. Mostly, test questions are written not to confuse readers, but what is simple for the test writer might be confusing to someone else. So, first understand the wording of the questions and, when you have done that, determine what you are supposed to do from there.

## Ignore Nothing

Do not ignore any part of the question. Some of the seemingly trivial details are sometimes crucial to the question and to determining the correct answer. Make a few notes, if required, and don't hesitate to go back to the question again if you need to.

## Look for Twists in the Question

Don't immediately assume that you know what a question is going to ask you after reading just the first few words of the question. A question could take a turn from what you are expecting, and this might cause you to answer it incorrectly. Try to look for twists in words that sound confusing, for example:

According to police regulations, which areas are nonnegotiable, where interference from the community is not allowed?

- ○  A.  Both B and C
- ○  B.  Personnel decisions
- ○  C.  Shift allocation
- ○  D.  Accountability systems

Answer A is correct because it is the most likely answer. You have to understand from the question that the most unlikely answer is D, so you are left with only one option. Often these questions will test your common sense rather than recall.

# Look for Clues

Sometimes it is useful to look for clues in the question. If, for example, the question asks for a plural answer and the options given have mixed singular and plural answers, rule out the singular answers. It is important for you to know that no test will be designed to accept grammatically wrong answers. So, in choosing from the grammatically correct options, you could be correct unless there has been a serious printing error.

# Predict the Correct Answer

At times it is helpful for you to predict the correct answers after reading the question without looking at the answer options. By doing this, you might be able to strike out the wrong answers as soon as you look at the options. You should cross out the options that you know are incorrect so that you can concentrate on the possibly correct answers. Eliminating incorrect answers will definitely make your task easier.

# Identify Qualifiers in Questions

You need to be careful about identifying qualifiers in questions because such words alter a sentence or statement. Some qualifiers are words such as *equal*, *always*, *most*, and *often*. Other words that are used in the same context are as follows:

- ► More, equal, less
- ► Little, great, no
- ► None, all, most, some
- ► Is, is not
- ► Good, bad
- ► Usually, sometimes, never, always

For example, assume that a question is given as "Which of the following models is never a general model of an organization?" You need to recognize from the way the question is written that you have to select the most unlikely option. You will do that only if you understand that the word *never* in the sentence changes what is being asked for and demands that you look at the option that can never be considered as a possible correct answer. Similarly, if the same question is posed as "Which of the following models is often a general model of organizations," you would notice the word *often* and know that you have to look at and identify the most likely answer. In both instances, the qualifier changed what was being asked in the question.

# Negatives

When reading through your exam questions, try to identify negatives in a question. The negative might be in the form of a word such as *none, no, not,* or *never*. The negative might also be used in the form of prefixes, such *un*interrupted, *dis*believe, *mis*interpret, *il*logical, *un*due, *ir*regular, and so forth. These words might change the meaning of the question. For example, assume that you are faced with a question that describes an incident, giving details of the persons present at the scene. You are asked, "Which of the following is not the perpetrator?" Here you have to look at the list of answer options and identify the least likely person or persons because the question asked you which one is NOT the perpetrator.

On the other hand, a sentence that uses two negatives, or a double negative, has generally the same meaning as it had without a negative in the statement. For example: "It is logical to presume that a high achiever is interested in his studies" is a simple statement without any negatives. Notice how the meaning remains the same if two negatives are placed in the sentence, such as, "It is illogical to presume that a high achiever is disinterested in his studies."

If you notice a single negative in a question, it generally implies that the opposite is being asked. If you see a negative in a sentence, carefully look at the sentence for a second negative. A double negative makes the question entirely different because its meaning is the same as a simple positive statement. Therefore, you should reply to it as you would reply to a statement without any negatives.

**CAUTION**

Questions with negatives and double negatives generally require some thinking in order to get to the actual meaning. You need to be careful about interpreting these types of questions.

# Recognize the Type of Question

During the test you will be faced with different types of questions. The most common question type is the standard multiple-choice true or false question, which presents a statement with two answer options: true and false.

For example:

An intrinsic reward is praise by the management, not a salary increase.

    ◯  A.  True
    ◯  B.  False

A is the correct answer because *intrinsic reward* means an award not based on material or tangible rewards.

The *single best answer* question is also a common type of multiple-choice question. It gives a statement or a stem followed by a number of items, and one or more of the items could be correct. Depending on the instructions of the question, there are some in which any or none of the answers could be correct. Here's an example of a single best answer question:

The goal of law enforcement and maintaining social order is

    ◯  A.  A due process model
    ◯  B.  Found in the Fourth Amendment
    ◯  C.  The crime control model
    ◯  D.  Impossible to meet

Here option C is correct because the other three options are definitely incorrect.

Some questions are designed to show a blank within the stem, which has to be filled in by one of the given options. For example:

A study shows that_____ is the most unpopular option given by police executives for training.

    ◯  A.  Legal information
    ◯  B.  Writing skills
    ◯  C.  Computers
    ◯  D.  Personnel management

B is correct because studies show very few police executives opt for writing skills training sessions.

In certain types of questions, a scenario is given that is based on a report of an incident; for example, a robbery or assault. After reading the account, the answer options give you possible responses to the incident that a police officer might take. To answer this type of question correctly, you have to recall policy and regulations and apply them to the situation. In the same type of questions, you might also be required to identify or pinpoint the perpetrator by reading through the given scene.

In certain types of questions, a summary or report might be given and you will be required to complete it by filling in the blank or blanks at the end. You do so by selecting a suitable word from the given options at the end. For example:

On October 15, 1999, the Chairman of X delivered a speech to the association of chiefs of police in which he said, "I know you are concerned about radar jammers. They are simply tools for law breaking. They should be _____ and I believe they should be regulated as heavily as we can."

Taxable, illegal, user friendly

Some questions require you to sequence the answer options according to the order in which they should happen. For example:

On receiving a call for help a police officer must

(Order according to the correct sequence)

- ○ A. Handle the call
- ○ B. Proceed to the scene
- ○ C. Acknowledge the call
- ○ D. Notify of his or her arrival

The correct order is C, B, D, A because these are the general rules of responding to a call.

In certain questions, a paragraph is given and you are required to match the statement that best supports the content of the paragraph. Examples of these types of questions have been given in the reading comprehension sample questions.

As part of your test, you might be faced with questions in which you are required to write a paragraph. This paragraph could be on a variety of topics, but it will most often be in the form of a report. It will be useful for you to go over the information in the report writing section of this book and practice writing some accounts of incidents that will help you for this type of questions in your test.

Although it is not common practice, during the test you might be faced with certain questions that require short answers. These answers will give the test grader the opportunity to get a greater measure of your knowledge than can be garnered from standard multiple choice questions. For this type of question, you are usually given a scenario followed by a series of related questions. You are expected to write short, focused answers to these questions. Try to give brief points in sequence rather than writing in an elaborate, essay-type style. Prepare for this type of question with regular practice, and follow the rules of good writing. Be brief, to the point, relevant, and stick to facts.

Remember that the questions you read could be about traffic maps, police directives, arithmetic questions, or they might be testing your language and problem-solving skills. Regardless of what a question asks, it will be based on one of the question formats I have mentioned. So, it is important for you to understand how the questions are designed and to be able to recognize the question type so that you are comfortable when you see your test.

# Maintain Speed

Your chance of attempting all questions depends on how well you maintain speed during your test. Be sure that while you are studying for the test that you are putting together an effective time management plan that you will use during the test. More on this topic is mentioned in Chapter 9, "Time Management."

**TIP**

If time is on your side, you should review all your answers. It's okay to be the last one in the room as long as you pass the exam.

# Review All Answers

No matter how hard-pressed you are for time, review your answers at least once to ensure that your response is the one most likely to be correct.

**TIP**

Save time at the end of the exam to review your test and make sure that you haven't left out any answers or parts of answers.

# Write Neatly

Even if you are not required to write much during your test, make sure that whatever marks you make are done in a neat manner. Most questions will require marks on correct answers, so that will be simple. But if you are faced with a question in which you are required to write, remember that neat and legible writing is always a plus point. If you have given some other marks for your reference or jotted down notes, it is always better that they are done in a neat and organized manner. If the test grader cannot understand what you have written, you might not get the credit you deserve.

# Let's Rehearse

Studies shows that it is very important for anyone participating in a competitive situation—be it sports events or any type of test—to rehearse all the steps first so that the competitor is mentally prepared for the ordeal. Let's go over the steps leading to and during your test so that you can form a visual picture of your experience.

▶ Be well rested, prepared, and relaxed on the day of the test.

▶ Know the exact location of the test venue. Also know the approximate amount of time it takes to get to the venue. It is advisable to be aware of traffic reports on the day of your exam. If the route you intended to take is blocked for some reason, it is best to know that before you get stuck in traffic. This also necessitates that you have a backup route to the test center in the event of a traffic problem. It is a good idea to make a practice drive to the test center prior to test day. This will help you by enabling you to know exactly how to get there, and knowing this ahead of time will reduce stress.

▶ Have all the necessary materials like pens, pencils, watch, and any other items you require for the test.

▶ You might or might not be given one hour of preparation in which you can refer to your notes.

▶ You enter the test hall and are given the test.

▶ Time yourself and spend 10 minutes reading through the test.

▶ Mark the easy questions, or the questions that you know the answer to, as you read through.

▸ After you have read through the test, determine the number of minutes you have in all and calculate how much time you can give to each question. Keep in mind the level of difficulty of the overall test and allocate time accordingly.

▸ Now read the instructions at the beginning very carefully.

▸ Begin the questions.

▸ Understand the question and what it demands.

▸ Recognize the type of question and what skill it wants you to exercise.

▸ Predict the answer before you read the options.

▸ If you know the answer, mark it immediately.

▸ If you do not know the answer, do the following:

Highlight the key words.

Look for twists in the question.

Keep a lookout for qualifiers.

Notice double negatives.

Eliminate as many answer options as possible.

Look for grammatical clues.

If you're still not sure, let the question pass. Answer all the questions that you know, and return to this question later. You might be surprised that by answering other questions, you've jogged your memory with the correct answers to the difficult questions. Do not worry about answering questions in order.

▸ Keep track of the time.

▸ Go back to the difficult questions a second time. Give extra time to predict the best answer option. Remember, you might have already found some clues in other questions.

▸ Answer as many questions as you possibly can. It is always better to answer all questions rather than skipping some if you are not sure of your answer. Your answers will have a good chance of being correct if you use your common sense to give the response.

▸ If you are sure that you have answered all the questions that you possibly could, and most of them are probably correct, go the questions you have left a third time.

▸ Apply your common sense and make an educated guess. Choose an answer based on theories you have learned so that there is a greater chance of it being correct. Compare the answers to similar situations you might have seen or read about before and give the most probable answer. It's better to give *any* answer than to give no answer at all (unless there is a loss of points for wrong answers).

▸ Keep track of the time.

▸ Review all answers.

▸ Change answers only when you're absolutely sure that you are changing it to the correct answer. Your first instinct is most often correct.

▸ Take one final look and hand in the test. Remember, you have done your best and that's all that matters!

# The Final Helpful Tip

Throughout the chapter, I have given you a set of suggestions to help better facilitate your test performance. But you must remember that no matter what advice you receive, each person has his or her own strengths and weaknesses. Build up your own strategies that work best for you. If you feel that it will be easier for you to tackle the tough questions first, do so. If you feel you would be able to perform better after you gain confidence by attempting all the easy questions first, do so. You are the best judge of your learning style and how you work under different situations. Good luck!

# PART V
## Practice Exams

# CHAPTER ELEVEN

# Practice Test 1

At the back of this book you'll find answer sheets you can use for the Practice Exams.

## Commonly Misspelled Words

Select the properly spelled word; choose all that apply.

1. ❏ A. Superseed
   ❏ B. Supersede
   ❏ C. Supercede
   ❏ D. Superceed

2. ❏ A. Iresistable
   ❏ B. Irrasistable
   ❏ C. Irresistible
   ❏ D. Irresistable

3. ❏ A. Dcvclopement
   ❏ B. Developmint
   ❏ C. Developemant
   ❏ D. Development

4. ❏ A. Seperate
   ❏ B. Separate
   ❏ C. Saperate
   ❏ D. Sepperate

5. ❏ A. Tyranny
   ❏ B. Tyrrany
   ❏ C. Tearrany
   ❏ D. Tearany

6. ❏ A. Harrass
   ❏ B. Harass
   ❏ C. Harress
   ❏ D. Haress

7. ❏ A. Desiccate
   ❏ B. Dessicate
   ❏ C. Dezicate
   ❏ D. Dessicait

8. ❏ A. Indispensible
   ❏ B. Indespensable
   ❏ C. Indispensable
   ❏ D. Indespsensible

9. ❏ A. Reseave
   ❏ B. Recieve
   ❏ C. Resieve
   ❏ D. Receive

10. ❏ A. Pursue
    ❏ B. Pursew
    ❏ C. Persue
    ❏ D. Persew

11. ❏ A. Reccomend
    ❏ B. Recommend
    ❏ C. Re-Comend
    ❏ D. Recomend

12. ❏ A. Desparate
    ❏ B. Despirate
    ❏ C. Desperate
    ❏ D. Disperate

13. ❏ A. Cemetery
    ❏ B. Cemetary
    ❏ C. Sematery
    ❏ D. Semetary

14. ❏ A. Subpoena
    ❏ B. Subpeona
    ❏ C. Supeona
    ❏ D. Subpena

15. ❏ A. Definately
    ❏ B. Defenately
    ❏ C. Definitely
    ❏ D. Defenitely

16. ❑ A. Ocassion
    ❑ B. Occasion
    ❑ C. Oakation
    ❑ D. Occation

17. ❑ A. Consensus
    ❑ B. Concensus
    ❑ C. Consentious
    ❑ D. Concentious

18. ❑ A. Inadvertant
    ❑ B. Inadverdent
    ❑ C. Inadverdant
    ❑ D. Inadvertent

19. ❑ A. Judgment
    ❑ B. Judgement
    ❑ C. Judgemant
    ❑ D. Judgmant

20. ❑ A. Drunkeness
    ❑ B. Drunkuness
    ❑ C. Drunkunness
    ❑ D. Drunkenness

21. ❑ A. Occurrence
    ❑ B. Occurrance
    ❑ C. Occurence
    ❑ D. Ocurence

22. ❑ A. Disippate
    ❑ B. Disapate
    ❑ C. Dissipate
    ❑ D. Dissapate

23. ❑ A. Wreckless
    ❑ B. Reckless
    ❑ C. Reckluss
    ❑ D. Recklass

24. ❑ A. Wierd
    ❑ B. Weard
    ❑ C. Weird
    ❑ D. Wird

25. ❑ A. Accadenly
    ❑ B. Accidently
    ❑ C. Accadentally
    ❑ D. Accidentally

# Choose the Correct Sentence or Sentences

In questions 26–40, choose the sentence or sentences that correctly use or uses the words defined before the sentences.

26. *Its* is a possessive pronoun. *It's* is a contraction of *it* and *is*. *You're* is a contraction of *you* and *are*. *Your* is a possessive pronoun.
    - ❑ A. Its time *you're* completing *your* test.
    - ❑ B. It's time *your* completing *you're* test.
    - ❑ C. It's time *you're* completing *your* test.
    - ❑ D. Its time *you're* completing *you're* test.

27. *They're* is a contraction of *they* and *are*. *Their* is a plural possessive pronoun. One use of *there* is to connote in, into, at, or to that place.
    - ❑ A. *They're* all safely in *their* places over *there*.
    - ❑ B. *There* all safely in *they're* places over *their*.
    - ❑ C. *Their* all safely in *there* places over *they're*.
    - ❑ D. *They're* all safely in *they're* places over *there*.

28. As a noun, *bow* can mean to lower one's head or body in respect, or something, such as a ribbon, bent into a curved shape. A *beau* is a sweetheart. A *bough* generally denotes the main branch of a tree.
    - ❑ A. Her *bow* tied a *beau* around the *bough* of the tree.
    - ❑ B. Her *bough* tied a *beau* around the *bow* of the tree.
    - ❑ C. Her *bow* tied a *bough* around the *beau* of the tree.
    - ❑ D. Her *beau* tied a *bow* around the *bough* of the tree.

29. *Were* is a form of the verb **to be**. *We're* is a contraction of *we* and *are*. *They're* is a contraction of *they* and *are*. *Their* is a plural possessive pronoun. One use of *there* is to suggest in, into, at, or to that place.
    - ❑ A. Were busy trying to determine if they we're there.
    - ❑ B. We're busy trying to determine if they were there.
    - ❑ C. Were busy trying to determine if they we're their.
    - ❑ D. We're busy trying to determine if they were they're.

30. *Than* is used to designate a difference of kind, manner, or identity or as an expression of inequality. *Then* is used to denote time.
    - ❑ A. A bicycle is often a faster mode of transportation *than* is a squad car, but *then* a bicycle can be maneuvered into smaller spaces.
    - ❑ B. At first, the officer decided he'd rather write a ticket *then* issue a warning *than* he changed his mind.
    - ❑ C. In the officer's opinion, it was more a time for issuing a verbal warning *than* one where he'd write a ticket that would *then* require the person to appear in court.

❑ D. It was decided to hold the briefing in the more private conference room rather *than* in the squad room, and *then* issue shift assignments after the meeting.

31. *To* means in a certain direction. *Too* indicates also or more than. *Two* is a number.

❑ A. *To* many people just don't realize that *too* or more theories can help further an initial investigation, *two*.

❑ B. *Two* many people just don't realize that *to* or more theories can help further an initial investigation, *too*.

❑ C. *Too* many people just don't realize that *two* or more theories can help further an initial investigation, *too*.

❑ D. *Too* many people just don't realize that *to* or more theories can help further an initial investigation, *two*.

32. *Who* refers to people. *Which* refers to one or more of a group, most often in a question.

❑ A. *Which* stole the car?
❑ B. *Who* stole the car?
❑ C. *Which* tools were used to break into the home?
❑ D. *Who* broke into the home?

33. *Who's* is a contraction of *who* and *is*. *Whose* is the possessive form of the pronoun *who*.

❑ A. The car title is in *who's* name?
❑ B. The car title is in *whose* name?
❑ C. *Who's* in charge here?
❑ D. *Whose* in charge here?

34. *Learn* means to acquire knowledge. *Teach* means to impart that knowledge.

❑ A. I know they *teach* an overwhelming number of topics at the police academy, but I intend to *learn* all that I can.

❑ B. Considering the number of topics they *teach* at the police academy, they'll *learn* mc as much as they can.

❑ C. Although they can't *teach* you everything you'll need to know when you're in uniform, take enough time to study so that you *learn* as many of the procedures they'll cover while you're at the academy.

❑ D. An instructor can *teach* me only so much; some things I'll need to *learn* through experience.

35. *All together* means as a group. *Altogether* means in total.

❑ A. Line up *altogether* against the wall.
❑ B. As we gather *all together* to prepare for the day, let's remember to "be safe out there."
❑ C. It is *all together* too risky to even contemplate.
❑ D. The recruits filed into the room. "*Altogether* now," said the sergeant, as he indicated they were to line up against the wall.

36. *All ready* is to be totally prepared. *Already* refers to something occurring prior to an exact time period.
   - ❑ A. It is *all ready* too late to register for the test.
   - ❑ B. The paperwork was *already* so that he was *all ready* properly registered for the test.
   - ❑ C. The paperwork was *all ready* so that he was *already* properly registered for the test.
   - ❑ D. The paperwork was *already* so that he was *already* properly registered for the test.

37. *Emigrate* is to leave a country. *Immigrate* is to enter a country.
   - ❑ A. He was ready to *immigrate* to a new country.
   - ❑ B. He was ready to *emigrate* to a new country.
   - ❑ C. She tried to *emigrate* into the USA, but her visa was rejected.
   - ❑ D. She tried to *immigrate* into the USA, but her visa was rejected.

38. To *imply* is to suggest, and to *infer* is to reach a conclusion based on reasoning.
   - ❑ A. When the prosecutor glared at the defendant and shook his head, he was trying to *infer* that the guy was guilty.
   - ❑ B. When the prosecutor glared at the defendant and shook his head, his intent was to *imply* that the guy was guilty.
   - ❑ C. When the prosecutor glared at the defendant and shook his head, his hope was that the jury would *infer* that the guy was guilty.
   - ❑ D. When the prosecutor glared at the defendant and shook his head, his hope was that the jury would *imply* that the guy was guilty.

**39.** *Accept* is to take what is offered, and *except* means to exclude.
   - ❑ A. He just couldn't *except* that he had to *accept* the consequences of his actions.
   - ❑ B. The department chose to *accept* all the recommendations *except* one.
   - ❑ C. He just couldn't *accept* that he had to *accept* the consequences of his actions.
   - ❑ D. The department chose to *except* all the recommendations *accept* one.

40. *Good* is an adjective used to reflect a favorable impression of the persons, places, or things it modifies. *Well* is an adverb used to reflect a favorable impression of the verbs, adjectives, or other adverbs it modifies.
   - ❑ A. Proper grammar and punctuation are part of the secret of writing well.
   - ❑ B. Proper grammar and punctuation are part of the secret of good writing.
   - ❑ C. Proper grammar and punctuation are part of the secret of writing good.
   - ❑ D. Proper grammar and punctuation are part of the secret of well writing.

# Choose the Correct Synonym

For questions 41–50, read the sample sentence and then choose the word that most closely defines the meaning of the italicized word.

41. Prior experience can often affect someone's *perception* of how law enforcement agencies operate. *Perception* can most closely be defined as meaning
    - ❑ A. Prejudice
    - ❑ B. Understanding
    - ❑ C. Belief
    - ❑ D. Definition

42. Despite the lack of evidence, Officer Williams was determined to *persevere* with the investigation. *Persevere* can most closely be defined as meaning
    - ❑ A. Persist
    - ❑ B. Continue
    - ❑ C. Strive
    - ❑ D. Resolve

43. Determined to reach a preliminary conclusion, Officer Miller set aside time to *reconcile* the evidence. *Reconcile* can most closely be defined as meaning
    - ❑ A. Coordinate
    - ❑ B. Organize
    - ❑ C. Delete
    - ❑ D. Resolve

44. One legal and common sense *perception* is that implementing a knock-and-announce policy when conducting an arrest reduces the potential for violence. *Perception* can most closely be defined as meaning
    - ❑ A. Fable
    - ❑ B. Myth
    - ❑ C. Falsehood
    - ❑ D. Observation

45. It is often difficult for an officer to determine which evidence is *pertinent* to a case. *Pertinent* can most closely be defined as meaning
    - ❑ A. Immaterial
    - ❑ B. Irrelevant
    - ❑ C. Relevant
    - ❑ D. Obsolete

46. Regardless of the spirit in which it's given, any acceptance of a free gift (even something as inconsequential as a free cup of coffee) could be considered graft, and therefore undermine the *integrity* of the department. *Integrity* can most closely be defined as meaning

    ❑  A.  Honesty
    ❑  B.  Dishonesty
    ❑  C.  Morale
    ❑  D.  Attendance

47. Officer Bryan's behavior was deemed to be *insubordination*. *Insubordination* can most closely be defined as meaning

    ❑  A.  Obedience
    ❑  B.  Compliance
    ❑  C.  Disobedience
    ❑  D.  Cooperative

48. Officer Stewart knew that his body would eventually *adapt* to working the overnight shift. *Adapt* can most closely be defined as meaning

    ❑  A.  Resist
    ❑  B.  Adjust
    ❑  C.  Defy
    ❑  D.  Dare

49. How an officer carries herself can affect the public's or a supervisor's *perception* of how well she can perform the job. *Perception* can most closely be defined as meaning

    ❑  A.  Opinion
    ❑  B.  Prejudice
    ❑  C.  Fallacy
    ❑  D.  Apprehension

50. Whether or not the department correctly conducted its firearms training program was the subject of *controversy*. *Controversy* can most closely be defined as meaning

    ❑  A.  Dispute
    ❑  B.  Agreement
    ❑  C.  Integrity
    ❑  D.  Publicity

# Police Vocabulary

Choose the most correct, complete definition; choose all that apply.

51. *Resisting arrest* is when

   ❏  A.  A person prevents, or attempts to prevent, an officer from making an unauthorized arrest

   ❏  B.  A person prevents, or attempts to prevent, an officer from making an authorized arrest of another

   ❏  C.  A person prevents, or attempts to prevent, someone from making a citizen's arrest

   ❏  D.  A person prevents, or attempts to prevent, an officer from making an illegal arrest

52. *Criminal mischief* is when

   ❏  A.  A person makes obscene phone calls to another

   ❏  B.  A person, without any legal right to do so, damages property belonging to another

   ❏  C.  A person makes harassing phone calls to another

   ❏  D.  A person, without any legal right to do so, tampers with the mail of another

53. In police work, *EMS* is an acronym most often used to indicate

   ❏  A.  Entitled (to) Meritorious Service

   ❏  B.  Engage Master Sergeant

   ❏  C.  Exempt Management Staff

   ❏  D.  Emergency Medical Services

54. *Adultery* is

   ❏  A.  The act of viewing a pornographic film

   ❏  B.  Engaging in reading sexual literature

   ❏  C.  Engaging in phone conversations with someone other than one's spouse

   ❏  D.  Engaging in sexual relations with someone other than one's living spouse

55. *Larceny* is

   ❏  A.  Providing a police officer with an incorrect phone number

   ❏  B.  Taking property belonging to another with the intent of keeping the property permanently for one's own use

   ❏  C.  Unlawful use of a service or property

   ❏  D.  Taking property back to a retail establishment with the intent to return it without a proper receipt

56. *Burglar's tools* are
    - ❑ A. Any instruments used in the commission of driving without a license
    - ❑ B. Any instruments used to complete faulty workmanship and then bill the client for work done
    - ❑ C. Any instruments used modify a vehicle so that it doesn't comply with environmental regulations
    - ❑ D. Any instruments used in the commission of a burglary, larceny, or theft of services

57. The suspect was charged with a misdemeanor. A *misdemeanor* is
    - ❑ A. A crime more serious than a felony
    - ❑ B. A crime less serious than a felony
    - ❑ C. Any willful attempt to use a gun to inflict serious bodily injury
    - ❑ D. Any willful attempt to use a gun to end another's life

58. A *homicide* is the criminal act of a human being taking the life of another human being through intentional or unintentional felonious means. Most state statutes classify a homicide as a Class A felony or first-degree murder when it involves
    - ❑ A. Recklessness
    - ❑ B. Premeditation
    - ❑ C. Passion
    - ❑ D. Unlicensed use of a handgun

59. *Menacing* is when, through physical threat, a person intentionally places, or attempts to place, another in fear of immediate
    - ❑ A. Loss of services
    - ❑ B. Loss of property
    - ❑ C. Loss of life
    - ❑ D. Physical injury

60. A person commits an *assault* when he or she
    - ❑ A. Intends to remove property belonging to another
    - ❑ B. Intends to hit another
    - ❑ C. Intends to destroy property belonging to another
    - ❑ D. Intends to cause physical injury to another, and commits an act that causes physical injury to that person or to another

# Sentence Ordering Questions

Determine the proper sequence for each of the five sentences.

61. The five sentences that follow are from a burglary report:

    **1.** I advised the suspect, "Police, don't move." At this time, I was able to subdue the suspect. I advised Officer Brown, who remained at the location until the owner could arrive while I transported the suspect to the station.

    **2.** While on routine patrol, a pedestrian flagged down my patrol car, and advised me that a burglary was taking place in a residence located at 753 West Market.

    **3.** I advised the station of the situation by radio and proceeded to that location.

    **4.** I exited my vehicle, and immediately observed that the front door to the business was slightly ajar. As I silently entered the store, I observed a white male, with his back to me, behind the counter, attempting to access the cash register.

    **5.** Officer Brown advised by radio that he had arrived at the rear of that location.

    ❑  A.  1, 2, 3, 4, 5
    ❑  B.  2, 3, 5, 4, 1
    ❑  C.  2, 3, 4, 5, 1
    ❑  D.  2, 3, 4, 1, 5

62. The five sentences that follow are from a missing-person report:

    **1.** Upon speaking with the woman, she advised that her daughter had failed to return home from a friend's house.

    **2.** I advised the dispatcher that although I was done questioning the woman, I was still out of service doing follow-up on the complaint and gave dispatch the description, requested that the description be given by radio to the other officers on patrol, and proceeded to the friend's residence.

    **3.** I was on routine patrol when a woman approached my patrol vehicle. I advised the dispatcher that I was out of service handling a pedestrian complaint.

    **4.** Upon further questioning, the woman further advised that she had called the friend's home, and spoke with her daughter's friend's mother, who'd said her daughter had left that residence an hour ago at the time specified by the mother.

    **5.** I obtained a description of the child, as well as directions to the friend's house, which the woman stated were also her daughter's logical route home.

    ❑  A.  3, 1, 4, 5, 2
    ❑  B.  3, 4, 1, 5, 2
    ❑  C.  3, 2, 1, 5, 4
    ❑  D.  3, 1, 2, 5, 4

63. The five sentences that follow are from an accident report:

    **1.** At 1640 hours date, dispatch advised me of a noninjury accident at the corner of Pine and Elmhurst.

    **2.** I obtained driver's license information from the drivers of both vehicles.

    **3.** I arrived at the scene and confirmed that neither driver was injured.

    **4.** Upon photographing the scene, I instructed the drivers to move their vehicles to the side of the roadway.

    **5.** Both drivers were given written statement forms to complete.

    ❏  A.  1, 5, 4, 3, 2
    ❏  B.  1, 2, 3, 4, 5
    ❏  C.  1, 3, 4, 2, 5
    ❏  D.  1, 4, 3, 2, 5

64. The five sentences that follow are from a traffic summons report:

    **1.** As I approached the intersection, I observed a blue late model Oldsmobile, westbound on Elm, fail to stop for the red traffic light at the intersection of Elm and Main.

    **2.** It was determined that the driver did not have a valid driver's license, so the driver was issued traffic citations for failure to stop at a red light and for driving without a license.

    **3.** At 1732 hours date, I was on routine southbound on Main Street approaching Elm.

    **4.** I subsequently stopped the vehicle in the 300 block of West Elm.

    **5.** I approached the driver of the vehicle and asked him for his driver's license and vehicle registration.

    ❏  A.  3, 4, 5, 1, 2
    ❏  B.  3, 1, 5, 2, 4
    ❏  C.  3, 2, 5, 4, 1
    ❏  D.  3, 1, 4, 5, 2

65. The five sentences that follow are from an incident report involving a loud music complaint:

    **1.** Upon approaching that location, I could hear loud music.

    **2.** As I stopped to exit my vehicle, person unknown immediately turned off the music.

    **3.** It was then observed that a number of cars were parked outside the garage at 523 East Eureka, and that a number of young males were standing around outside at that location.

    **4.** I checked the ID of all subjects at that location and subsequently issued a warning, advising that further loud music complaints this night would result in a summons.

**5.** At 2123 hours, I received a dispatch to the 500 block of East Eureka regarding a loud music complaint coming from an unknown address at that location.

- ❏  A.  5, 1, 3, 2, 4
- ❏  B.  5, 3, 2, 1, 4
- ❏  C.  5, 4, 2, 3, 1
- ❏  D.  5, 3, 1, 2, 4

66. The five sentences that follow are from a shoplifting complaint report:

**1.** Mr. Brookhart confronted the young male by yelling at him to stop and attempting to approach him, but he wasn't able to reach the male before he exited the store and proceeded to run away from the store in a southerly direction.

**2.** Mr. Brookhart advised that while he was waiting on another customer, he had observed a young male attempt to hide several comic books in his backpack.

**3.** I obtained further description of the suspect.

**4.** At 1224 hours date, while on routine patrol in the Bayview Shopping Plaza parking lot, this officer was flagged down by Mr. Arthur Brookhart outside the Collector's Corners Comic Book Shop.

**5.** The young male then proceeded toward the door of the store.

- ❏  A.  4, 5, 2, 1, 3
- ❏  B.  4, 3, 5, 2, 1
- ❏  C.  4, 2, 5, 1, 3
- ❏  D.  4, 5, 3, 1, 2

67. The five sentences that follow are from a possible child abuse report:

**1.** While on routine patrol, I noticed an adult female on foot, leaving the area of Springdale Park.

**2.** When the female was questioned regarding the rough way she was holding the child by the arm, she advised that the child had fallen and she was attempting to rush him home to treat his injuries. She was rude and abrupt with this officer, and told me this was a personal matter and the police weren't needed.

**3.** As I approached, the female was observed to grab a young male child by the arm.

**4.** I determined that this could possibly be a possible child abuse situation, and requested that the sergeant meet me at the scene.

**5.** Upon exiting my vehicle and approaching the female and child, it was further observed that the child was bleeding from a cut above his left eyebrow and appeared to have bruises beginning to form on his face.

❏ A. 1, 5, 3, 2, 4
❏ B. 1, 3, 5, 2, 4
❏ C. 1, 5, 3, 4, 2
❏ D. 1, 2, 3, 4, 5

68. The five sentences that follow are from a possible domestic violence report:

**1.** Without waiting for the officers to advise him of any complaint, the male apologized for the noise and said they would "keep it down" and attempted to close the door.

**2.** At 2343 hours date, Officer Miller in Unit 101 and I were dispatched to the scene of a possible domestic violence incidence. Dispatch advised loud shouting and other noises were heard to be coming from Apt. A at 503 West Spring.

**3.** Upon arrival at the residence, a white male responded to our knock at the door.

**4.** Upon entering the apartment, it was determined that the only other occupant was a white female.

**5.** Officer Miller blocked the door and advised we wished to speak to all parties inside the apartment.

❏ A. 2, 3, 5, 1, 4
❏ B. 2, 5, 1, 4, 3
❏ C. 1, 2, 3, 4, 5
❏ D. 2, 3, 1, 5, 4

69. The five sentences that follow are from a man-with-a-gun and possible-robber report:

**1.** I observed a white male brandishing a gun, obviously involved in a heated confrontation with the other white male.

**2.** While on routine patrol in Quadrant D, at 1956 hours I was flagged down by a pedestrian who advised that a white male appeared to be holding another white male at gunpoint in the 300 block of Birch near Pine.

**3.** I produced my service revolver and shouted, "Police!"

**4.** After calling for backup, I proceeded to the area and took cover behind my vehicle.

**5.** Upon observing my weapon, the suspect dropped his gun.

❏ A. 2, 4, 1, 3, 5
❏ B. 2, 1, 4, 5, 3
❏ C. 2, 4, 5, 3, 1
❏ D. 2, 4, 3, 1, 5

70. The five sentences that follow are from a call for emergency services report:

    **1.** I advised the station I would be outside the vehicle, investigating the incident.

    **2.** I radioed the dispatcher and requested a rescue squad.

    **3.** While on routine patrol, I observed what I believed to be an elderly man falling down the steps in front of 574 North West Street.

    **4.** On further observation, the male regained consciousness, but was dazed and unable to answer questions.

    **5.** I approached the male and observed that he appeared to be unconscious.

    ❏  A.  3, 5, 4, 1, 2
    ❏  B.  3, 5, 4, 2, 1
    ❏  C.  3, 1, 5, 4, 2
    ❏  D.  3, 4, 5, 1, 2

# Arithmetic and Arithmetic Formula Questions

Choose the correct answer.

71. Officer Trisel completes a robbery report. The victim states that the following property was stolen from him:

    One wristwatch, valued at $325

    Two gold chains, valued at $950 each

    One ring, valued at $1925

    Cash in the amount of $440

In addition to those items, the robbery victim also tells the officer that his laptop computer in a leather case valued at $2,550 was also taken.

When Officer Trisel prepares his report on the robbery, which of the following will be the total value of the stolen property and cash?

    ❏  A.  $6,190
    ❏  B.  $6,700
    ❏  C.  $7,140
    ❏  D.  $9,065

72. Officer Schultz responded to the scene of an apartment burglary. Once there, the victim advised the officer the following items were taken from the apartment:

One DVD player, valued at $125

One television, valued at $325

One answering machine, valued at $125

One portable phone, valued at $95

One ring, valued at $675

As Officer Schultz was preparing his report, the victim phoned the station to advise that he'd found the ring on the floor under a table where the burglar had evidently dropped it; however, on further inspection of the apartment, he discovered that a second portable phone valued at $125 was also missing.

When Officer Schultz completes his report, what will be the proper total for the stolen property?

❑   A. $1,470

❑   B. $795

❑   C. $825

❑   D. $1,270

73. Officer Purdy responds to the scene of a burglary of the high school football stadium concession stand. Upon investigation, the PTA representative for concession sales, Mrs. Gale Miller, advises that earlier the day before she'd accepted a delivery of new products, which had not yet been cataloged and put away. Based on comparing what remained with the invoice for the shipment, it appeared that all items taken were from that shipment and they were as follows:

22 boxes of candy bars, each valued at $6

10 12-packs of bottled water, each valued at $4.50

8 12-packs of power drinks, each valued at $7.50

10 boxes of potato chips, each valued at $9.00

6 boxes of corn chips, each valued at $9.00

1 box of ketchup packets, valued at $2.50

1 box of mustard packets, valued at $2.50

1 box of pickle relish, valued at $3.50

14 8-count packages of hot dog buns, each valued at $0.65

Mrs. Miller advised that all other items appeared to be accounted for. Upon determining the total wholesale value of the stolen property, that total would be

❑   A. $397.60

❑   B. $398.10

❑   C. $239.16

❑   D. $398.60

74. While on routine patrol, Officer Williams is flagged down by female pedestri- an who advises that person unknown stole her purse. She advised the purse and its contents were as follows:

> One Prada handbag, valued at $175
>
> One Prada billfold, valued at $125
>
> One manicure set, valued at $25
>
> Miscellaneous makeup in a leather case valued at $250
>
> Cash, valued at approximately $425
>
> One leather checkbook case, valued at $95

Officer Williams also made a note of additional property for which a set value could not be determined, such as credit cards. The known value of stolen items was

- ❑  A.  $1,095
- ❑  B.  $1,085
- ❑  C.  $2,015
- ❑  D.  $1,195

75. Officer Cooper responded to the scene of a burglary of a doctor's office. Upon investigation, it was determined that the perpetrators had been unable to access the outer lobby, and thus only the only items taken were from the lobby and reception area. The items reported stolen were

> Four paintings, each valued at $350
>
> One phone, valued at $1,225
>
> One computer system, valued at $2,950
>
> One laser printer, valued at $1,750
>
> One photocopier, valued at $2,225

As Officer Cooper was later completing his report, he received a call from the doctor's receptionist, who advised him that because of its proprietary software, she'd ascertained the actual value of the computer system to be $4,950. She also reported they discovered that a radio valued at $45 was also missing. The total value of the stolen property was

- ❑  A.  $13,495
- ❑  B.  $11, 595
- ❑  C.  $14,545
- ❑  D.  $10,495

76. Upon his arrival at a reported burglary in progress, Officer Bailey failed to secure his patrol car. Upon his return to the vehicle, he discovered that person or persons unknown had removed several items from the vehicle. The property taken and the values were

    One clipboard, valued at $10

    One cell phone, valued at $95

    One scarf, valued at $25

    One pair of leather gloves, valued at $35

    The total value of the items removed from the squad car was

    ❑  A. $165
    ❑  B. $155
    ❑  C. $160
    ❑  D. $175

77. Officer Bollenbacher arrived at the scene of burglary at the Ye Olde Homestyle Cafe and was advised that sometime overnight person or persons unknown had broken into the premises and had removed $350 from the cash register. In addition, the following property was also taken:

    One portable television, valued at $350

    One police scanner, valued at $250

    One radio, valued at $50

    The owner of the cafe also advised that the cash register would have to be replaced; the value of the cash register was $1,950. The total value of property stolen was

    ❑  A. $2,950
    ❑  B. $650
    ❑  C. $2,550
    ❑  D. $1,000

78. Officer Sutton responded to the scene of an appliance store burglary. Upon speaking with the manager, it was determined that the following property was stolen:

    Three portable televisions, each valued at $225

    Five air conditioners, each valued at $365

    Four sets of stereo speakers, each valued at $175

    While on station completing his report, Officer Sutton received a call from the store manager who advised that they'd found one of the air conditioners, still in the box and undamaged, outside behind the store. The total value of the stolen property would be

    ❑  A. $2,835
    ❑  B. $3,200
    ❑  C. $3,565
    ❑  D. $2,855

79. Officer Meyers was flagged down by a subject in front of the Fifty-First National Bank branch at the corner of Old Towne Road and Highway 30. Upon further investigation, it was learned that the manager of the Grocery Goodies Supermarket had been robbed at gunpoint by person unknown as he was attempting to use the night deposit box. Upon consulting his notes, the manager advised that the contents of the deposit bag had been

   73 quarters

   84 dimes

   96 nickels

   15 pennies

   75 $1 bills

   96 $20 bills

   84 $5 bills

   97 $10 bills

   3 $100 bills

   The total amount stolen was determined to be

   ❏  A. $5,523.35

   ❏  B. $3,850.40

   ❏  C. $3,716.60

   ❏  D. $4,548.20

80. Officer Roode was dispatched to the scene of a yard sale. Upon arrival, he was advised that four persons unknown had walked up to the display tables and each had grabbed a variety of items, run back to their waiting car, and had left the area without paying for their purchases. As near as the operator of the yard sale, Mrs. Martha Florence, could determine, the following items of approximate value were taken:

   Five costume jewelry necklaces, each valued at $5

   Four costume jewelry bracelets, each valued at $3

   One crystal liquor decanter, valued at $45

   One crystal vase, valued at $55

   Two boxes baseball cards, each valued at $125

   One quilt, valued at $325

   Two quilted pillow shams, each valued at $75

   Upon arriving on station to complete his report, Officer Roode received a phone call from Mrs. Florence, who advised that she had also determined that two full-sized bed sheet sets each valued at $20 had also been taken. The total amount of the stolen items was

   ❏  A. $807

   ❏  B. $902

   ❏  C. $682

   ❏  D. $777

81. While on routine patrol, Officer Hampton was flagged down by a pedestrian who advised that he had been robbed at gunpoint. Upon further investigation, it was determined that the items stolen were

    One wallet, valued at $50

    ~~Cash in wallet $24

    One wedding ring, valued at $325

    One watch, valued at $55

    The total value of the items stolen was

    ❑  A. $455
    ❑  B. $454
    ❑  C. $474
    ❑  D. $424

82. Officer Bishop responded to the scene of a new house construction, and was advised by Brandon Miller, the contractor, that overnight person or persons unknown had removed some materials from the site. The inventory of the property taken and its value was determined to be

    2,000 square feet oak hardwood flooring valued at $6,000

    20 oak floor grates, each valued at $16.49

    One 13-ft. multi-position aluminum ladder valued at $99

    2 4' steel scaffolds, each valued at $99

    The value of the stolen property was determined to be

    ❑  A. $60,950
    ❑  B. $61,175
    ❑  C. $6,626.80
    ❑  D. $6,627.80

83. Officer Parker investigated a burglary of a residence at 23581 West Mayberry, where it was determined the following items had been taken:

    One 12-piece service of sterling flatware in a wooden storage case, valued at $12,000

    One sterling silver tea service, valued at $6,000

    Two sterling silver candlesticks, each valued at $750

    Two paintings, each valued at $7,500

    Two paintings, each valued at $12,500

    While on station completing his report, Officer Parker received word from the owner of the stolen property that he'd also discovered two crystal vases, each valued at $225, to be missing, as well as a sterling silver tray valued at $1,225. The total value of the stolen items was determined to be

    ❑  A. $60,950
    ❑  B. $61,175
    ❑  C. $28,200
    ❑  D. $49,175

84. While conducting an investigation of a burglary to Angela's Antiques at 850 East Ohio Avenue, Officer Williams was advised that the following items were determined to be missing:

> One Daisy butter churn, valued at $1,225
>
> One yelloware bowl, valued at $225
>
> One hand-pieced quilt, valued at $2,575
>
> One crock, valued at $250

The total value of the stolen items was

- ❑ A. $4,225
- ❑ B. $4,275
- ❑ C. $5,275
- ❑ D. $5,325

85. While on routine patrol, Officer Stevens was flagged down by a pedestrian who advised that he and his wife had been robbed at gunpoint. During the course of the investigation, it was determined that the following items had been taken:

> One black eel skin wallet, valued at $75
>
> One red leather purse, valued at $125
>
> Cash, in the amount of $565
>
> One man's wedding ring with diamond, valued at $2,500
>
> One lady's wedding ring set, valued at $9,500
>
> One man's watch, valued at $950
>
> One woman's watch, valued at $1,250
>
> Miscellaneous contents of woman's purse valued at $375

The total value of the stolen items was determined to be

- ❑ A. $13,090
- ❑ B. $20,515
- ❑ C. $15,240
- ❑ D. $15,340

86. Officer Jackson was dispatched to the scene of a burglary of a freezer in the garage at 755 East Maple. The owner, Mr. Albert Cartwright, advised that he'd just stocked his freezer in anticipation of the neighborhood block party and cookout. During the course of the investigation, it was determined the following items had been stolen:

> 25 pounds of frozen steaks, valued at $8.99 a pound
>
> 2 whole pork tenderloins, each valued at $30
>
> 20 pounds baby back ribs, valued at $3.99 a pound
>
> 15 whole chickens, each valued at $4
>
> 3 beef briskets, each valued at $35

Mr. Cartwright later advised that he'd failed to tell the officer about 10 packages of hotdogs valued at $0.99 each and five packages of bratwurst valued at $3.75 each that had also been taken. The total value of the stolen frozen food was

- ❑   A.  $558.29
- ❑   B.  $558.20
- ❑   C.  $542.80
- ❑   D.  $576.95

87. Officer Davidson answered a shoplifting complaint at the Tracy's Treasures Gift Shop. Mrs. Tracy Edwards, the shop owner, advised that while she was waiting on another customer, she observed an unknown female exit the store with several items without paying for them. Determined to have been taken were

   One Tracy's Treasures original scrapbook, valued at $69.95

   Two decorated candles, each valued at $29.95

   Two gift books, each valued at $14.95

   The total value of the stolen items was

- ❑   A.  $114.85
- ❑   B.  $144.80
- ❑   C.  $159.75
- ❑   D.  $129.80

88. While investigating an armed robbery of the Quick Stop Carryout, Officer Kildare determined the following items had been stolen:

   Cash in the total of $879.54

   Five cartons of cigarettes, each valued at $35.00

   Three lighters, each valued at $1.49

   Six packages of beef jerky, each valued at $0.99

   The total value of the items stolen were

- ❑   A.  $1,064.95
- ❑   B.  $1,066.45
- ❑   C.  $1,061.98
- ❑   D.  $1,054.95

89. Officer Walters was investigating a burglary at a residence at 305 East Hope, where he ascertained that the following items were determined to be missing:

   1 laptop computer, valued at $1,250

   125 CDs, each valued at $12

   1 briefcase, valued at $250

   1 laptop case, valued at $99

   1 calculator, valued at $35

   1 cordless phone and base, valued at $95

The total value of the items stolen was

- ❑  A. $1,741
- ❑  B. $3,229
- ❑  C. $1,873
- ❑  D. $1,774

90. Officer Frank responded to the report of a burglary at a warehouse at 22537 East Aberdeen. Upon arrival, the owner of the warehouse, Mr. Dennis Hitchens, advised that overnight person or persons unknown had removed six old cars that were being kept in the warehouse until they could be restored. Mr. Hitchens produced ownership papers for the vehicles, which were determined to be

One 1987 Oldsmobile 98, valued at $550

One 1985 Buick Riviera, valued at $350

One 1989 Chevrolet Impala, valued at $675

One 1995 Buick Skylark, valued at $1,650

One 1990 Chevrolet Suburban, valued at $4,500

One 1990 Chevrolet Caprice, valued at $625

The total value of the vehicles stolen was

- ❑  A. $8,250
- ❑  B. $8,450
- ❑  C. $8,550
- ❑  D. $8,350

Questions 91–96 involve comparing an original composite sketch to four other drawings, three of which show how the suspect might possibly disguise his or her appearance. The assumption is made that the suspect has not undergone any cosmetic surgery. From the four supplemental composites, choose the one that is not of the original suspect.

91.

❑ A.

❑ B.

❑ C.

❑ D.

92.

❑ A.

❑ B.

❑ C.

❑ D.

93.

☐ A.

☐ B.

☐ C.

☐ D.

94.

☐ A.

☐ B.

☐ C.

☐ D.

95.

❏ A.

❏ B.

❏ C.

❏ D.

For question 96, compare the original sketch to the four sketches shown in A-D. Choose the sketch that matches the original.

96.

❏ A.

❏ B.

❏ C.

❏ D.

In questions 97–100 compare the original sketch with the four shown in A–D. Choose the sketch that is different from the original.

97.

❑ A.

❑ B.

❑ C.

❑ D.

98.

❑ A.

❑ B.

❑ C.

❑ D.

99.

❑ A.

❑ B.

❑ C.

❑ D.

100.

❑ A.

❑ B.

❑ C.

❑ D.

CHAPTER TWELVE

# Answer Key to Practice Test 1

| | | |
|---|---|---|
| **1.** B, C | **19.** A | **37.** B, D |
| **2.** C | **20.** D | **38.** B, C |
| **3.** D | **21.** A | **39.** B, C |
| **4.** B | **22.** C | **40.** A, B |
| **5.** A | **23.** B | **41.** B |
| **6.** B | **24.** C | **42.** A |
| **7.** A | **25.** D | **43.** D |
| **8.** C | **26.** C | **44.** D |
| **9.** D | **27.** A | **45.** C |
| **10.** A | **28.** D | **46.** A |
| **11.** B | **29.** B | **47.** C |
| **12.** A | **30.** A, C, D | **48.** B |
| **13.** A | **31.** C | **49.** A |
| **14.** A | **32.** B, C, D | **50.** A |
| **15.** C | **33.** B, C | **51.** C |
| **16.** B | **34.** A, C, D | **52.** B |
| **17.** A | **35.** B | **53.** C, D |
| **18.** D | **36.** C | **54.** D |

| | | |
|---|---|---|
| **55.** B, C | **71.** C | **87.** C |
| **56.** D | **72.** B | **88.** A |
| **57.** B | **73.** D | **89.** B |
| **58.** B | **74.** A | **90.** D |
| **59.** D | **75.** B | **91.** C |
| **60.** D | **76.** A | **92.** A |
| **61.** B | **77.** D | **93.** B |
| **62.** A | **78.** A | **94.** C |
| **63.** C | **79.** C | **95.** D |
| **64.** D | **80.** B | **96.** A |
| **65.** A | **81.** B | **97.** B |
| **66.** C | **82.** C | **98.** D |
| **67.** B | **83.** B | **99.** A |
| **68.** D | **84.** B | **100.** D |
| **69.** A | **85.** D | |
| **70.** C | **86.** B | |

1. **Answers B and C are correct:** Supersede; Supercede
2. **Answer C is correct:** Irresistible
3. **Answer D is correct:** Development
4. **Answer B is correct:** Separate
5. **Answer A is correct:** Tyranny
6. **Answer B is correct:** Harass
7. **Answer A is correct:** Desiccate
8. **Answer C is correct:** Indispensable
9. **Answer D is correct:** Receive
10. **Answer A is correct:** Pursue
11. **Answer B is correct:** Recommend
12. **Answer C is correct:** Desperate

13. **Answer A is correct**: Cemetery

14. **Answer A is correct**: Subpoena

15. **Answer C is correct**: Definitely

16. **Answer B is correct**: Occasion

17. **Answer A is correct**: Consensus

18. **Answer D is correct**: Inadvertent

19. **Answer A is correct**: Judgment

20. **Answer D is correct**: Drunkenness

21. **Answer A is correct**: Occurrence

22. **Answer C is correct**: Dissipate

23. **Answer B is correct**: Reckless

24. **Answer C is correct**: Weird

25. **Answer D is correct**: Accidentally

26. **Answer C is correct**. The sentence consists of two contractions and a possessive pronoun. *It's (it is)* time *you're (you are)* completing *your (possessive pronoun)* test. Answer A is incorrect because it uses the possessive pronoun Its rather than the proper contraction *It's*. Answer B reserves the proper usage of *you're* and *your*. Answer D improperly uses the contraction *you're* instead of the possessive pronoun *your*.

27. **Answer A is correct**. The sentence consists of a contraction, a possessive pronoun, and an adverb. *They're (They are)* all safely in *their (possessive pronoun)* places over *there (adverb)*. Answer B is incorrect because it begins with the adverb *There* instead of the correct contraction *They're*, uses the contraction *they're* instead of the correct possessive pronoun *their*, and the possessive pronoun *their* instead of the correct adverb *there*.

28. **Answer D is correct**. Proper use of the words is illustrated in **D**: Her *beau (sweetheart)* tied a *bow (ribbon bent in a curved shape)* around the *bough (branch)* of the tree. Answers A, B, and C incorrectly use those three words.

29. **Answer B is correct**. This sentence properly uses the contraction *We're (We are)*, the verb *were*, and the adverb *there*: *We're* busy trying to determine if they *were there*. Sentence A incorrectly uses the verb *Were* instead of the correct contraction *We're* and the contraction *we're* instead of the correct verb *were*; the adverb *there* is correct. Sentence C

uses the verb *Were* instead of the correct contraction *We're*, the contraction *we're* instead of the correct verb *were*, and the possessive pronoun *their* instead of the correct adverb *there*. Sentence D properly uses the contract *We're* and verb *were*, but uses the contraction *they're* instead of the proper adverb *there*.

30. **Answers A, C, and D are correct**. Sentence B incorrectly reverses the two defined words: At first, the officer decided he'd rather write a ticket *then* (*than* should have been used to designate a difference) issue a warning *than* (*then* should have been used to denote time) he changed his mind.

31. **Answer C is correct**. The correct sentence uses the adverb *Too* to indicate *more than* or an *excessive degree*, *two* to designate a *number*, and *too* as an adverb to convey *also*. Sentence A incorrectly uses the preposition *To* instead of the correct adverb *Too*, the adverb *too* instead of the number *two*, and the number *two* instead of the correct adverb *too*. Sentence B incorrectly uses the number *Two* instead of the correct adverb *Too* and the preposition *to* instead of the correct number *two*. Sentence D incorrectly uses the preposition *to* instead of the number *two* and then uses the number *two* instead of the correct adverb *too*.

32. **Answers B, C, and D are correct**. Sentence A uses the adjective *Which* without providing a noun for it to modify.

33. **Answers B and C are correct**. Sentence A incorrectly uses the contraction *who's* instead of the correct possessive pronoun *whose*. Sentence D incorrectly uses the possessive pronoun *Whose* instead of the correct contraction for *Who* and *is*, which is *Who's*.

34. **Answers A, C, and D are correct**. In the phrase "they'll learn me as much as they can," sentence B incorrectly uses the verb *learn* instead of the correct one, which is *teach*.

35. **Answer B is correct**. "Line up *altogether*" in sentence A refers to doing something as a group, so the correct word choice would be *all together*. In sentence C, "*all together* too risky" refers to something "in total too risky," so the proper word choice would be *altogether*. "*Altogether* now" in sentence D refers to something to be done as a group, so the correct word choice would be *all together*.

36. **Answer C is correct**. The context for sentence A is that of something that had occurred in the past, so *already* would be the proper word choice instead of *all ready*. The context of "paper was *all ready*" in sentence B should be to convey that something is totally prepared, thus *already* is the proper word choice; the context for "so he was *all ready*

properly registered" refers something that's occurred prior to the time period conveyed, thus *already* is the proper word choice. In sentence D, "the paperwork was *already*" describes something that is totally prepared, so the proper word choice would be *all ready*.

37. **Answers B and D are correct.** In sentence A, *immigrate* is incorrect because the sentence refers to somebody who is ready to leave a country. In sentence C, *emigrate* is incorrect because the sentence refers to somebody who tried to enter a country.

38. **Answers B and C are correct.** In sentence A, *infer* is incorrect because the sentence refers to somebody who is making a suggestion. In sentence D, the prosecutor is performing an action in the hope that the jury will arrive at a conclusion based on his action, thus the proper word choice would be *infer*.

39. **Answers B and C are correct.** In sentence A, the context in "couldn't *except*" is "take what is offered," so *accept* is the correct word choice. In sentence B, the context of "chose to *except*" is "to take what is offered," so the correct word is *accept*, and the context of "*accept* one" is to exclude one, so the correct word is *except*.

40. **Answers A and B are correct.** Sentence C is incorrect because the adjective *good* is used instead of the correct adverb *well*. Sentence D is incorrect because the adjective *good* would be more appropriate in that context than is the adverb *well*.

41. **Answer B is correct.** A *perception* is an understanding reaching through discernment. Answer A is incorrect because a *prejudice* is an opinion formed without justification or with preconceived bias. Answer C is incorrect because *belief* is a conviction rather than a formed understanding, which is a subtle, but important, distinction. Answer D is incorrect because a *definition* refers to something's meaning or essential nature.

42. **Answer A is correct.** To *persevere* is to *persist*. Answer B is incorrect because to *continue* means more to go with the flow. Answer C is incorrect because although to *strive* requires devoting energy to overcome opposition, it isn't the best word in the context of the sample sentence. Answer D is incorrect because to *resolve* more closely means to reach a resolution and is not correct in the context of the sample sentence.

43. **Answer D is correct.** In the context of the sample sentence, *reconcile* means to reach a conclusion by analysis of the evidence or to *resolve* based on the substance of the evidence. Answer A is incorrect because to *coordinate* in this context would mean to organize without reaching

any conclusions—to simply arrange the evidence in some sort of order. Answer B is incorrect for the same reason. Answer C is incorrect because to *delete* the evidence would mean to somehow get rid of it.

44. **Answer D is correct**. In the context of this sentence, *perception* could most closely be defined as an *observation*, or an understanding reached through experience. Answer A is incorrect because a *fable* can be a short, cautionary tale or a falsehood. Answer B is incorrect because a *myth* in this context would mean an incorrect perception. Answer C is incorrect because a *falsehood* is an untrue statement or a lie.

45. **Answer C is correct**. Answer A is incorrect because *immaterial* means unimportant. Answer B is incorrect because *irrelevant* means something is not relevant. Answer D is incorrect because *obsolete* means something is no longer current, useful, or relevant.

46. **Answer A is correct**. Answer B is incorrect because *dishonesty* means fraud or intent to deceive. Answer C is incorrect because *morale* refers to spirit of, or the emotional or mental condition of those involved. Answer D is incorrect because *attendance* refers to the act of attending or the number of people attending.

47. **Answer C is correct**. Answer A is incorrect because *obedience* means compliance with the rules or laws. Answer B is incorrect because *compliance* means to follow the rules or laws. Answer D is incorrect because *cooperative* means a willingness to work with others within the established rules.

48. **Answer B is correct**. Answer A is incorrect because to *resist* means to take a stand against something. Answer C is incorrect because to *defy* is to resist or challenge the established order. Answer D is incorrect because *dare* means to perform an act because of courage, not, as in the context of this sentence, because of shift assignment.

49. **Answer A is correct**. Answer B is incorrect because *prejudice* is an opinion formed without justification or with preconceived bias, not because of a supervisor's observation of behavior as is implied in the context of the example sentence. Answer C is incorrect because a *fallacy* is a falsehood. Answer D is incorrect because *apprehension* means comprehending, or the legal process of an arrest.

50. **Answer A is correct**. Answer B is incorrect because *agreement* means in accord. Answer C is incorrect because *integrity* refers to someone's honest and high standards. Answer D is incorrect because *publicity* refers to getting what is generally assumed to be favorable public attention or distributing favorable information to the press.

51. **Answer C is correct.** Answer A is incorrect because it refers to an *unauthorized* arrest. Answer B is incorrect because it is in no way related to the described charge of *resisting arrest.* Answer D is incorrect because it refers to an *illegal arrest.*

52. **Answer B is correct.** Answers A, C, and D are incorrect because they refer to other criminal acts other than criminal mischief.

53. **Answers C and D are correct.** Answers A and C are incorrect because they are fictitious explanations of the acronym.

54. **Answer D is correct.** Answers A, B, and C are incorrect definitions.

55. **Answers B and C are correct.** Answers A and D are incorrect definitions.

56. **Answer D is correct.** Answers A, B, and C are incorrect definitions.

57. **Answer B is correct.** Answer A is incorrect because it states that a misdemeanor is *more* serious than a felony. Answers C and D are incorrect because they define other crimes.

58. **Answer B is correct.** Answers A, C, and D are incorrect because *recklessness, passion,* and *unlicensed use of a handgun* are not parts of the primary definition for Class A felony homicide or first-degree murder.

59. **Answer D is correct.** Answers A, B, and C are incorrect because *loss of services, loss of property,* and *loss of life* are not parts of the charge of menacing.

60. **Answer D is correct.** Answers A, B, and C are incorrect because they do not describe the charge.

61. **Answer B is correct.** Answers A, C, and D do not place the sentences in their logical order.

62. **Answer A is correct.** Answers B, C, and D do not place the sentences in their logical order.

63. **Answer C is correct.** Answers A, B, and D do not place the sentences in their logical order.

64. **Answer D is correct.** Answers A, B, and C do not place the sentences in their logical order.

65. **Answer A is correct.** Answers B, C, and D do not place the sentences in their logical order.

66. **Answer C is correct.** Answers A, B, and D do not place the sentences in their logical order.

67. **Answer B is correct.** Answers A, C, and D do not place the sentences in their logical order.

68. **Answer D is correct.** Answers A, B, and C do not place the sentences in their logical order.

69. **Answer A is correct.** Answers B, C, and D do not place the sentences in their logical order.

70. **Answer C is correct.** Answers A, B, and D do not place the sentences in their logical order.

71. **Answer C is correct.** $325 + (2 \times $950) + $1,925 + $440 + $2,550 = $7,140; therefore answers A, B, and D are incorrect.

72. **Answer B is correct.** $125 + $325 + $125 + $95 + 675 − $675 + $125 = $795; therefore answers A, C, and D are incorrect.

73. **Answer D is correct.** $(22 \times $6) + (10 \times $4.50) + (8 \times $7.50) + (10 \times $9) + (6 \times $9) + $2.50 + $2.50 + (14 \times $.65) = $398.60; therefore answers A, B, and C are incorrect.

74. **Answer A is correct.** $175 + $125 + $25 + $250 + $425 + $95 = $1,095; therefore answers B, C, and D are incorrect.

75. **Answer B is correct.** $(4 \times $350) + $1,225 + $2,950 + $1,750 + $2,225 + ($4,950 − $2,950) + $45 = $11,595; therefore answers A, C, and D are incorrect.

76. **Answer A is correct.** $10 + $95 + $25 + $35 = $165; therefore answers B, C, and D are incorrect.

77. **Answer D is correct.** $350 + $350 + $250 + $50 = $1,000; therefore answers A, B, and C are incorrect.

78. **Answer A is correct.** $(3 \times $225) + (5 \times $365) + (4 \times $175) − $365 = $2,835; therefore answers B, C, and D are incorrect.

79. **Answer C is correct.** $(73 \times $.25) + (84 \times $.10) + (96 \times $.05) + (15 \times $.01) + (75 \times $1) + (96 \times $20) + (84 \times $5) + (97 \times $10) + (3 \times $100) = $3,716.60; therefore answers A, B, and D are incorrect.

80. **Answer B is correct.** $(5 \times $5) + (4 \times $3) + $45 + $55 + (2 \times $125) + $325 + (2 \times $75) + (2 \times $20) = $902; therefore answers A, C, and D are incorrect.

81. **Answer B is correct.** $50 + $24 + $325 + $55 = $454; therefore answers A, C, and D are incorrect.

82. **Answer C is correct.** $6,000 + (20 \times $16.49) + $99 + (2 \times $99) = $6,626.80; therefore answers A, B, and D are incorrect.

83. **Answer B is correct.** $12,000 + $6,000 + (2 × $750) + (2 × $7,500) + (2 × $12,500) + (2 × $225) + $1,225 = $61,175; therefore answers A, C, and D are incorrect.

84. **Answer B is correct.** $1,225 + $225 + $2,575 + $250 = $4,275; therefore answers A, C, and D are incorrect.

85. **Answer D is correct.** $75 + $125 + $565 + $2,500 + $9,500 + $950 + $1,250 + $375 = $15,340; therefore answers A, B, and C are incorrect.

86. **Answer B is correct.** (25 × $8.99) + (2 × $30) + (20 × $3.99) + (15 × $4) + (3 × $35) + (10 × $.99) + (5 × $3.75) = $558.20; therefore answers A, C, and D are incorrect.

87. **Answer C is correct.** $69.95 + (2 × $29.95) + (2 × $14.95) = $159.75; therefore answers A, B, and D are incorrect.

88. **Answer A is correct.** $879.54 + (5 × $35.00) + (3 × $1.49) + (6 × $.99) = $1,064.95; therefore answers B, C, and D are incorrect.

89. **Answer B is correct.** $1,250 + (125 × $12) + $250 + $99 + $35 + $95 = $3,229; therefore answers A, C, and D are incorrect.

90. **Answer D is correct.** $550 + $350 + $675 + $1,650 + $4,500 + $625 = $8,350; therefore answers A, B, and C are incorrect.

91. **Answer C is correct.** The subject in C has a different hairline, eyebrows, eyes, and nose than the subject in the original sketch; therefore answers A, B, and D are incorrect because those figures show the original subject in disguise.

92. **Answer A is correct.** The female shown in A has a different hairline, eyebrows, eyes, nose, and mouth than the subject in the original sketch; therefore answers B, C, and D are incorrect because those sketches show the original subject in disguise.

93. **Answer B is correct.** The male shown in B has a lighter complexion and different eyebrows, eyes, nose, and mouth than the subject in the original sketch; therefore answers A, C, and D are incorrect because they show the original subject in disguise.

94. **Answer C is correct.** The subject in C has a thinner face, eyes that are more slanted than the original sketch subject's, and a narrower nose; therefore answers A, B, and D are incorrect because they show the original subject in disguise.

95. **Answer D is correct.** The subject in D has a different hairline, age lines, eyes, and nose than does the original sketch subject; therefore answers A, B, and C are incorrect because they show the original subject in disguise.

96. **Answer A is correct**. The subjects shown in B, C, and D have different eyebrows, eyes, noses, and mouths than does the subject shown in the original sketch.

97. **Answer B is correct**. The subject in B has a smaller mole. The sketches in A, C, and D match the original sketch, and therefore are incorrect.

98. **Answer D is correct**. The female in D doesn't have a scar on her chin. The sketches in A, B, and C match the original sketch, and therefore are incorrect.

99. **Answer A is correct**. The male shown in A is missing the moles to the right of his nose. The sketches in B, C, and D match the original sketch, and therefore are incorrect.

100. **Answer D is correct**. The male shown in D is missing the scar to the right of his nose that is shown in the original sketch. The sketches in A, B, and C all show that scar, and therefore are incorrect.

# 13

# Practice Test 2

## Using Maps and Face Recognition

1. You are advised of a report of a suspicious Middle Eastern male seen loitering near the area of the city power plant, reportedly also occasionally taking pictures. The subject is described as being shorter than 5'6", slender, and 20–25 years of age. He is further described as having a semi-narrow nose, black medium-length hair with slight curl, slightly angled jaw, very thick lips, and brown eyes. He is described as clean-shaven, but with razor burns as if he'd just shaved off a lot of facial hair.

   Choose the police drawing of a Middle Eastern male that most closely matches the described individual:

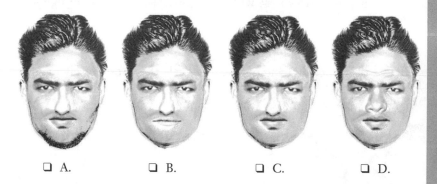

   ❏ A.          ❏ B.          ❏ C.          ❏ D.

2. You are advised of a report of a suspicious person seen loitering near the playground area at City Park. The suspect is described as a black male, just under 6' tall. He is further described as having a heavy build, probably weighing more than 250 pounds. The reporting party said the man looked to be about 30 years of age, has a very wide nose, very curly and matted black hair—long on top but not really extending below his ears, an extremely rounded jaw, very thick lips, dark eyes, and thick eyebrows.

Choose the police drawing of a African-American male that most closely matches the described individual:

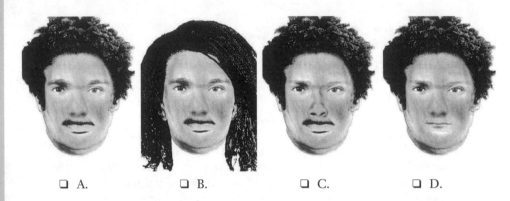

❑ A.          ❑ B.          ❑ C.          ❑ D.

3. You receive a report that the suspect in a missing or abducted child report is a white female described as being 5' 8" and slender, weighing about 125 pounds. She is further described as being 20 years old and as having a slightly narrow nose with flared nostrils, long straight light-brown hair with a slight wave at the temples, wide-set dark brown eyes, slightly angled jaw, medium slightly upturned lips, thin angled eyebrows, and a light complexion.

Choose the police drawing of a white female that most closely matches the described individual:

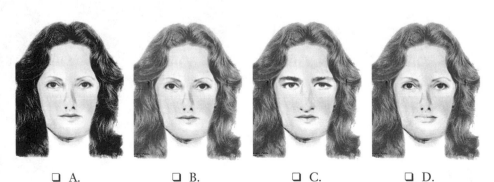

❑ A.          ❑ B.          ❑ C.          ❑ D.

**Directions:** After studying the original composite sketch, compare it to the four sketches that follow question 4 to determine which one is not of the original suspect.

4. Compare this original composite sketch of a white male with thick hair parted on the side, bushy mustache, neatly trimmed beard, straight narrow nose, thick eyebrows, and medium height and build with the following four drawings, three of which are drawings showing how the suspect might possibly disguise his appearance. The assumption is made that the suspect has not undergone any cosmetic surgery. From the four supplemental composites, choose the one that is not of the original suspect.

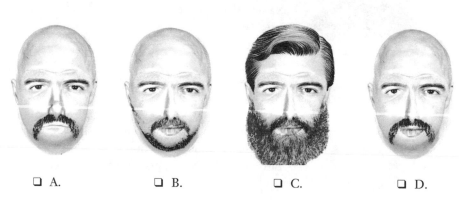

❏ A.              ❏ B.              ❏ C.              ❏ D.

**Directions:** Before answering questions 5–16, study the four wanted posters for five minutes. Be sure to pay attention to both the mug shot drawings and the additional information that accompanies the posters.

Wanted – Escaped Prisoner
Name: Muhammad Robb
Age: 36
Height: 5'10"
Eyes: Brown
Scars: Gall bladder surgery scar
Race: Black
Weight: 185
Hair: Bald
Facial hair: Mustache, goatee
Tattoos: None

Serving a sentence for felony assault. Subject is known to have a short temper.

Wanted – Escaped Prisoner
Name: Abasi Turner
Age: 24
Height: 5'6"
Eyes: Brown
Scars: Knife scar on left cheek
Race: Black
Weight: 115
Hair: Black, short, tightly curled (short afro)
Facial hair: None (See note)
Tattoos: Thin chains, just above both biceps

Serving a sentence for armed robbery. Subject sometimes goes several days without shaving. Considered armed and dangerous. No known weapons preference; however, upon arrest, he had a .22 in his possession.

Wanted – Escaped Prisoner
Name: Kayin Bishop
Age: 28
Height: 6'2"
Eyes: Brown
Scars: None
Race: Black
Weight: 225
Hair: Black, short curly
Facial hair: None
Tattoos: Prison tattoos, 1" star on each upper forearm

Serving a sentence for extortion and theft. Known to prey on older females. Gains entry into home by posing as a Medicare-supplement insurance salesman. Generally dresses well, in dark slacks, short-sleeved shirt, and tie. Articulate with good vocabulary.

Wanted – Escaped Prisoner
Name: Solomon Simpson
Age: 42
Height: 5'10"
Eyes: Brown
Scars: None
Race: Black
Weight: 190
Hair: Black, short, curly
Facial hair: None
Tattoos: USMC and bulldog on upper part of right arm

Serving a sentence for aggravated assault. Known to carry a switchblade in the past. Former Marine with hand-to-hand combat skills. Use caution.

**Directions:** After studying the wanted posters and information for five minutes, set that information aside and answer the following questions by selecting the proper mug shot:

5. Which subject is 28 years old?

❏  A.          ❏  B.          ❏  C.          ❏  D.

6. Which subject has a surgery scar?

❏  A.          ❏  B.          ❏  C.          ❏  D.

7. Which subject has a bulldog tattoo on the upper part of his right arm?

❏  A.          ❏  B.          ❏  C.          ❏  D.

8. Which subject has a facial scar?

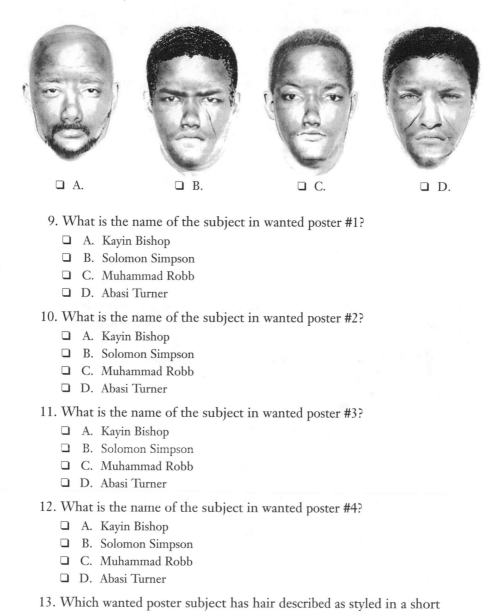

❏ A.                ❏ B.                ❏ C.                ❏ D.

9. What is the name of the subject in wanted poster #1?
   ❏ A. Kayin Bishop
   ❏ B. Solomon Simpson
   ❏ C. Muhammad Robb
   ❏ D. Abasi Turner

10. What is the name of the subject in wanted poster #2?
   ❏ A. Kayin Bishop
   ❏ B. Solomon Simpson
   ❏ C. Muhammad Robb
   ❏ D. Abasi Turner

11. What is the name of the subject in wanted poster #3?
   ❏ A. Kayin Bishop
   ❏ B. Solomon Simpson
   ❏ C. Muhammad Robb
   ❏ D. Abasi Turner

12. What is the name of the subject in wanted poster #4?
   ❏ A. Kayin Bishop
   ❏ B. Solomon Simpson
   ❏ C. Muhammad Robb
   ❏ D. Abasi Turner

13. Which wanted poster subject has hair described as styled in a short afro?
   ❏ A. Kayin Bishop
   ❏ B. Solomon Simpson
   ❏ C. Muhammad Robb
   ❏ D. Abasi Turner

14. Which wanted poster subject has a mustache and a goatee?
   - ❏ A. Kayin Bishop
   - ❏ B. Solomon Simpson
   - ❏ C. Muhammad Robb
   - ❏ D. Abasi Turner

15. Which wanted poster subject is described as weighing 190 pounds?
   - ❏ A. Kayin Bishop
   - ❏ B. Solomon Simpson
   - ❏ C. Muhammad Robb
   - ❏ D. Abasi Turner

16. Which wanted poster subject is described as being 6'2"?
   - ❏ A. Kayin Bishop
   - ❏ B. Solomon Simpson
   - ❏ C. Muhammad Robb
   - ❏ D. Abasi Turner

**Directions:** Before answering questions 17–28, study the four wanted posters for five minutes. Be sure to pay attention to both the mug shot drawings and the additional information that accompanies the posters.

Wanted – Escaped Prisoner
Name: Abdul Ryad
Age: 24
Height: 5'8"
Eyes: Brown
Scars: Small, over inside right eyebrow
Race: Middle Eastern
Weight: 145
Hair: Black, short, parted on left
Facial hair: None
Tattoos: None

Wanted poster #1.

Subject was serving a sentence for hijacking a fertilizer truck. Subject has been known to use Hispanic aliases in the past. Subject should be considered armed and dangerous.

Wanted – Escaped Prisoner
Name: Daniel Patterson
Age: 23
Height: 5'7"
Eyes: Brown
Scars: None
Race: Asian-American
Weight: 145
Hair: Black, short, no part
Facial hair: None
Tattoos: Dragon, upper part of left arm

Wanted poster #2.

Subject was serving a sentence for aggravated assault. Subject's mother, Kim Patterson, is divorced from the subject's father and still resides in town at 2345 South Brown Street. Originally from Thailand, subject's mother has been known to help obtain janitorial or dishwasher employment in area Thai restaurants for her son. Subject has been diagnosed with bipolar disorder and was on prison hospital-moderated medications.

Wanted – Escaped Prisoner
Name: Nathaniel (Nate) Christie
Age: 27
Height: 5'10"
Eyes: Brown
Scars: None
Race: Native American
Weight: 180
Hair: Black, thick on top, combed to the left
Facial hair: None
Tattoos: None

Wanted poster #3.

Subject was serving a sentence for arson. Bragged to fellow inmates that it is his intent to die "riddled by bullets" like a "Cherokee outlaw" that he claims is a distant relative (a part of his family tree). Has previously served time for armed robbery. Subject should therefore be considered armed and dangerous.

Wanted – Escaped Prisoner
Name: Roberto Garcia
Age: 29
Height: 5'9"
Eyes: Brown
Scars: None
Race: Hispanic
Weight: 190
Hair: Black
Facial hair: None
Tattoos: None

Wanted poster #4.

Subject was serving a sentence for burglary and forgery. Subject's MO is to break into the homes of insurance adjusters and insurance offices and steal blank checks, which he then forges and passes at banks in neighboring cities.

**Directions:** After studying the wanted posters and information for five minutes, set that information aside and answer the following questions by selecting the proper mug shot:

17. Which subject told fellow inmates that he wants to die full of bullet holes?

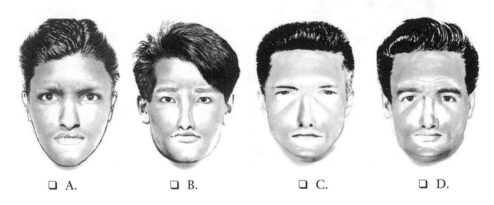

❏ A.          ❏ B.          ❏ C.          ❏ D.

18. Which subject was serving a sentence for forgery?

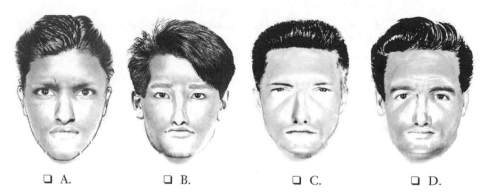

&#9744; A.                &#9744; B.                &#9744; C.                &#9744; D.

19. Which subject was serving a sentence for aggravated assault?

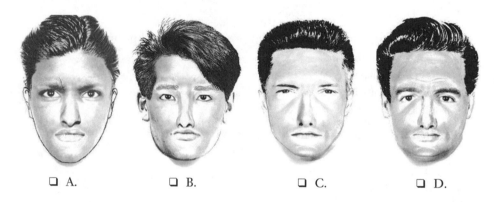

&#9744; A.                &#9744; B.                &#9744; C.                &#9744; D.

20. Which subject sometimes uses Hispanic aliases?

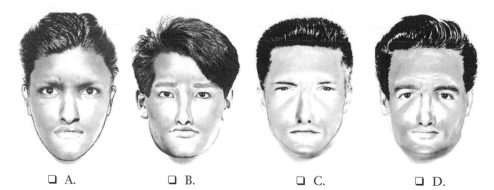

&#9744; A.                &#9744; B.                &#9744; C.                &#9744; D.

21. What is the name of the escaped prisoner in wanted poster #1?
    - ❏ A. Roberto Garcia
    - ❏ B. Nathaniel (Nate) Christie
    - ❏ C. Daniel Patterson
    - ❏ D. Abdul Ryad

22. What is the name of the escaped prisoner in wanted poster #2?
    - ❏ A. Roberto Garcia
    - ❏ B. Nathaniel (Nate) Christie
    - ❏ C. Daniel Patterson
    - ❏ D. Abdul Ryad

23. What is the name of the escaped prisoner in wanted poster #3?
    - ❏ A. Roberto Garcia
    - ❏ B. Nathaniel (Nate) Christie
    - ❏ C. Daniel Patterson
    - ❏ D. Abdul Ryad

24. What is the name of the escaped prisoner in wanted poster #4?
    - ❏ A. Roberto Garcia
    - ❏ B. Nathaniel (Nate) Christie
    - ❏ C. Daniel Patterson
    - ❏ D. Abdul Ryad

25. Which escaped prisoner has a dragon tattoo?
    - ❏ A. Roberto Garcia
    - ❏ B. Nathaniel (Nate) Christie
    - ❏ C. Daniel Patterson
    - ❏ D. Abdul Ryad

26. Which escaped prisoner is 29 years old?
    - ❏ A. Roberto Garcia
    - ❏ B. Nathaniel (Nate) Christie
    - ❏ C. Daniel Patterson
    - ❏ D. Abdul Ryad

27. Which escaped prisoner has a scar over his right eyebrow?
    - ❏ A. Roberto Garcia
    - ❏ B. Nathaniel (Nate) Christie
    - ❏ C. Daniel Patterson
    - ❏ D. Abdul Ryad

28. Which escaped prisoner is 5'10"?
    - ❏ A. Roberto Garcia
    - ❏ B. Nathaniel (Nate) Christie
    - ❏ C. Daniel Patterson
    - ❏ D. Abdul Ryad

**Directions:** Before answering questions 29–40, study the four likenesses and supporting information for five minutes.

You are advised of four Failure to Appear (FTA) warrants, and are given photocopies of the likenesses of the four subjects for whom the warrants were issued.

Name: Vicki Patterson
Age: 29
Height: 5'9"
Eyes: Blue
Scars: 3" scar, right knee
Race: White
Weight: 135
Hair: Blonde
Facial hair: None
Tattoos: Butterfly, left ankle

FTA warrant subject #1.

FTA to answer for the charge of Driving Under the Influence of Drugs and Alcohol.

Name: Deb Johnson
Age: 24
Height: 5'6"
Eyes: Hazel
Scars: None
Race: White
Weight: 195
Hair: Brown, dark
Facial hair: None
Tattoos: None

FTA warrant subject #2.

FTA to answer for the charge of Public Intoxication and Disorderly Conduct.

Name: Amy Chandler
Age: 27
Height: 5 ' 5 "
Eyes: Brown
Scars: Appendectomy scar
Race: Asian
Weight: 120
Hair: Black
Facial hair: None
Tattoos: None

FTA warrant subject #3.

FTA to answer for the charge of Passing Bad Checks.

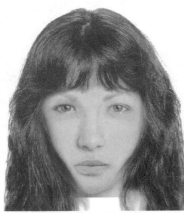

Name: Tiffany Calloway
Age: 18
Height: 5 ' 6 "
Eyes: Brown
Scars: None
Race: White
Weight: 130
Hair: Brown
Facial hair: None
Tattoos: Heart tattoo, lower back

FTA warrant subject #4.

FTA to answer for the charge of Petty Theft (Shoplifting).

Set the drawings aside and then answer the following questions:

29. Which subject has a heart tattoo?

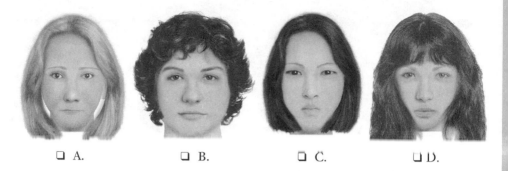

❑ A.            ❑ B.            ❑ C.            ❑ D.

30. Which subject has a warrant for Passing Bad Checks?

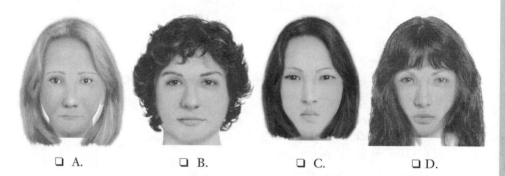

❑ A.            ❑ B.            ❑ C.            ❑ D.

31. Which subject has a surgery scar?

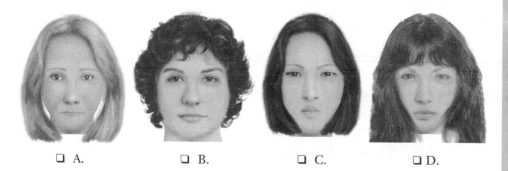

❑ A.            ❑ B.            ❑ C.            ❑ D.

32. Which subject has hazel eyes?

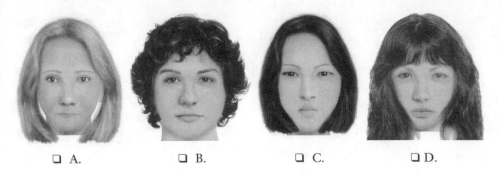

❏ A.              ❏ B.              ❏ C.              ❏ D.

33. What is the name of FTA warrant subject #1?
    ❏  A.  Vicki Patterson
    ❏  B.  Deb Johnson
    ❏  C.  Amy Chandler
    ❏  D.  Tiffany Calloway

34. What is the name of FTA warrant subject #2?
    ❏  A.  Vicki Patterson
    ❏  B.  Deb Johnson
    ❏  C.  Amy Chandler
    ❏  D.  Tiffany Calloway

35. What is the name of FTA warrant subject #3?
    ❏  A.  Vicki Patterson
    ❏  B.  Deb Johnson
    ❏  C.  Amy Chandler
    ❏  D.  Tiffany Calloway

36. What is the name of FTA warrant subject #4?
    ❏  A.  Vicki Patterson
    ❏  B.  Deb Johnson
    ❏  C.  Amy Chandler
    ❏  D.  Tiffany Calloway

37. Which warrant subject failed to appear to answer to the charge of Petty
    Theft?
    ❏  A.  Vicki Patterson
    ❏  B.  Deb Johnson
    ❏  C.  Amy Chandler
    ❏  D.  Tiffany Calloway

38. Which warrant subject is 27 years old?
  - ❑ A. Vicki Patterson
  - ❑ B. Deb Johnson
  - ❑ C. Amy Chandler
  - ❑ D. Tiffany Calloway

39. Which warrant subject is the heaviest?
  - ❑ A. Vicki Patterson
  - ❑ B. Deb Johnson
  - ❑ C. Amy Chandler
  - ❑ D. Tiffany Calloway

40. Which warrant subject is the tallest?
  - ❑ A. Vicki Patterson
  - ❑ B. Deb Johnson
  - ❑ C. Amy Chandler
  - ❑ D. Tiffany Calloway

## TIP

When patrolling or looking for a suspect, it is critical you pay attention to detail. What may at first seem like the smallest, inconsequential feature, such as a tattoo or clothing, will often be the element you need to help you.

**Directions**: Compare the information given by witnesses and use the process of elimination to determine the most logical answer. (This process of elimination is based on the assumption that the information mentioned most frequently is probably the correct information.)

41. Officer Kray arrives at the scene of an armed robbery at a gas station. Upon interviewing four witnesses, he obtains the following four suspect descriptions. Which description is most likely correct?
  - ❑ A. Black male, 25, blue jeans, red T-shirt, 5'8"
  - ❑ B. Black male, 30, dark slacks, red T-shirt, 5'8"
  - ❑ C. Middle Eastern male, 25, blue jeans, red T-shirt, 6'
  - ❑ D. Black male, 25, blue jeans, red T-shirt, 5'8"

42. Officer Cooper responds to the scene of a bank robbery. Upon interviewing four witnesses, he gets the following vehicle descriptions. Which description is most likely correct?
  - ❑ A. Dark blue Chevy, four-door sedan, right rear taillight broken, Ohio license plate
  - ❑ B. Dark blue Buick, four-door sedan, left rear taillight broken, Ohio license plate
  - ❑ C. Dark blue Chevy, two-door sedan, right rear taillight broken, Ohio license plate
  - ❑ D. Black Ford, four-door sedan, right rear taillight out, Ohio license plate

43. Officer Smith responds to the scene of a hit-and-run car accident. Upon interviewing four witnesses to the accident, he obtains four license plate numbers. Which license plate number is most likely correct?

- ❏ A. KLM 883
- ❏ B. KKM 783
- ❏ C. KLM 783
- ❏ D. LKM 783

44. Officer Murphy responds to the scene of a purse snatching. Upon interviewing the victim and three witnesses, she gets the following descriptions. Which description is most likely correct?

- ❏ A. Male, white, 25, 5'10", 160 pounds, long brown hair, armed with a gun
- ❏ B. Male, white, 18, 5'10", 160 pounds, long brown hair, armed with a gun
- ❏ C. Male, white, 18, 5'8", 160 pounds, long blond hair, armed with a gun
- ❏ D. Male, white, 18, 5'10", 160 pounds, long brown hair, armed with a knife

**Directions:** Refer to the following figure and the following instructions to answer questions 45–56.

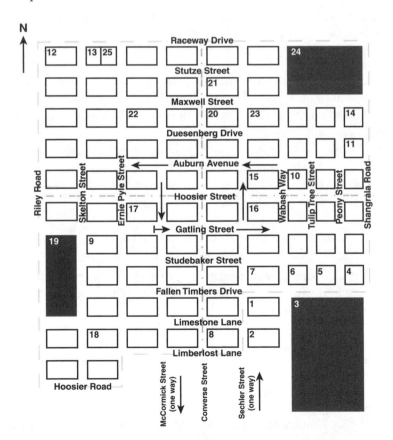

The preceding figure is of the fictional town of Utopia, Indiana. Points of interest include the following:

1. Shangrala State College Football Stadium

2. Shangrala State College Campus Parking

3. Shangrala State College Campus

4. Shangrala Apartments

5. Letterman Apartments

6. Campus Corners Apartments

7. Stadium View Apartments

8. Campus Corners Shopping Plaza

9. Utopia Community Medical Center

10. Rayburn Law Offices (southwest corner)

11. Utopia Public Library

12. Kadiddlehopper Korners

13. Founder's Park

14. Shangrala Seniors Apartments

15. Utopia Municipal Office Complex

16. Utopia Safety Building

17. Veterans' Park

18. Limberlost Grade School

19. Utopia Community Hospital

20. Utopia High School

21. Utopia Schools Sports Complex

22. Utopia Middle School

23. Lincoln Grade School

24. Cardinal Center Mall

25. Utopia Community Gardens

Shangrala State College, which is noted for its Challenger Memorial Celestial Observatory, is outside the city limits, as are the Shangrala State College Football Stadium and Shangrala State College Campus Parking. The campus, football stadium, and parking are within the jurisdiction of the Indiana Sheriff's Office; however, patrolling the campus is handled by the Shangrala State College Campus Police.

Shangrala Road south of Hoosier Street is also known as *State Route 133* and is under the jurisdiction of the Indiana State Police; however, complaints at private and commercial property along the west section of Shangrala Road are handled by the Utopia Police Department. All other state routes within the city limits are under the jurisdiction of the Utopia Police Department.

The city limits for Utopia are represented on the map by the light-gray broken lines. Except where otherwise noted, all areas on the map outside of the city limits are under the jurisdiction of the Shangrala County Sheriff's Department. Those areas include the west side of Riley Road, the north side of Raceway Drive, the east side of Shangrala Road, parts of the south side of Limberlost Lane, and the south side of Hoosier Road.

Utopia itself is divided into four patrol quadrants:

▶ The section of town to the city limits from the north side of Hoosier Street west of Converse Street and from the west side of Converse Street north of Hoosier Street is assigned as Unit 1.

▶ The section of town to the city limits from the north side of Hoosier Street east of Converse Street and from the east side of Converse Street north of Hoosier Street is assigned as Unit 2.

▶ The section of town to the city limits from the south side of Hoosier Street west of Converse Street and from the west side of Converse Street south of Hoosier Street is assigned as Unit 3.

▶ The section of town to the city limits from the south side of Hoosier Street east of Converse Street and from the east side of Converse Street south of Hoosier Street is assigned as Unit 4.

Three roving units also patrol Utopia. The patrol unit for the entire city limits area north of Hoosier Street is assigned as Unit A. The patrol unit for the entire city limits area south of Hoosier Street is assigned as Unit B. Unit C patrols the downtown area and is assigned to calls only when another unit is busy and can't respond or when it's needed for prisoner transport.

Auburn Avenue is one-way, westbound, from Shangrala Road to Riley Road.

Gatlin Street carries two-way traffic west of McCormick Street, and carries one-way traffic from McCormick Street east to Shangrala Road.

The emergency room entrance and exit for the Utopia Community Hospital are on Gatling Street.

Based on this information, answer questions 45 to 56:

45. There's a report of an armed robbery in progress at the Utopia Community Bank, which is located on the southeast corner of the Campus Corners Shopping Plaza. Which agency should respond to the call?
    - ❏  A.  Shangrala State College Campus Police
    - ❏  B.  Utopia Police Department
    - ❏  C.  Shangrala County Sheriff's Office
    - ❏  D.  Indiana State Police

46. Officer Murphy is flagged down by a pedestrian at the corner of Tulip Tree Street and Duesenberg Drive. The pedestrian reported seeing a suspicious male approaching some playground equipment. Which is the most likely location for where this suspicious person was seen?
    - ❏  A.  Limberlost Grade School
    - ❏  B.  Founder's Park
    - ❏  C.  Lincoln Grade School
    - ❏  D.  Veterans' Park

47. The Rayburn Law Offices are located at the corner of which streets?
    - ❏  A.  Wabash Way and Auburn Avenue
    - ❏  B.  Wabash Way and Hoosier Street
    - ❏  C.  Tulip Tree Street and Auburn Avenue
    - ❏  D.  Tulip Tree Street and Hoosier Street

48. Which apartment complex can be described as northwest of the Shangrala State College campus?
    - ❏  A.  Shangrala Apartments
    - ❏  B.  Letterman Apartments
    - ❏  C.  Campus Corners Apartments
    - ❏  D.  Utopia Community Gardens

49. Officer Grant is flagged down by a motorist who asks for directions to the planetarium. Which is the most logical location for the planetarium?

   ❑  A.  Cardinal Center Mall

   ❑  B.  Shangrala State College Campus

   ❑  C.  Founder's Park

   ❑  D.  Utopia Gardening Center

50. The Utopia Police Department receives a report of an altercation taking place near the emergency room entrance at the Utopia Community Hospital. Which units are most likely to be assigned to respond?

   ❑  A.  Unit A and Unit 1

   ❑  B.  Unit B and Unit 2

   ❑  C.  Unit B and Unit 3

   ❑  D.  Unit C and Unit 3

51. Officer Stewart is in Unit 2, traveling southbound on Converse Street approaching Auburn Avenue when he receives a call to respond to the northwest corner parking lot of Utopia Public Library. Assuming that there is no road construction and all traffic signals and routes are equal, what is his most logical route of travel?

   ❑  A.  Continue south on Converse Street, turn right on Auburn Street, go north on Ernie Pyle Street to Raceway Drive, and then west on Raceway Drive

   ❑  B.  Continue south on Converse Street, turn east on Hoosier Street to Shangrala Road, go south on Shangrala Road to Maxwell Street, and then west on Maxwell Street

   ❑  C.  Continue south on Converse Street, turn east on Hoosier Street, north on Shangrala Road, and then west on Maxwell Street

   ❑  D.  Continue south on Converse Street, turn east on Hoosier Street, north on Peony Street, and then east on Maxwell Street

52. Dispatch receives a report of an accident that occurred in the northbound lane of Shangrala Road just south of Hoosier Street. Which agency should respond?

   ❑  A.  Indiana State Police

   ❑  B.  Utopia Police Department

   ❑  C.  Shangrala County Sheriff's Department

   ❑  D.  Shangrala State College Campus Police

53. Because it involves a fight and it's unknown whether weapons are involved, the rescue squad requests that an officer respond with them to a complaint at the Shangrala Road entrance to Shangrala Apartments. Which agency should respond?

   ❏ A. Utopia Police Department
   ❏ B. Indiana State Police
   ❏ C. Shangrala County Sheriff's Department
   ❏ D. Shangrala State College Campus Police

54. Unit A is tied up on another call. Dispatch receives a call of a fight taking place at the Utopia Schools Sports Complex. Which units should respond?

   ❏ A. Unit C and Unit 1
   ❏ B. Unit C and Unit 2
   ❏ C. Unit C and Unit 3
   ❏ D. Unit C and Unit 4

55. Units A, B, and C are all tied up on other calls. Unit 3 is assigned to a complaint at Veterans' Park and requests backup. Which unit should respond?

   ❏ A. Unit 1
   ❏ B. Unit 2
   ❏ C. Unit 4
   ❏ D. Unable to determine from the information given

56. Unit B is at the Campus Corners Shopping Plaza. Where is Kadiddlehopper Korners in relation to Unit B's location?

   ❏ A. Northeast
   ❏ B. Southeast
   ❏ C. Northwest
   ❏ D. Southwest

**Directions:** Use the following key for the maps used to answer questions 57–59:

| Key Element | Figure |
|---|---|
| Moving vehicle | ⬆ |
| Parked vehicle | ⬆ |
| Pedestrian at a stationary location | O |
| Pedestrian on the move; arrow indicates direction in which the pedestrian is walking | ⬆ |

57. Officer Davis was traveling eastbound on Freyburg Road and just east of Cable Road when he observed an accident. The accident occurred when a vehicle traveling northbound on River Road failed to stop for the stop sign at the intersection of Freyburg Road, and subsequently struck a vehicle that had the right of way and was traveling westbound on Freyburg Road. Officer Brown's patrol unit is not shown in the sketch. Which sketch is correct?

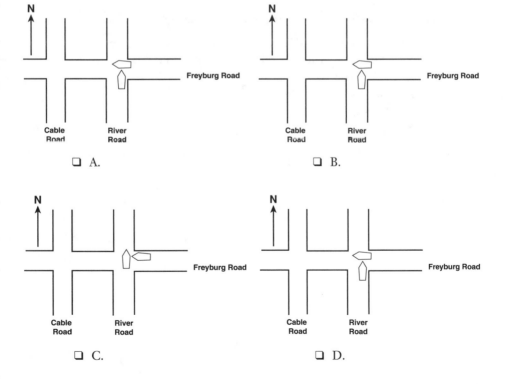

❏ A.

❏ B.

❏ C.

❏ D.

58. Officer Frank investigates an automobile accident that occurred when a vehicle traveling northbound on O'Hara Street ran a red light at the intersection with Baxter Street and struck a four-door sedan broadside on the driver's side rear door; this vehicle was traveling westbound on Baxter and had the right of way. This information was confirmed by a witness who was standing facing northbound while she waited at the bus stop on Baxter, which is located at the southwest side of O'Hara Street at Baxter. Which sketch accurately portrays this accident?

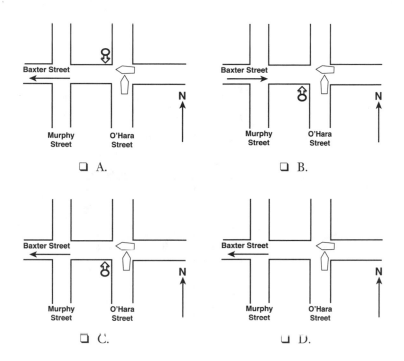

59. Officer Peters investigates an auto accident that occurred when, according to the parties involved and confirmed by witnesses, vehicle 1 pulled out of a parking place on Elizabeth Street (a northbound one-way street) and established its right of way, vehicle 2 changed lanes. As vehicle 2 pulled into the right lane, it clipped the driver's side rear bumper of vehicle 1, which pushed vehicle 1 into a car illegally parked northbound in a no parking zone on Elizabeth Street just south of Main Street. The drivers of which vehicle or vehicles were cited for this accident?

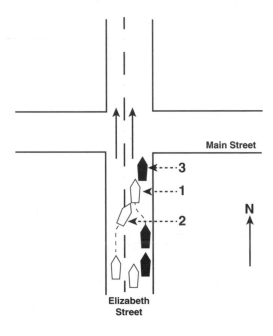

❏  A.  Vehicle 1
❏  B.  Vehicle 2
❏  C.  Vehicle 3
❏  D.  Vehicles 2 and 3

# Fractions

**Directions:** Select the best answer for the following questions.

60. 8 1/4 + 17 1/2 + 18 1/4 = X. Which of the following equals X?
❏  A.  43 3/4
❏  B.  43 2/4
❏  C.  44
❏  D.  43

61. 16 3/8 – 5 1/8 = X. Which of the following equals X?
   - ❑  A.  11 1/2
   - ❑  B.  11 1/4
   - ❑  C.  11 1/8
   - ❑  D.  10 2/8

62. To add numbers like 3/8 + 1/6, you need to find the *lowest common denominator* (LCD) of 8 and 6. What is the LCD of that equation?
   - ❑  A.  48
   - ❑  B.  8
   - ❑  C.  6
   - ❑  D.  24

63. What is the answer to the problem in question #62?
   - ❑  A.  13/24
   - ❑  B.  1/2
   - ❑  C.  4/6
   - ❑  D.  26/48

64. 1/6 + 1/4 = X. What is the value of X if it's reduced to a proper fraction that cannot be reduced further?
   - ❑  A.  10/24
   - ❑  B.  5/12
   - ❑  C.  8/12
   - ❑  D.  10/2

65. 6 3/4 – 1 1/4 = X. What is the value of X if it's reduced to a proper fraction that cannot be reduced further?
   - ❑  A.  5 2/4
   - ❑  B.  7 4/4
   - ❑  C.  5 1/2
   - ❑  D.  4 1/2

66. 7/8 × 5/8 = X. What is the value of X if it's reduced to a proper fraction that cannot be reduced further?
   - ❑  A.  35/64
   - ❑  B.  56/40
   - ❑  C.  40/56
   - ❑  D.  7/5

67. 3/4 × 1 1/9 = X. What is the value of X if it's reduced to a proper fraction that cannot be reduced further?
   - ❑  A.  30/36
   - ❑  B.  10/12
   - ❑  C.  5/6
   - ❑  D.  1 4/36

68. $5 \times 6\ 2/3 = X$. What is the value of X if it's reduced to a proper fraction that cannot be reduced further?

    ❑   A.  33 2/3
    ❑   B.  33 1/3
    ❑   C.  30 2/3
    ❑   D.  23 1/3

69. $7\ 2/3 \div 1/3 = X$. What is the value of X if it's reduced to a proper fraction that cannot be reduced further?

    ❑   A.  23
    ❑   B.  2 1/3
    ❑   C.  22 2/3
    ❑   D.  2 1/2 (2.5278 reduced to the closest fraction)

# Percentages

**Directions:** Select the best answer for the following questions.

70. The Big City Police Department has a total of 80 safety flares in inventory, of which there are 3 in each of 20 different squad cars. What is the percentage of the flares that remain in the equipment room?

    ❑   A.  60%
    ❑   B.  40%
    ❑   C.  25%
    ❑   D.  75%

71. In one year, detectives at the Big City Police Department investigated 23 homicides, 146 robberies, 346 burglaries, and 13 questionable deaths. Of the questionable deaths, 10 were ruled suicides, 2 were ruled to be of natural causes, and 1 was ruled a homicide. During that year, the detectives were able to solve 387 of the crimes. Rounded to the nearest three decimal places, what is their clearance rate (percentage of crimes solved) for the crimes?

    ❑   A.  73.295%
    ❑   B.  75%
    ❑   C.  73.574%
    ❑   D.  73.156%

72. The Big City Police Department has 73 white male officers, 34 white female officers, 26 Hispanic male officers, 16 Hispanic female officers, 36 African-American male officers, 34 African-American female officers, and 14 male and 3 females of other ethic origins on the department.

    To the nearest three decimal places, what percentage of the officers are male?

    ❏  A.  .063%
    ❏  B.  63.135%
    ❘❘  ❘⁻  6.314%
    ❏  D.  63.136%

73. To the nearest two decimal places, what percentage of the African-American officers are female?

    ❏  A.  48.57%
    ❏  B.  49.61%
    ❏  C.  94.44%
    ❏  D.  94.45%

74. To the nearest percent, what is the percentage of nonwhite females on the department?

    ❏  A.  23%
    ❏  B.  22%
    ❏  C.  30%
    ❏  D.  28%

75. The Big City Police Department expects to spend 23.5% of its $5,000.00 incidentals budget on firearms maintenance. How much has it budgeted to spend?

    ❏  A.  $1,275.25
    ❏  B.  $1,174.00
    ❏  C.  $1,176.50
    ❏  D.  $1,175.00

76. The Big City Police Department expects to spend 56% of its $25,000.00 vehicles maintenance budget on tires. How much did it spend?

    ❏  A.  $14,000.00
    ❏  B.  $15,000.00
    ❏  C.  $13,000.00
    ❏  D.  Not enough information given to form an answer

# Decimals

**Directions:** Select the best answer for the following questions.

77. Add 674.935 + 896.22. What is the total?
   - ❑ A. 7345.57
   - ❑ B. 1571.155
   - ❑ C. 734.557
   - ❑ D. 1570.155

78. Multiply 84.95 × .235. What is the total?
   - ❑ A. 361.48936
   - ❑ B. 1996.325
   - ❑ C. 19.96325
   - ❑ D. 19963.25

79. 145 ÷ 8.62 = X. To the two nearest decimal points, which of the following equals X?
   - ❑ A. 0.17
   - ❑ B. 1.68
   - ❑ C. 16.82
   - ❑ D. 168.21

80. Convert the fraction 15/26 into a decimal. Which answer is correct rounded off to four decimals?
   - ❑ A. 576923076923076923076923076923308
   - ❑ B. 0.5769
   - ❑ C. 1.7333
   - ❑ D. 0.1733

# Ratios and Proportions

**Directions:** Select the best answer for the following questions.

81. If there is 1 officer on patrol for every 3,600 citizens, and there are currently 23 officers on patrol, what is the population of the city?
   - ❑ A. 8,280
   - ❑ B. 828,000
   - ❑ C. 82,800
   - ❑ D. Not enough information given to form an answer

82. If Big City has a population of 85,000 and there is one officer on patrol for every 3,400 citizens, and the department has officers who cover three eight-hour shifts in a given day, what is the total number of officers in the police department?

❑　A.　25

❑　B.　15

❑　C.　35

❑　D.　Not enough information given to form an answer

83. If turning a screw 21 times advances it 3 inches, which of the following ratios correctly states the relationship?

❑　A.　21:3

❑　B.　8:1

❑　C.　7:1

❑　D.　Not enough information given to form an answer

84. If a vehicle can travel ten miles in 10 minutes, and assuming that it maintains the same speed, how many miles can the vehicle travel in 40 minutes?

❑　A.　80 miles

❑　B.　40 miles

❑　C.　20 miles

❑　D.　Not enough information given to form an answer

# Memory and Observation

**Directions:** Set a timer for five minutes. Study the picture for five minutes, and five minutes only. (Remember: The purpose of these tests is to aid you in taking your actual exam; therefore, you need to gauge your ability to commit things to memory and your observation skills. Take notes if you wish, but also remember that you also need to set those notes aside at the end of the five minutes.)

Notes regarding the picture:

▶ Broad Avenue is an east-west, two-way street.

▶ 42nd Street is a north-south, two-way street.

Each window in the Historic District Apartments represents an apartment condominium, with the exception of the top floor; the entire top floor is the penthouse apartment condominium.

**Additional directions:** At the end of five minutes, set the drawing and your notes aside. Re-create your notes on a new, blank sheet of paper, if desired. Then answer the following questions.

85. A fire hydrant is closest to which of the following?
   - ❑   A.  Historic District Apartments
   - ❑   B.  Southeast corner of Broad and 42nd
   - ❑   C.  Charlie's Collectibles
   - ❑   D.  Tony's Deli

86. The United States Postal Service mail collection box is close to which of the following?
   - ❑   A.  1125 42nd Street
   - ❑   B.  1220 Broad Street
   - ❑   C.  1220 Broad Avenue
   - ❑   D.  1125 42nd Avenue

87. According to the drawing, which vehicle is committing a traffic violation?
   - ❑   A.  The four-door sedan
   - ❑   B.  The convertible
   - ❑   C.  The Fed Ex truck
   - ❑   D.  The motorcycle

88. Which of the items below is not on the sign in the window at Charlie's Collectibles?
    - ❑ A. Autographs
    - ❑ B. Comic Books
    - ❑ C. Rare Books
    - ❑ D. Memorabilia

89. What is the name of the north-south street?
    - ❑ A. Broad Avenue
    - ❑ B. Broad Street
    - ❑ C. 42nd Street
    - ❑ D. 42nd Avenue

90. Where is there a dog in the sketch?
    - ❑ A. 42nd Street, on the sidewalk beside the Fed Ex truck
    - ❑ B. 42nd Street, in front of Big City Cinemas
    - ❑ C. 42nd Street, beside Historic District Apartments
    - ❑ D. 42nd Street, in front of Charlie's Collectibles

91. What is the license plate number on the convertible?
    - ❑ A. ECG 637
    - ❑ B. ECG 367
    - ❑ C. EGC 736
    - ❑ D. EGC 637

92. In which direction is the Fed Ex truck headed?
    - ❑ A. North
    - ❑ B. South
    - ❑ C. East
    - ❑ D. West

93. Which of the following best describes the pedestrian in front of Courtney's Cookies?
    - ❑ A. A woman pushing a baby stroller
    - ❑ B. A man walking a dog
    - ❑ C. An elderly woman
    - ❑ D. A man carrying a motorcycle helmet

94. What time is shown on the clock?
    - ❑ A. 4 o'clock
    - ❑ B. 2 o'clock
    - ❑ C. 7 o'clock
    - ❑ D. 10 o'clock

95. What is the address of Taylor's Art Emporium?
   - ❏ A. 1220 Broad Street
   - ❏ B. 1220 Broad Avenue
   - ❏ C. 1230 Broad Avenue
   - ❏ D. 1230 Broad Street

96. Which business is closest to the male pedestrian walking alone?
   - ❏ A. Big City Theater
   - ❏ B. Charlie's Collectibles
   - ❏ C. Taylor's Art Emporium
   - ❏ D. Courtney's Cookies

97. What is the license plate number on the Fed Ex truck?
   - ❏ A. ECG 637
   - ❏ B. ECG 367
   - ❏ C. EGC 736
   - ❏ D. None given

98. What business is at 1135 North 42nd Street?
   - ❏ A. Charlie's Collectibles
   - ❏ B. Big City Cinemas
   - ❏ C. Jemma's Jewelry
   - ❏ D. Tony's Deli

99. How many apartment condominiums are in the Historic District Apartments building?
   - ❏ A. 10
   - ❏ B. 9
   - ❏ C. 8
   - ❏ D. 7

100.Which of the following vehicles is in front of the convertible?
   - ❏ A. Four-door sedan
   - ❏ B. Fed Ex truck
   - ❏ C. Motorcycle
   - ❏ D. Two-door sedan

# 14

CHAPTER FOURTEEN

# Answer Key to Practice Test 2

| | | |
|---|---|---|
| 1. C | 19. B | 37. D |
| 2. A | 20. A | 38. C |
| 3. B | 21. D | 39. B |
| 4. A | 22. C | 40. A |
| 5. C | 23. B | 41. D |
| 6. A | 24. A | 42. A |
| 7. D | 25. C | 43. C |
| 8. B | 26. A | 44. B |
| 9. C | 27. D | 45. B |
| 10. D | 28. B | 46. C |
| 11. A | 29. D | 47. B |
| 12. B | 30. C | 48. D |
| 13. D | 31. C | 49. B |
| 14. C | 32. B | 50. C |
| 15. B | 33. A | 51. D |
| 16. A | 34. B | 52. A |
| 17. C | 35. C | 53. A |
| 18. D | 36. D | 54. B |

| | | |
|---|---|---|
| 55. D | 71. B | 87. A |
| 56. C | 72. D | 88. B |
| 57. B | 73. A | 89. C |
| 58. C | 74. A | 90. A |
| 59. B | 75. D | 91. D |
| 60. C | 76. D | 92. A |
| 61. B | 77. B | 93. C |
| 62. D | 78. C | 94. B |
| 63. A | 79. A | 95. B |
| 64. B | 80. B | 96. B |
| 65. C | 81. C | 97. D |
| 66. A | 82. D | 98. C |
| 67. A | 83. C | 99. B |
| 68. B | 84. B | 100. C |
| 69. A | 85. D | |
| 70. C | 86. C | |

1. **Answer C is correct.** Unlike the reported suspect, the person illustrated in drawing A has a light beard; the person in drawing B has thin lips; the person in drawing D has thick lips and age lines on his forehead that probably wouldn't be present on somebody who's only around 25.

2. **Answer A is correct.** Unlike the reported suspect, the person in drawing B has hair that extends below his ears; the person in drawing C has narrow, crooked nose with flared nostrils; the person in drawing D has thin lips and thinner eyebrows.

3. **Answer B is correct.** The person depicted in drawing A has hair that's darker than what could be described as *light brown hair*; the person depicted in drawing C has thick eyebrows and a wide nose; the person depicted in drawing D has thick lips.

4. **Answer A is correct.** The subject in composite drawing A has darker skin tones and a wide nose, and is therefore different from the suspect. The composite shown in drawing B is the same person with a shaved head. Drawing C is the same person with a bushier beard and mustache, and drawing D shows the same person with a shaved head, no beard, and a fuller mustache.

5. **Answer C is correct.** The subject in wanted poster C is 28, and therefore is the correct answer. The subject in wanted poster A is 36, the subject in wanted poster B is 24, and the subject in wanted poster D is 42.

6. **Answer A is correct.** The subject in wanted poster A has a gall bladder surgery scar. The subject in wanted poster B has a scar, but it's from a knife wound. The subjects in wanted posters C and D do not have scars.

7. **Answer D is correct.** The subject in wanted poster D has a bulldog tattoo under a USMC tattoo on his upper part of his right arm. The person in wanted poster A does not have any tattoos. The subject in wanted poster B has tattoos of thin chains above both biceps. The subject in wanted poster C has prison tattoos of 1" stars on each upper forearm.

8. **Answer B is correct.** The subject in wanted poster B has a knife-wound scar on his left cheek. The subject in wanted poster A has a scar, but it's from gall bladder surgery. The subjects in wanted posters C and D do not have any scars.

9. **Answer C is correct.**

10. **Answer D is correct.**

11. **Answer A is correct.**

12. **Answer B is correct.**

13. **Answer D is correct.** Abasi Turner is the only one whose hair is described as being a short afro.

14. **Answer C is correct.** Muhammad Robb is the only one of the four subjects who has facial hair—a mustache and a goatee.

15. **Answer B is correct.** The subject in B weighs 190 pounds; A weighs 225, C weighs 185, and D weighs 115.

16. **Answer A is correct.** The subject in A is described as 6'2"; B is 5'10", C is also 5'10", and D is 5'6".

17. **Answer C is correct.** "Riddled by bullets" is essentially "full of bullet holes"; therefore, the answer is the subject in C.

18. **Answer D is correct.**

19. **Answer B is correct.**

20. **Answer A is correct.**

21. **Answer D is correct.**

22. **Answer C is correct.**

23. **Answer B is correct.**

24. **Answer A is correct.**

25. **Answer C is correct.**

26. **Answer A is correct.**

27. **Answer D is correct.**

28. **Answer B is correct.**

29. **Answer D is correct.** The subject in A has a tattoo, but it's of a but terfly. The subjects in B and C do not have tattoos.

30. **Answer C is correct.**

31. **Answer C is correct.** The subject in A has a 3" scar on her right knee, but it's not indicated how she got the scar. The subjects in B and D do not have any scars.

32. **Answer B is correct.** The subject in A has blue eyes, and the subjects in C and D have brown eyes.

33. **Answer A is correct.**

34. **Answer B is correct.**

35. **Answer C is correct.**

36. **Answer D is correct.**

37. **Answer D is correct.**

38. **Answer C is correct.**

39. **Answer B is correct.** Subject A weighs 135 pounds, B weighs 195, C weighs 120, and D weighs 130; therefore, B is the heaviest.

40. **Answer A is correct.** Subject A is 5'9", B is 5'6", C is 5'5", and D is also 5'6"; therefore, A is the tallest.

41. **Answer D is correct.** Witnesses A, B, and D describe the subject as a black male. Witnesses A, C, and D describe the subject as age 25. Witnesses A, C, and D describe him as wearing blue jeans. All witnesses say he was wearing a red T-shirt, but only A, B, and D describe him as being 5'8". The correct answer is D because it best matches the majority descriptions.

42. **Answer A is correct.** Witnesses A, B, and C describe the robbery suspect as leaving the scene in a dark-blue vehicle; witnesses A and C describe it as a Chevy. Witnesses A, B, and D describe it as a four-door sedan. Witnesses A, C, and D report that the right rear taillight

was out. All four say the vehicle has Ohio plates. The correct answer is A because it best matches the majority description.

43. **Answer C is correct.** Witnesses A, B, and C give the first letter of the license plate as K. Witnesses A and C say the second letter is L, and witnesses B and D say it's K. All witnesses give the third letter as M. Only witness A says the numbers on the plate are 883, whereas B, C, and D say that it's 783. Therefore, C is the logical choice because it matches the majority description.

44. **Answer B is correct.** Witnesses A, B, C, and D all describe the suspect as a white male who weighs 150 pounds. Witnesses A, B, and D say he's 5'10". Witnesses A, B, and D say he has long brown hair. Witnesses A, B, and C say he was armed with a gun. The description in B is the logical choice because it matches the majority description.

45. **Answer B is correct.** The Utopia Community Bank is within the city limits, and therefore under the jurisdiction of the Utopia Police Department (B).

46. **Answer C is correct.**

47. **Answer B is correct.** Rayburn Law Offices is at the southwest corner of location 10 on the map, which is the corner named in B. A is the northwest corner, C is the northeast corner, and D is the southeast corner.

48. **Answer D is correct.** A, B, and C are directly north of the campus.

49. **Answer B is correct.** A planetarium is a model of the solar system. Shangrala State College is noted for its Challenger Memorial Celestial Observatory. So, based on the information given, it would be the most logical place for a planetarium.

50. **Answer C is correct.** The hospital emergency room entrance is located in the quadrant of the city handled by Unit 3; it is also in the southern half of the city, which is handled by Unit B.

51. **Answer D is correct.**

52. **Answer A is correct.** The accident occurred on the section of Shangrala Road that is also known as State Route 133, which is under the jurisdiction of the Indiana State Police.

53. **Answer A is correct.** The apartment complex itself is under the jurisdiction of the Utopia Police Department.

54. **Answer B is correct.** The Utopia Sports Complex is in the northeast quadrant, which is handled by Unit 2. Unit C is a roving unit that responds where needed when another unit for an area is tied up elsewhere.

55. **Answer D is correct.** Without knowing the nature or seriousness of the complaint or the location of the other units, there isn't enough information available to know which other unit should provide backup.

56. **Answer C is correct.**

57. **Answer B is correct.** Freyburg Road is spelled incorrectly in A and D. The directions of the vehicles are reversed in C.

58. **Answer C is correct.** The pedestrian in A is at the wrong location. The direction of the one-way sign is pointed in the wrong direction in B. The pedestrian isn't indicated in D.

59. **Answer B is correct.** A is incorrect because vehicle 1 wasn't at fault; it had already established its right of way when vehicle 2 switched lanes. D and C are incorrect because despite being illegally parked, the vehicle did not cause the accident and therefore would not be cited for that offense.

60. **Answer C is correct.** To solve 8 1/4 + 17 1/2 + 18 1/4, you must first find the *least common denominator* (LCD) for the fractions. In this case, that would be 8 2/8 + 17 4/8 + 18 2/8, which equals 43 8/8 or 43 + 1, or 44.

61. **Answer B is correct.** 16 3/8 – 5 1/8 is simple subtraction: 3/8 – 1/8 = 2/8 and 16 – 5 = 11, so the solution for X is 11 2/8; reducing 2/8 to its LCD, the final answer is 11 1/4.

62. **Answer D is correct.** 24 is the LCD because it is the smallest number that is divisible by 8 and 6.

63. **Answer A is correct.** 3/8 + 1/6 = 9/24 + 4/24 = 13/24.

64. **Answer B is correct.** 1/6 + 1/4 = 2/12 + 3/12 = 5/12.

65. **Answer C is correct.** 6 3/4 – 1 1/4 = 5 2/4. Reducing 2/4 to a proper fraction that cannot be reduced further makes the correct answer 5 1/2.

66. **Answer A is correct.** To multiply 7/8 × 5/8, the product of the numerators is divided by the products of the denominators, or

```
Numerator: 7 × 5 = 35
Denominator: 8 × 8 = 64
```

67. **Answer A is correct.**

```
3/4 × 1 1/9 =
3 × 10 = 30 = 10/12 = 5/6
4 × 9 = 36
```

B and C are correct answers, but they are incorrect here because they have not been reduced to a proper fraction that cannot be reduced further.

68. **Answer B is correct.**

    5 × 6 2/3 =
    5 × 20 = 100 = 33 1/3
    1 × 3 = 3

69. **Answer A is correct.** To divide fractions or fractions and mixed numbers, you need to convert the divisor to its reciprocal (reverse numerator and denominator) and then multiply, or

    7 2/3 ÷ 1/3 =
    23 × 3 = 69 = 23
    3 × 1 = 3

70. **Answer C is correct.** A percentage shows what portion of 100 a number represents. There are 60 (3 × 20) flares in use; therefore, there are 20 (80 – 60) remaining in inventory. 20/80 = .25 or 25%.

71. **Answer B is correct.** The department investigated 23 homicides + 146 robberies + 346 burglaries + 13 questionable deaths. So, based on the numbers given, the department conducted 528 investigations. However, of the questionable deaths, 10 were ruled to be suicides, two were ruled to be natural causes, and only one was ruled a homicide. The question specifically asks for the clearance rate for the crimes, stating that the detectives were able to solve 387 of them. The additional homicide brings that total to 24 for the year, so 24 homicides + 146 robberies + 346 burglaries = 516 crimes. 387/516 = .75 or 75%. The question also asks that the figured be rounded to the nearest three decimals, but that isn't necessary because the result does not have a decimal component.

72. **Answer D is correct.** To arrive at the answer for this question, you divide the total number of male officers (149) by the total number of officers (236), or 149/236 = 0.63135593220338983050847457627119, which is 63.136% when rounded off to the nearest three decimal places.

73. **Answer A is correct.** To arrive at the answer for this question, you divide the total number of African-American female officers (34) by the total number of African-American officers (36 + 34, or 70), or 34/70 = 0.48571428571428571428571428571429, which when rounded off to the two nearest decimal places is 48.57%.

74. **Answer A is correct.** To arrive at the answer for this question, you divide the total number of nonwhite females (16 Hispanic female officers + 34 African-American female officers + 3 females of other ethic origins, or 53) by the total number of officers in the department (236) or 53/236 = 0.224576, which is 22.4576%. When rounded to the nearest percent, the result is 23%.

75. **Answer D is correct.** To calculate 23.5% of $5,000.00, you multiply .235 by $5,000.00, or .235 × 5000.00 = $1,175.00.

76. **Answer D is correct.** The answer to this question is unknown because while the expected budget is given, the actual cost of tires is not.

77. **Answer B is correct.** When adding decimals, remember to line up the decimal points. Therefore, to arrive at the correct answer for this problem:

$$\begin{array}{r} 674.935 \\ +\ \underline{896.22\ } \\ 1571.155 \end{array}$$

78. **Answer C is correct.** To arrive at the correct answer, remember to account for all decimal places.

79. **Answer A is correct.** To arrive at this answer, you add two decimal places to the dividend to account for the two removed from the divisor; this provides a quotient with the proper number of decimal places. 145 ÷ 8.62 = 0.168. Rounding 0.168 to the nearest two decimal points, you arrive at the answer of 0.17.

80. **Answer B is correct.**

81. **Answer C is correct.** To arrive at the answer, you multiply 23 (officers on patrol) by 3600 (number of citizens each officer serves to protect).

82. **Answer D is correct.** This problem doesn't give enough information to reach a conclusion because it doesn't take into account the number of officers on days off, on sick leave, or on vacation.

83. **Answer C is correct.** Answer A (21:3) states the ratio as it's expressed in the problem; however, it is incorrect because like a fraction, it should be reduced as low as possible. Therefore, treating that ratio like a fraction, 21/3 can be reduced to 7/1, or 7:1, answer C.

84. **Answer B is correct.** To solve this problem, first establish the ratios, and then state the ratios as a proportion to calculate the unknown:

RATIO 1      $\dfrac{10 \text{ miles}}{10 \text{ minutes}}$     RATIO 2     $\dfrac{X \text{ miles}}{40 \text{ minutes}}$

Stated as a proportion:

$$\frac{10 \text{ miles}}{10 \text{ minutes}} = \frac{X \text{ miles}}{40 \text{ minutes}}$$

or      $\dfrac{10X}{10} =$      $\dfrac{X \times 40}{10}$

or      $X = \dfrac{10 \times 40}{10}$    or    $X = \dfrac{400}{10}$

or      $X = 40$

85. **Answer D is correct.**

86. **Answer C is correct.** The street names are Broad Avenue and 42nd Street; therefore, B and D are incorrect. The United States Postal Service mail collection box is in front of Taylor's Art Emporium at 1220 Broad Avenue.

87. **Answer A is correct.** The four-door sedan is pulling into the intersection in violation of a red light.

88. **Answer B is correct.** *Comic books* are not shown on the sign, so A, B, and D—which are mentioned on the sign—are incorrect.

89. **Answer C is correct.** The street names are Broad Avenue and 42nd Street; therefore, B and D are incorrect. Broad Avenue is an east-west street, so A is incorrect.

90. **Answer A is correct.** The dog is on the side of the street where no buildings are shown, so the nearest landmark is the Fed Ex truck.

91. **Answer D is correct.**

92. **Answer A is correct.**

93. **Answer C is correct.**

94. **Answer B is correct.**

95. **Answer B is correct.** The street names are Broad Avenue and 42nd Street; therefore, A and D are incorrect. Answer C is the address for Courtney's Cookies.

96. **Answer B is correct.** Answer A is incorrect because the business name is Big City Cinemas, not Big City Theater. Answers C and D are incorrect because they are on Broad Avenue and the male pedestrian walking alone is on 42nd Street, therefore B (Charlie's Collectibles) is correct.

97. **Answer D is correct.** The graphic doesn't show a license plate for the Fed Ex truck.

98. **Answer C is correct.**

99. **Answer B is correct.** Each window in the building represents a condominium apartment, except for the top floor; the penthouse condominium apartment has two windows. There are 10 windows, or 8 apartment condominiums and 1 penthouse apartment condominium, for a total of 9. Therefore, answers A, C, and D are incorrect.

100. **Answer C is correct.**

# 15

# Practice Test 3

## Military Time

Most law enforcement agencies use military time, which follows a twenty-four hour time clock. This is done because it is a better way to distinguish between a.m. and p.m. In other words, stating time as what's shown on a standard clock face means that each time will be repeated twice a day. This requires that it be known whether an event occurred at, say, 3:00 in the morning (a.m. or "overnight") or 3:00 in the afternoon (p.m., or as some might state it, "during the day"). Therefore, there's a distinct advantage to using military time for recording the exact time of an occurrence or crime: It leaves no room for ambiguity or doubt. When military time is used, the numbers used to state a given time occur only once a day.

Military time begins at midnight (0000 hours, as shown on the following table). Thereafter, except for the omission of the colon used when stating standard time and the addition of a zero before the time when stating military time, military time follows a regular clock-style notation of time for the first 12 hours.

**Standard Time Notation**          **Military Time Notation**
2:00 a.m.                           0200 hours

The more noticeable difference occurs after noon, when the time is represented by adding 12 hours to what's shown on the clock face.

**Standard Time Notation**          **Military Time Notation**
2:00 p.m.                           1400 hours

Learning how to pronounce military times correctly takes some getting used to as well. The following table provides some examples.

| Time | Military Time | Pronunciation of Military Time |
|---|---|---|
| 12:00 midnight | 0000 | Zero hundred hours |
| 1:00 a.m. | 0100 | Zero one hundred hours |
| 1:32 a.m. | 0132 | Zero one hundred thirty-two hours |
| 12:00 noon | 1200 | Twelve hundred hours |
| 1:00 p.m. | 1300 | Thirteen hundred hours |
| 1:32 p.m. | 1332 | Thirteen, thirty-two hours |
| 2:00 p.m. | 1400 | Fourteen hundred hours |
| 3:00 p.m. | 1500 | Fifteen hundred hours |
| 4:00 p.m. | 1600 | Sixteen hundred hours |
| 5:00 p.m. | 1700 | Seventeen hundred hours |
| 6:00 p.m. | 1800 | Eighteen hundred hours |
| 7:00 p.m. | 1900 | Nineteen hundred hours |
| 8:00 p.m. | 2000 | Twenty hundred hours |
| 8:32 p.m. | 2032 | Twenty, thirty-two or twenty, thirty-two hours |
| 9:00 p.m. | 2100 | Twenty-one hundred hours |
| 10:00 p.m. | 2200 | Twenty-two hundred hours |
| 11:00 p.m. | 2300 | Twenty-three hundred hours |

**Directions**: Using the information concerning military time you just covered, answer the following questions:

1. You need to write 12:00 noon in military time. How would you do so?
   - ❏  A.  12:00 hours
   - ❏  B.  12:00 p.m.
   - ❏  C.  1200 p.m.
   - ❏  D.  1200 hours

2. Based on the description of military time, what is the most significant reason for stating time as military time?
   - ❏  A.  It does away with the colon.
   - ❏  B.  A time occurs only once a day.
   - ❏  C.  It saves the bother of writing or knowing whether a time is a.m. or p.m.
   - ❏  D.  It makes it easier to express the accurate time verbally.

3. How is 3:45 stated verbally in military time?
   - ❏ A. Zero three hundred, forty-five hours
   - ❏ B. Zero three hundred and forty-five hours
   - ❏ C. Zero three hundred hours and forty-five minutes
   - ❏ D. Zero three hundred hours, forty-five minutes

4. Based on the information given, how is 6:16 p.m. written as military time?
   - ❏ A. 1416 hours
   - ❏ B. 1616 hours
   - ❏ C. 1816 hours
   - ❏ D. 2016 hours

5. How is twenty-three minutes after noon stated in civilian time and military time?
   - ❏ A. 12:23 a.m. and 1223 hours
   - ❏ B. 12:23 p.m. and 1223 hours
   - ❏ C. 12:23 a.m. and 0023 hours
   - ❏ D. 12:23 p.m. and 0023 hours

# 25-Minute Recall Test

**Directions**: For this test, spend 15 minutes reading the narrative that follows. The objective is to commit to memory as many of the facts given in the narrative as you can. Do not take notes. For this test, you are to rely entirely on your recall of facts gathered only from reading.

**Memory Narrative**

As one of 20 swing shift police officers assigned to work the perimeter of Veteran's Memorial Civic Center, you report for roll call at 6:30 a.m. on October 19.

At roll call training prior to leaving the station house, Sergeant Wright advises that this special swing shift detail is assigned to cover a job fair being held at the civic center from 9:00 a.m. until 3:00 p.m. Possible trouble is expected from two groups opposed to military recruiters being at the event.

The two groups opposing the military recruiters' presence at the job fair have been known to cause disturbances in the past. One group, which goes by the name of Developmental Underground, holds radical antiwar beliefs; this group has used violence in the past to further its cause. The second group is an association known as the Progressive Pathfinders; this group is against private ownership rights, believing that a collective government-controlled country can better ensure animal rights and address environmental concerns. According to their literature and website, the Progressive Pathfinders is antimilitary because they profess it is under the control of big business.

A third group, known as the Freedom Republic Warriors, has a permit for 5 to 10 people to be present at the benches at Veteran's Memorial Flag Park during the hours of the job fair. The permit specifies their purpose there is for a "support the troops" gathering. This group is known to display flags, unobtrusive signs, and banners bearing their "support the troops" messages.

The only known vehicle associated with the Developmental Underground is a gray Chevy four-door sedan, bearing license plate number DVU 837. The Progressive Pathfinders is known to use two vehicles: One is an older red Oldsmobile four-door sedan with vanity plate PROPATH; the other is a white Dodge panel truck, bearing the license plate number AXM 648.

Note that in the past the Progressive Pathfinders have had members show up wearing white jumpsuits and carrying painting paraphernalia, so that it appears they are workers on their way to a job. This was how the members who threw paint on ladies wearing fur disguised themselves before the attack last winter that occurred in front of the Big City Philharmonic. You are advised that in that case they were better able to pull off this scenario because it was known that remodeling was taking place in the law offices adjacent to the philharmonic; they appeared to be workers on their way to that site. In that instance, they left the area after being picked up in the above-described panel truck, which was later stopped several blocks away. You are also told that Incident Report #2004-012319245 has further details about this offense and subsequent arrests.

The Veteran's Memorial Civic Center covers the entire block and is bordered by Market Street to the north, by Walnut Street to the east, by Main Street to the south, and by Maple Street to the west—all of which are two-way streets. Three-fourths of the block is covered by the Veteran's Memorial Civic Center building itself; the southeast quadrant of the block houses Veteran's Memorial Flag Park—an area set aside for lawn, garden, flagpole, and benches that face the street and are just inside the sidewalk area.

The Big City Parking Garage takes up the entire block directly west of the civic center, and is bordered by Elm Street to the west.

The Hamilton County Courthouse is across the street from the civic center, which places it at the southwest corner of Main and Walnut. The Big City Administration Building is at the northeast corner, and the Big City Safety

Building, which headquarters the Big City Police and Fire Departments, is at the southeast corner.

You are advised that at 8:00 a.m., you and Officer Stanley are to report to the civic center, where you are assigned to foot patrol along the south side of the center. Officers Gentry and Parker are assigned to the east side, Officers Graham and Williams to the north side, and Officers Phillips and Bentley to the west side. The remaining 12 officers will be in six patrol units, and are assigned to patrol the immediate vicinity.

**Additional directions.** Remember, study the narrative for 15 minutes, and 15 minutes only. At the end of the 15 minutes, do not refer to the story again while you take 10 minutes to answer the following questions.

6. In military time, at what time are you to report to the location of your foot patrol?
   - ❑ A. 2000 hours
   - ❑ B. 0700 hours
   - ❑ C. 0800 hours
   - ❑ D. 1900 hours

7. What is the surname of the officer with whom you're assigned to work?
   - ❑ A. Gentry
   - ❑ B. Parker
   - ❑ C. Williams
   - ❑ D. Stanley

8. Which group is known to use a white panel truck?
   - ❑ A. Progressive Pathfinders
   - ❑ B. Freedom Republic Warriors
   - ❑ C. Progressive Underground
   - ❑ D. Developmental Underground

9. Which group has a permit that allows them to congregate in the Veteran's Memorial Flag Park?
   - ❑ A. Progressive Pathfinders
   - ❑ B. Freedom Republic Warriors
   - ❑ C. Freedom Underground
   - ❑ D. Developmental Underground

10. What is the location of the Hamilton County Courthouse?
   - ❑ A. Southeast corner of Main and Walnut
   - ❑ B. Southwest corner of Main and Elm
   - ❑ C. Southeast corner of Main and Maple
   - ❑ D. Southwest corner of Main and Walnut

11. Who is the officer that conducts roll call?

   ❏  A. Sergeant Stanley
   ❏  B. Sergeant Graham
   ❏  C. Sergeant Wright
   ❏  D. Sergeant Bentley

12. The vehicle known to be associated with the Developmental Underground is a

   ❏  A. Gray Chevy four-door sedan
   ❏  B. Gray Chevy two-door sedan
   ❏  C. White Dodge panel truck
   ❏  D. Red Oldsmobile four-door sedan

13. What is the report referenced in the roll call briefing?

   ❏  A. Accident Report #2004-012319648
   ❏  B. Incident Report #2004-012319245
   ❏  C. Incident Report #2004-012319648
   ❏  D. Accident Report #2004-012319245

14. The permit obtained by the Freedom Republic Warriors allows how many people to gather at the location named in the permit?

   ❏  A. 1–10
   ❏  B. 5–10
   ❏  C. 5–15
   ❏  D. 1–20

15. What building is at the northeast corner of Main and Walnut?

   ❏  A. Big City Safety Building
   ❏  B. Big City Parking Garage
   ❏  C. Big City Administration Building
   ❏  D. Big City Fire Department

# Timed Test: 25-Minute Time Limit

**Directions**: For this test, first spend 15 minutes reading the following narrative. The objective is to commit to memory as many of the facts given in the narrative as you can. Do not take notes. For this test, you are to rely entirely on your recall of facts gathered only from reading.

You are one of two officers assigned to Unit 102, the patrol vehicles assigned to patrol district two in Small Town, Ohio. Your tour of duty is on the second shift on July 25, and begins at 4:00 p.m. and ends at 12:00 midnight. The other officer in Unit 102 is to be Officer Sullivan.

Included in your patrol district is Buckeye Plaza, a strip mall that is on the east edge of the city limits, and which is adjacent to the northbound and southbound entrances to I-75. Less than a mile south of the southbound I-75 entrance are the exits to State Route 303, an eastbound and westbound four-lane highway.

Small Town, Ohio usually has a low crime rate; however, there has recently been a series of four armed robberies, all occurring at Buckeye Plaza.

All the armed robberies, except one, have occurred on a Friday night, shortly before or after the businesses close at 9:00 p.m. Speculation is that the perpetrator chooses this time so that his getaway vehicle will better blend in with the other vehicles exiting the strip mall. Also, it is at this time that traffic tends to be busiest on the highways near the mall.

The first armed robbery occurred at 9:08 p.m. on June 13 at the Sweet Things Bakery Shoppe. At that time, only one employee was on duty at closing. The store now employs two people on Friday evenings. It does not have an alarm system.

The second robbery occurred shortly before 9:00 p.m. on June 27 at Caroline's Jewelry Store. Since that date, the store has updated its security system, which includes a silent alarm. The store has also installed both a listening device and video camera system that are monitored and maintained by Acme Security Associates.

The third robbery occurred on July 4 at Joe's Quick Stop Gas Station, and is the only exception to the usual 9:00 p.m. robbery time. In this instance, the robbery occurred at 10:05 p.m.—which was the time of a fireworks display at Founder's Park. One perpetrator robbed the gas station cashier and another, the driver of an older model blue Ford pickup with a temporary tag, robbed one of the cashiers in the drive-through beer and wine carryout attached to the service station. This business does not have an alarm system; however, it has installed video cameras.

The fourth robbery took place on July 18 shortly before 9:00 p.m. at the Speedy Loan and Check Cashing Center. This business has an audible alarm.

After the first robbery, the others occurred either when alarms were triggered at other businesses across town or when other incidents requiring backup were taking place and took officers out of their regular patrol area. This has led to speculation that the perpetrators now employ additional parties whose job it is to create a diversion. For that reason, you are advised that should an occasion arise that requires you to leave your patrol area during your shift, you are not to do so until another unit can cover for you.

The Officer in Charge (OIC) for your shift—Lt. Griffin—has advised that you are to make sure that each business in the strip mall is aware of your additional patrol in the vicinity. Early in your shift, you and Officer Sullivan are to patrol the strip mall on foot and advise each business proprietor or employee of your presence.

The Midway County Sheriff's Department and the Ohio State Highway Patrol have been advised of the prior robberies, and they have additional units scheduled for patrol on the adjoining highways and area roads on this date.

**Additional Directions**: Take 10 minutes to answer the following 10 questions without referring to the narrative.

16. How many robberies have occurred at, on, or near 2200 hours?
   - ❏  A.  1
   - ❏  B.  2
   - ❏  C.  3
   - ❏  D.  4

17. Of the four businesses that have been the scene of an armed robbery, which one still does not have an alarm system?
   - ❏  A.  Caroline's Jewelry Store
   - ❏  B.  Sweet Things Bakery Shoppe
   - ❏  C.  Joe's Quick Stop Gas Station
   - ❏  D.  Speedy Loan and Check Cashing Center

18. What is the surname of the officer assigned to work with you?
   - ❏  A.  Sylvan
   - ❏  B.  Griffin
   - ❏  C.  Griffon
   - ❏  D.  Sullivan

19. Which business has an alarm monitored and maintained by Acme Security Associates?
   - ❏  A.  Caroline's Jewelry Store
   - ❏  B.  Sweet Things Bakery Shoppe
   - ❏  C.  Joe's Quick Stop Gas Station
   - ❏  D.  Speedy Loan and Check Cashing Center

20. What was the date of the third robbery?
   - ❏  A.  June 13
   - ❏  B.  June 20
   - ❏  C.  June 27
   - ❏  D.  July 4

21. Which store now has two employees working on Friday evenings?
    - ❏ A. Caroline's Jewelry Store
    - ❏ B. Sweet Things Bakery Shoppe
    - ❏ C. Joe's Quick Stop Gas Station
    - ❏ D. Speedy Loan and Check Cashing Center

22. In addition to an alarm system, which business also has a listening device?
    - ❏ A. Caroline's Jewelry Store
    - ❏ B. Sweet Things Bakery Shoppe
    - ❏ C. Joe's Quick Stop Gas Station
    - ❏ D. Speedy Loan and Check Cashing Center

23. Who is your OIC for this shift?
    - ❏ A. Lt. Sullivin
    - ❏ B. Lt. Sullivan
    - ❏ C. Lt. Griffin
    - ❏ D. Lt. Griffon

24. Which business has an audible alarm?
    - ❏ A. Caroline's Jewelry Store
    - ❏ B. Sweet Things Bakery Shoppe
    - ❏ C. Joe's Quick Stop Gas Station
    - ❏ D. Speedy Loan and Check Cashing Center

25. What is the date of your shift?
    - ❏ A. July 4
    - ❏ B. July 11
    - ❏ C. July 18
    - ❏ D. July 25

# Timed Test: 25-Minute Time Limit

**Directions**: For this test, spend 10 minutes reading the following narrative. The objective is to commit to memory as many of the facts given in the narrative as you can. Do not take notes. For this test, you are to rely entirely on your recall of facts gathered only from reading.

According to George Schiro, a forensic scientist for the Louisiana State Police Crime Laboratory, "[t]he most important aspect of evidence collection and preservation is protecting the crime scene."

Protecting the crime scene involves ensuring that the pertinent evidence remains uncontaminated until investigators can collect and record it. That's why the protection of a crime scene begins when the first police officer arrives at the scene and doesn't end until the scene is released from police custody. Part of this protection includes the first officer's notes at the scene; these notes might be needed later to provide valuable information about what or who was at the scene, to establish times, and to supply other pertinent information.

The ideal scenario would be to have the first officer who arrives at the scene of a crime approach the scene slowly and methodically; however, in many instances, this just isn't possible or practical. This ideal scenario can be disrupted when that first officer to arrive is also involved in such common police occurrences as

▸ Arresting a suspect

▸ Performing life-saving measures on an injured victim

Regardless, the first officer at the scene should either make mental note of, or if practical, take written notes about the condition of the scene. These notes should include information about how the scene was upon the officer's arrival and after the scene was stabilized.

Those officer notes need to include the significant times involved in responding to the crime scene:

▸ Information to identify the officer (for example, badge number)

▸ Time dispatched to the scene

▸ Time left to respond to the scene

▸ Time of arrival at the scene

▸ Time of arrival of other officers and support personnel (for example, rescue squad) to respond to the scene

▸ Time left the scene

The officer crime scene notes should also indicate

▸ Any occurrence in which the officer had to alter something at the crime scene

▸ Any occurrence in which anyone else, such as EMS or fire personnel, may have altered the scene

▸ Any odors present

▸ The condition of the doors, windows, and natural or other lighting

▶ Any observed characteristics about the suspects, victims, or witnesses, which can include notes about visible injuries, intoxication (or the odor of alcohol about a person), mental condition, physical condition, and state (such as cleanliness or disarray) of clothing

▶ The names and identifying information of anyone else other than the reporting officer who recorded descriptions or took statements

▶ The names of suspects, victims, and witnesses

▶ The names of anyone else who might have entered or been at the scene

Upon first arriving at a crime scene, it can sometimes be difficult to determine exactly what will end up being the most important information. That's why the first officer at the scene must be diligent about remembering and noting anything he or she observes on arrival. Any signs of activity or what might at first appear to be a trivial observation about a victim or the scene itself could later provide a valuable lead for solving the crime.

**Additional Directions:** Take 15 minutes to answer the following 10 questions without referring to the narrative.

26. Choose the correct statement.
    - ❑ A. The first officer to arrive at the scene of a crime is the only one who takes notes.
    - ❑ B. The first officer to arrive at the scene needs to record the time of his arrival.
    - ❑ C. The first officer to arrive at the scene of a crime should prevent anyone else from entering the crime scene.
    - ❑ D. The first officer to arrive at the scene of a crime should be a supervisor.

27. According to the narrative, which of the following is the first step in preserving a crime scene?
    - ❑ A. The notes and observations of the first officer to arrive at the scene
    - ❑ B. Surrounding the area with crime scene tape
    - ❑ C. To place anyone present under arrest
    - ❑ D. To chase anyone present away from the scene

28. According to the narrative, the notes taken by the first officer to arrive at the scene should include specific names. Choose the answer that was not indicated in the narrative.
    - ❑ A. The names and identifying information on anyone else other than the reporting officer who recorded descriptions or took statements
    - ❑ B. The names of suspects, victims, and witnesses
    - ❑ C. The names of anyone else who might have entered or been at the scene
    - ❑ D. The name of the dispatcher who advised the officer to respond to the scene

29. According to George Schiro, a forensic scientist for the Louisiana State Police Crime Laboratory, which of the following is the most important aspect of evidence collection and preservation?
    - ❑ A. Ensuring that the news media photographs the scene
    - ❑ B. Keeping witnesses together in one place
    - ❑ C. Protecting the crime scene
    - ❑ D. Using regulation labels on all evidence collection bags

30. According to the narrative, a crime scene can sometimes be unavoidably disrupted when the first officer to arrive is also involved in such common police occurrences as when that first officer must
    - ❑ A. Chase looters away from the scene
    - ❑ B. Perform life-saving measures on an injured victim
    - ❑ C. Talk to the press
    - ❑ D. Pose for newspaper photographs

31. According to the narrative, the first officer to arrive at a crime scene is to make immediate mental and then, as soon as possible, written notes about *any observed characteristics* about specific individuals at the scene. Select the incorrect answer from the choices that follow.
    - ❑ A. Victims
    - ❑ B. Emergency personnel
    - ❑ C. Witnesses
    - ❑ D. Suspects

32. According to the narrative, the first officer to arrive at a crime scene should record *significant times involved in responding to the crime scene*. Which of the following answers is not one of those times?
    - ❑ A. Time central dispatch received the call
    - ❑ B. Time dispatched to the scene
    - ❑ C. Time of arrival at the scene
    - ❑ D. Time left the scene

33. According to information provided in the narrative, choose the correct instruction from those that follow.
    - ❑ A. Upon first arriving at a crime scene, the officer should first determine exactly what will end up being the most important information.
    - ❑ B. Upon first arriving at a crime scene, the first officer to arrive at the scene should include only information that his supervisor tells him to put in his notes.
    - ❑ C. Upon first arriving at a crime scene, it can sometimes be difficult to determine exactly what will end up being the most important information.
    - ❑ D. Upon first arriving at a crime scene, an experienced officer always find it easy to determine exactly what will end up being the most important information at the scene.

34. According to information in the narrative, which of the statements that follow is true?

   ❑ A. Beginning officers are too often guilty of including unessential information in their notes.

   ❑ B. After a supervisor has arrived at the scene of a crime, all notes need to be turned over to him or her.

   ❑ C. An officer's notes should include only leads determined by his or her supervisor to be valuable for solving the crime.

   ❑ D. A trivial observation about a victim or the scene itself could later provide a valuable lead for solving the crime.

35. According to the narrative, which of the following statements is true?

   ❑ A. The first officer at the scene must be diligent about remembering and noting anything he or she observes on arrival.

   ❑ B. When the supervisor arrives at the scene, the first officer at the scene must provide the supervisor with a written report of what he or she observed on arrival at the scene.

   ❑ C. The first officer at the scene is responsible only for taking the names of those present.

   ❑ D. The first officer at the scene must be negligent about remembering and noting anything he or she observes on arrival.

# Steps to Preserve a Crime Scene Timed Test: 30-Minute Time Limit

**Directions**: For this test, first spend 15 minutes reading the narrative that follows. The objective is to commit to memory as many of the facts given in the narrative as you can. Do not take notes. For this test, you are to rely entirely on your recall of facts gathered only from reading.

The officer who is placed in charge of preserving a crime scene will depend on the number of officers or other department personnel involved in the investigation and the nature of the crime. Regardless of who is in charge, there are certain measures that need to be taken into consideration in order to make the best effort possible to protect the evidence.

One important thing to keep in mind is that regardless of who is placed in charge of the investigation itself, any officer present may be asked to contact additional investigators and other personnel needed at the scene. Under no circumstances whatsoever should the officer making such contacts use the telephone at the scene.

After the crime scene itself has been stabilized, special attention should also be paid to any other areas that might yield valuable evidence. These areas can include stairways, driveways, sidewalks or other pathways, and the yard and gardens. To prevent potential contamination of any evidence these areas might yield, the areas should be roped off to prevent unauthorized people from entering them.

After the crime scene is secured, do not discuss the events or the crime with witnesses or bystanders or let the witnesses discuss these events. In fact, somebody should be put in charge of separating witnesses and suspect(s). While this separation is in progress, the officer doing so should listen attentively but discreetly, and then record in his notes anything that was overheard.

While assessing the situation at the crime scene, a concerted effort should be made to disturb as little as possible. In fact, measures should be taken to protect evidence—especially evidence located on the floor, which is particularly vulnerable. Safety measures need to be put in place to preserve any evidence that might be in danger of being destroyed; however, any actions taken to do so should be reported to the investigators.

Many times the arrival of additional personnel causes problems in protecting the scene. Therefore, it's important that only those people responsible for the immediate investigation of the crime, securing the crime scene, and processing the crime scene be allowed to enter the scene. Nonessential personnel can include other police officers, district attorney investigators, federal agents, politicians, and the news media. Unless they can add something (other than contamination) to the crime scene investigation, they should not be permitted access to the scene.

The best way to discourage unnecessary people from entering the crime scene is to establish a single entrance and exit point. This way, an officer can be placed at that point; this officer should have a notebook or crime scene log on which to record the names, times of arrival, and times of departure of everyone who enters the crime scene, including the names and times of the investigators themselves. The officer posted at the entrance should be prepared to inform anyone allowed entrance that he is noting these details because by entering the crime scene they might pose a problem by adding potential contamination. She or he should explain that the reason for taking names is in case the crime scene investigators need to obtain elimination fingerprints, or collect evidence from their shoes or person, such as fibers, blood, saliva, pulled head hair, and/or pulled pubic hair from all who enter the crime scene. In fact, this declaration is sometimes enough to discourage nonessential personnel from entering the crime scene. When someone normally considered as nonessential does need to enter the scene, the officer needs to make sure that person is escorted by someone working the scene to make sure that they will not inadvertently destroy any valuable evidence or leave any worthless evidence.

Never allow any drinking, eating, or smoking at a crime scene. Not only does it introduce a risk of contaminating a crime scene, it can also be a health hazard.

When the on-scene investigation will require some time to complete, set up a command post somewhere outside the restricted areas. This command post can be established in a place as simple as a vehicle, or as complex as a hotel room or a tent erected specifically for that purpose. The command post can be used as the gathering place for noninvolved personnel. It can also be a place where investigators take breaks, eat, drink, or smoke. Should the need arise, it can serve as a communication center or a place for press conferences. A well-established separate command post keeps extraneous activity away from the crime scene.

Remember that protection of the crime scene also includes protection of the crime scene investigators. Never leave anyone alone while processing the scene. This is especially important when the suspect has not been apprehended. There should always be at least two people working the scene, at least one of whom should have a radio and a firearm.

Using these special measures to preserve a crime scene helps ensure that the evidence collected is uncontaminated. The successful prosecution of a case often hinges on the state of the physical evidence. Therefore, proper crime scene measures mean the evidence is as unspoiled as possible at the time it is collected.

**Additional Directions:** Take 15 minutes to answer the following 10 questions without referring to the narrative.

36. According to the narrative, which area from where evidence is collected is especially vulnerable to contamination?
    - ❑  A.  Hallways
    - ❑  B.  The floor
    - ❑  C.  Driveways
    - ❑  D.  On clothing

37. Which of the following answers would most likely be an essential person at a homicide crime scene investigation?
    - ❑  A.  Coroner
    - ❑  B.  News photographer
    - ❑  C.  District attorney investigator
    - ❑  D.  Prosecutor

38. According to the narrative, a successful prosecution of a crime can often hinge on which of the following?
    - ❑  A.  Contaminated evidence
    - ❑  B.  Circumstantial evidence
    - ❑  C.  Uncontaminated evidence
    - ❑  D.  Lack of evidence

39. Which activity is permitted at a crime scene?
    - ❑  A.  Evidence collection
    - ❑  B.  Smoking
    - ❑  C.  Drinking
    - ❑  D.  Eating

40. According to the narrative, which crime scene area location would work best for the site of a press conference?
    - ❑  A.  The crime scene
    - ❑  B.  An off-site command post
    - ❑  C.  The coroner's office
    - ❑  D.  The prosecutor's or attorney general's office

41. The officer chosen to be in charge of a crime scene can depend on a number of factors. Based on the narrative, which of the following answers is not one of those factors?
    - ❑  A.  The number of officers involved in the investigation
    - ❑  B.  The number of other department personnel involved in the investigation
    - ❑  C.  The nature of the crime
    - ❑  D.  The number of years the officer has been employed by the department

42. When an officer is placed at a crime scene entrance, his responsibility includes maintaining a log in which he records specific information about anyone who enters the crime scene. Which answer that follows is not a part of the information needed for each person?
    - ❑  A.  Name
    - ❑  B.  Time of arrival
    - ❑  C.  Date of birth
    - ❑  D.  Time of departure

43. According to the narrative, after the crime scene itself has been stabilized, certain areas should be roped off to prevent unauthorized people from entering them. Which answer that follows is not normally one of those areas?
    - ❑  A.  Roadways
    - ❑  B.  Stairways
    - ❑  C.  Hallways
    - ❑  D.  Pathways

44. According to the context of the narrative, the protection of a crime scene means protecting several things. Which answer that follows is not one of those things?

   ❑  A.  Crime scene investigators
   ❑  B.  News media access
   ❑  C.  Evidence
   ❑  D.  Essential personnel access

45. According to the narrative, which statement that follows is true?

   ❑  A.  When the on-scene investigation can be completed quickly, set up a command post somewhere outside the restricted areas.
   ❑  B.  When the on-scene investigation will attract the media, set up a command post somewhere outside the restricted areas.
   ❑  C.  When the on-scene investigation will require that a suspect be charged and prosecuted for the crime, set up a command post somewhere outside the restricted areas.
   ❑  D.  When the on-scene investigation will require some time to complete, set up a command post somewhere outside the restricted areas.

# Collection of Evidence at a Crime Scene Timed Test: 60-Minute Time Limit

**Directions**: For this test, spend 40 minutes reading the following narrative. The objective is to commit to memory as many of the facts given in the narrative as you can. Do not take notes. For this test, you are to rely entirely on your recall of facts gathered only from reading.

# Types of Evidence

The information that follows is a breakdown of the types of evidence encountered and how that evidence is normally handled. It should be noted that packaging instructions assume that the item has already been processed for fingerprints at the scene or has had any other on-site investigative procedures (such as photographs) completed prior to the item being packaged.

## Fingerprints, Palm Prints, and Bare Footprints

Fingerprints, palm prints, and bare footprints are the best evidence to place an individual at the scene of a crime. Collecting fingerprints at a crime scene requires very few materials, which makes it ideal from a cost-effectiveness standpoint. All immovable items at a crime scene should be processed at the scene using the appropriate powder specified by your crime lab and department's evidence collection guidelines. Photographs are taken before prints are lifted, and often include those taken using a detachable flash and a camera that can make one-to-one photographs of prints; one-to-one photographs are especially important for those prints that cannot be easily lifted.

Paper bags or envelopes are used for items small enough to be transported and sent to the crime lab for processing; however, whenever possible, collecting the prints at the crime scene should be every investigator's top priority. Fingerprints from the suspect and elimination fingerprints from the victim will be needed for comparison; this is also necessary for palm and bare footprints.

## Bite Marks

Bite marks are most often associated with sexual assaults, but can be used whenever they are found at a crime scene for matching back to the individual who did the biting. Prior to collecting the bite mark, it should be photographed—the more photographs taken under a variety of conditions, the better. So, a number of Polaroid, color, and black-and-white photos are generally taken. Older bite marks that are no longer visible on the skin can sometimes be made visible and photographed by the use of UV light and alternative light sources. A cast can sometimes be taken of a deep bite mark that has left an impression. Casts and photographs of the suspect's teeth and maybe the victim's teeth will be needed for comparison. Consult with the forensic odontologist associated with the crime lab to ascertain specific bite mark photograph and collection information.

## Broken Fingernails

Similar to how a bullet has unique striations on it, natural fingernails also have individualizing striations on them. A broken fingernail found at a crime scene has been known to be matched to a suspect it came from months after the crime was committed. Dry, broken fingernails should be placed in a paper packet that is then to be placed in a paper envelope. When submitted to the crime lab for analysis, try to provide known samples from the suspect and the victim, and, if needed, elimination fingernails (for example, when it is known that an officer broke a fingernail at the crime site before donning rubber gloves and the scene was processed); these samples will be needed for comparison. Broken fingernails can also sometimes contain other trace evidence, such as skin that remains on a fingernail that was broken when the victim scratched the perpetrator, or vice versa.

## Questioned Documents

Handwriting samples are usually analyzed by an expert known as a *questioned documents examiner*. Questioned documents include those that include writing known to belong to a suspect and exemplars believed to be of the suspected person's handwriting. Documents successfully matched back to the individual who produced them can be another important piece of prosecutorial evidence. Confirmed handwriting samples must be submitted for comparison to the unknown samples. Questioned documents can also be processed for fingerprints. All dry questioned documents should be collected in paper containers.

## Blood and Body Fluids

DNA analysis can match blood and seminal fluid to an individual with a high degree of probability. DNA technology is evolving, and collection details about how to collect and handle such evidence is an evolving process as well. DNA testing is also expensive, so it isn't always used; however, in most cases, crime labs have procedures in place to ensure blood and body fluid evidence is collected and preserved in such a manner that it can be submitted for DNA analysis later if need be. The collection of liquid or dried blood and other body fluids or stains require detailed, specific steps. Fingerprint tape can sometimes be used to lift dried blood or stains from items too large to transport to the crime lab. Other times, dried evidence can be transferred to threads first soaked in distilled water. To avoid the contamination or breakdown of the evidence due to microorganisms or mold, such threads or any other evidence that's wet should not be held in plastic or paper containers for more than two hours. If it isn't practical to air-dry evidence at the scene, follow departmental crime lab procedures to see that it's done as soon as possible after transport of that evidence.

Transport of liquid or dried blood and other body fluids or stains also requires specific steps to ensure that no cross-contamination of evidence occurs. When in doubt, contact the crime lab that will be processing the evidence to be sure that all steps in the evidence collection, transportation, storage, and shipping process are handled correctly.

## Firearms

Bullets and casings found at the crime scene can be examined at the crime lab; this examination will sometimes reveal to an investigator what make and model of weapon expended the casing or bullet. Bullets and casings can also positively match back or rule out a link to a gun found to be in the possession of a suspect. A bullet found at the crime scene sometimes can even be matched to a lot of ammunition found to be in a suspect's possession.

When processing a firearm at the scene or packaging it for delivery to the crime lab, always observe departmental and common sense firearm safety procedures. Never attempt to lift a weapon by placing a pencil or other object inside the barrel or the trigger guard; doing so is not only unsafe, it could also damage potential evidence.

Before picking up a gun—by the textured surface on the grips to avoid placing unnecessary fingerprints on the weapon—make sure that the gun barrel is not pointed at anyone. Keep notes on the condition of the weapon as it was found. Also record any steps taken to make it as safe as possible without damaging potential evidence. After it has been determined to be safe, the firearm can then be processed for prints, and finally rendered completely safe. (A firearm must be in verified safe condition before it is packaged and submitted to the crime lab.) A firearm should be packaged in an individual envelope or paper bag, separate from any ammunition. The ammunition (and/or magazine) should be placed in its own paper envelope or bag. It is also important to submit any ammunition found in the gun to the crime lab, too. Any boxes of similar ammunition found in a suspect's possession should be placed in a paper container and sent to the crime lab. Any bullets and casings found at the crime scene should be packaged separately by placing them in paper envelopes or small cardboard pillboxes.

## Shoeprints and Tire Tracks

Even before they're positively matched to a pair of shoes or to tires in a suspect's possession, shoeprints and tire tracks can sometimes tell investigators what type of shoes or tires to look for when searching a suspect's residence or vehicles. Accepted general guidelines for collecting this type of evidence include the following:

▶ Before actually collecting any shoeprints or tire tracks at the scene, take one-to-one photographs using a tripod, ruler, and level and with a flash held at about a 45-degree angle from the surface containing the impression.

▶ When deep enough, take casts of shoeprints or tire tracks using dental stone. After the cast has hardened, it can be packaged in paper to be submitted to the lab.

▶ Photographs taken of shoeprints on a hard flat surface should be done using the flash as side lighting.

▶ Shoeprints on hard, flat surfaces sometimes can be lifted like a fingerprint and/or lifted with an electrostatic dustprint lifter.

## Toolmarks

Toolmarks can be positively matched to a tool in the suspect's possession. If a knife (or other sharp object) is being submitted to the lab for toolmarks, fingerprints, or other reason, the blade and point should be wrapped in stiff immovable cardboard and placed in a paper bag or envelope. The container should be labeled to warn that the contents are sharp and precautions should be taken. This is to prevent anyone from being injured.

## Fibers

Fibers from carpeting, clothing, and other parts of a residence or vehicle are usually collected in a paper packet and placed in an envelope. When suspects have been determined, similar fibers should be collected from them and submitted to the lab for comparison.

## Fracture Matches

Fracture matches are the "reassemble a jigsaw puzzle"-style type of evidence, and can be used to provide links between broken pieces at the scene and pieces found in the possession of a suspect. Fracture matches include such things as headlight fragments from the scene of a hit-and-run accident that are positively matched to a broken headlight on a suspect's vehicle. Smaller fragments can be placed in a paper packet and then placed in an envelope. The size of larger fragments (such as an entire bumper left behind at the scene of a hit-and-run accident) determine how such evidence is collected and stored.

## Hair

Hair can come from the head, body, or pubic region. Hair found at the scene should be placed in a paper packet and then placed in an envelope. When the hair has a root sheath attached, DNA analysis can be performed on the hair to determine that it's from a certain percentage of the population. When hair with the root attached is found at the scene, pulled hair should be taken from the suspect whenever possible. (A whole blood sample should also be collected from the suspect.) If there isn't a root sheath, rather than being able to determine that hair came from a particular individual, microscopic analysis can still determine whether the hair has the same characteristics as the suspect's hair and is similar to his or her hair. If this type of microscopic examination will be required, 15–20 representative hairs to be submitted to the lab for comparison should be collected from the suspect.

## Paint

Paint fragments should be collected in a paper packet and placed in an envelope. When suspects have been determined, representative paint chips or samples should be collected as is appropriate from them and submitted to the lab for comparison.

## Glass

Small glass fragments from the scene or suspect should be placed in a paper packet and then in an envelope. To prevent further breakage, larger pieces need to be wrapped securely in paper or cardboard and then placed in a padded cardboard box.

## Other Forms of Trace Evidence

Other forms of trace evidence that can sometimes be transferred to a perpetrator from the scene or from the perpetrator to the scene are fragments or pieces of things such as insulation, sheetrock, soil, and so on. The type of trace evidence determines how it is collected, but its collection usually follows the same guidelines as those for collecting and storing paint and fibers.

# Evidence Chain of Custody

Chain of custody for the evidence collected at a crime scene generally starts with the collection done by the investigator-technician. Marking and labeling that evidence is the starting point for the control and custody for those items of evidence. *Chain of custody* is defined as the witnessed, written record of all people who maintained unbroken control over the items of evidence. This *chain of custody* establishes the proof that items of evidence collected at the crime scene are the same evidence being presented when introduced in a court of law.

Chain of custody establishes the following:

- ▶ Any dates and times the evidence was handled
- ▶ Circumstances for the evidence being handled
- ▶ Changes, if any, that were made to the evidence
- ▶ Who had contact with the evidence

If a search warrant was obtained, that information is noted as well.

Other important considerations regarding the collection of evidence are as follows:

▶ Evidence recovered should be listed in chronological order, beginning with the first item recovered.

▶ Notations should include the exact location of recovery and time of recovery for each piece of evidence.

▶ Notations should also include measurements when it will aid in establishing from where the evidence was recovered (for example, in relation to the distance from a body).

# Tagging Evidence

The crime scene investigator or evidence recovery technician tags and marks items taken into evidence so that she can easily identify those items at a later date. This labeling, marking, and tagging of the evidence also adds credibility and control to this later identification of an item.

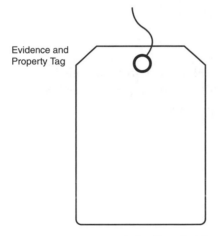

Evidence and
Property Tag

**FIGURE 15.1**  Evidence tag.

All evidence collected at the crime scene should be labeled, marked, or tagged in a consistent manner. Include the following information:

▶ Any serial number or garment information

▶ Brand name

▶ Collector's name and identifier

▶ Date

▶ Description of item

> ▶ Location of collection

> ▶ Police case number or identifier

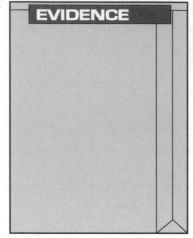

**FIGURE 15.2**   Evidence package.

Similar, but more extensive, information also needs to be included on the outside of the packaging materials, such as envelopes, into which the evidence is placed. Include the following information:

> ▶ Collector's name and identifier information

> ▶ Date

> ▶ Item description

> ▶ Location of collection

> ▶ Police case number or identifier

> ▶ Serial number or garment identifier

> ▶ Type of case

> ▶ Where item is to be routed to for analysis

Well-organized evidence procedures greatly aid in the identification of evidence when it is presented in a court of law—usually months, and sometimes years, after that evidence was gathered. Most departments establish specific steps for effective crime scene management, evidence collection, evidence labeling, and chain of evidence maintenance for that reason. Consistency provides a way to remain organized. An organized approach lends itself to an efficient, effective approach, which helps ensure that all steps are put into place in order for the evidence to stand up in court. This improves the chances for the successful prosecution of the crime.

**Additional Directions:** Take 20 minutes to answer the following 20 questions without referring to the narrative.

46. Based on the information provided in the narrative, select the correct reason why a fingerprint is a valuable piece of evidence:
    - ❏ A. It doesn't smear
    - ❏ B. Provides proof a specific person has been at the scene of the crime
    - ❏ C. Every person has them
    - ❏ D. Fingerprints are usually unique to a person

47. Other forms of trace evidence are always collected and stored the same as
    - ❏ A. Paper
    - ❏ B. Paint
    - ❏ C. Fiber
    - ❏ D. In a manner determined by the type of evidence

48. According to the narrative, there are specific primary reasons why wet evidence should not be permanently stored in plastic or paper. Of the reasons that follow, which one is incorrect?
    - ❏ A. Contamination of the evidence due to microorganisms
    - ❏ B. Potential for eventual leakage onto other evidence
    - ❏ C. Contamination of the evidence due to mold
    - ❏ D. Breakdown of the evidence due to microorganisms or mold

49. According to the narrative, evidence recovered should be listed in what order?
    - ❏ A. Alphabetical
    - ❏ B. Numerical
    - ❏ C. Chronological
    - ❏ D. Size

50. Based on the information provided in the narrative, which of the following choices can logically be deduced to be an incorrect statement about what is established by the evidence chain of custody?
    - ❏ A. Any dates and times the evidence was handled
    - ❏ B. The date and time the evidence was collected
    - ❏ C. Who had contact with the evidence
    - ❏ D. The exact time the crime occurred

51. For which type of evidence should handwriting samples be collected from the victim and any suspects?
    - ❏  A.  Fingerprints
    - ❏  B.  Questioned documents
    - ❏  C.  Evidence labeling tags
    - ❏  D.  Evidence envelopes

52. Which statement that follows is false?
    - ❏  A.  When submitting broken fingernails to the crime lab, also provide known samples from the suspect, from the victim, and, if needed, elimination fingernails
    - ❏  B.  Dry, broken fingernails should be placed in a paper packet
    - ❏  C.  Broken fingernails should be stored in a container of formaldehyde
    - ❏  D.  Broken fingernails can also sometimes contain other trace evidence

53. According to the narrative, the collection of one type of evidence is "ideal from a cost-effectiveness standpoint" because it requires very few materials to collect. Which is it?
    - ❏  A.  Fingerprints
    - ❏  B.  Whole blood
    - ❏  C.  Blood stains
    - ❏  D.  Firearms

54. Which statement that follows is true?
    - ❏  A.  DNA technology is evolving.
    - ❏  B.  DNA testing is inexpensive.
    - ❏  C.  DNA testing is often done on hair without the root attached.
    - ❏  D.  DNA testing can be performed only on whole blood samples.

55. Which of the items that follow is least likely to be transported to the crime lab and entered directly into the evidence chain of custody?
    - ❏  A.  Broken glass
    - ❏  B.  Pubic hair
    - ❏  C.  Bumper from a car
    - ❏  D.  Paint chips

56. Based on the narrative, three of the statements that follow can logically be deduced to be false. Which one of the statements that follow is true?
    - ❏  A.  Always excise the skin around a bite mark and store the evidence in a jar of formaldehyde.
    - ❏  B.  Always excise the skin around a bite mark and store the evidence in a jar of saline solution.
    - ❏  C.  Always excise the skin around a bite mark and store the evidence in a paper envelope.
    - ❏  D.  Bite marks are often associated with a sexual assault.

57. Based on the narrative, which is the proper way to lift a firearm when an officer enters it into evidence?

  ❑  A.  By placing a pencil or other straight object in the barrel of the gun
  ❑  B.  By lifting it by the textured surface on the grips
  ❑  C.  By placing a pencil or other straight object in the trigger guard of the gun
  ❑  D.  By lifting it by the trigger guard

58. Based on the narrative, three of the statements that follow are false. Which one of the statements that follow is true?

  ❑  A.  Shoeprints on a hard, flat surface sometimes can be lifted like a finger-print.
  ❑  B.  Shoeprints on a hard, flat surface sometimes can be lifted by making a dental stone impression of the imprint.
  ❑  C.  Shoeprints on a soft, wet surface sometimes can be lifted like a finger-print.
  ❑  D.  Shoeprints on a hard, grassy or carpeted surface sometimes can be lift-ed like a fingerprint.

59. Based on the narrative, which of the statements that follow is false?

  ❑  A.  Hair can come from the head, body, or pubic region.
  ❑  B.  To prevent further breakage, larger pieces of cardboard need to be wrapped securely in paper or cardboard.
  ❑  C.  To prevent further breakage, larger pieces of glass need to be wrapped securely in paper or cardboard.
  ❑  D.  Paint chips should be collected in a paper packet and placed in an envelope.

60. Which of the evidence items that follow would most likely not be con-sidered a *fracture match* piece of evidence?

  ❑  A.  Broken fingernail
  ❑  B.  Headlight fragments
  ❑  C.  Taillight fragments
  ❑  D.  Shredded documents

61. Based on the narrative, which of the statements that follow is true?

  ❑  A.  When hair is pulled from the suspect, 15–20 strands are needed for testing.
  ❑  B.  When representative hair is recovered from the suspect for a micro-scopic examination, 15–20 strands are required.
  ❑  C.  A hair must be absent the root sheath in order for DNA testing to be performed.
  ❑  D.  Even when a search warrant that includes mention of suspect hair sam-ples is involved, it is considered to be cruel and unusual punishment to expect a suspect to agree to submit pubic hair.

62. What information is usually recorded on the outside of evidence packaging material?
   - ❑  A.  Collector's name and identifier information
   - ❑  B.  Date
   - ❑  C.  Police case number or identifier
   - ❑  D.  All of the above

63. Based on information provided in the narrative, which of the statements that follow is not true?
   - ❑  A.  Bullets and casings found at the crime scene can be examined at the crime lab.
   - ❑  B.  Bullets and casings can be positively matched back to a gun.
   - ❑  C.  Bullets and casings are unnecessary evidence if the gun used in the perpetration of the crime is positively identified.
   - ❑  D.  Bullets and casings can be used to rule out a gun.

64. Based on the information provided in the narrative, choose the statement that follows that is true.
   - ❑  A.  Take a one-to-one photograph before collecting a victim's shoes
   - ❑  B.  Take a one-to-one photograph before collecting the suspect's shoes
   - ❑  C.  Take a one-to-one photograph before collecting tires from a vehicle
   - ❑  D.  Take a one-to-one photograph before collecting a shoeprint at the scene

65. Based on the information provided in the narrative, which of the answers that follow is not generally a part of the identifying information on an evidence tag?
   - ❑  A.  Brand name
   - ❑  B.  Date
   - ❑  C.  Suspect's name and identifier
   - ❑  D.  Police case number or identifier

# What Terrorist Threat Colors Mean Timed Test: 25-Minute Time Limit

**Directions**: For this test, spend 15 minutes reading the following narrative. The objective is to commit to memory as many of the facts given in the narrative as you can. Do not take notes. For this test, you are to rely entirely on your recall of facts gathered only from reading.

From the Homeland Security website:

http://www.whitehouse.gov/homeland/

Threat Conditions and Associated Protective Measures

The world has changed since September 11, 2001. We remain a Nation at risk to terrorist attacks and will remain at risk for the foreseeable future. At all Threat Conditions, we must remain vigilant, prepared, and ready to deter terrorist attacks. The following Threat Conditions each represent an increasing risk of terrorist attacks. Beneath each Threat Condition are some suggested Protective Measures, recognizing that the heads of Federal departments and agencies are responsible for developing and implementing appropriate agency-specific Protective Measures:

Low Condition (Green) This condition is declared when there is a low risk of terrorist attacks. Federal departments and agencies should consider the following general measures in addition to the agency-specific Protective Measures they develop and implement:

1. Refining and exercising as appropriate preplanned Protective Measures

2. Ensuring personnel receive proper training on the Homeland Security Advisory System and specific preplanned department or agency Protective Measures

3. Institutionalizing a process to assure that all facilities and regulated sectors are regularly assessed for vulnerabilities to terrorist attacks, and all reasonable measures are taken to mitigate these vulnerabilities

Guarded Condition (Blue). This condition is declared when there is a general risk of terrorist attacks. In addition to the Protective Measures taken in the previous Threat Condition, Federal departments and agencies should consider the following general measures in addition to the agency-specific Protective Measures that they will develop and implement:

1. Checking communications with designated emergency response or command locations

2. Reviewing and updating emergency response procedures

3. Providing the public with any information that would strengthen its ability to act appropriately

Elevated Condition (Yellow). An Elevated Condition is declared when there is a significant risk of terrorist attacks. In addition to the Protective Measures taken in the previous Threat Conditions, Federal departments and agencies should consider the following general measures in addition to the Protective Measures that they will develop and implement:

1. Increasing surveillance of critical locations

2. Coordinating emergency plans as appropriate with nearby jurisdictions

3. Assessing whether the precise characteristics of the threat require the further refinement of preplanned Protective Measures

4. Implementing, as appropriate, contingency and emergency response plans

High Condition (Orange). A High Condition is declared when there is a high risk of terrorist attacks. In addition to the Protective Measures taken in the previous Threat Conditions, Federal departments and agencies should consider the following general measures in addition to the agency-specific Protective Measures that they will develop and implement:

1. Coordinating necessary security efforts with Federal, State, and local law enforcement agencies or any National Guard or other appropriate armed forces organizations

2. Taking additional precautions at public events and possibly considering alternative venues or even cancellation

3. Preparing to execute contingency procedures, such as moving to an alternate site or dispersing their workforce

4. Restricting threatened facility access to essential personnel only.

Severe Condition (Red). A Severe Condition reflects a severe risk of terrorist attacks. Under most circumstances, the Protective Measures for a Severe Condition are not intended to be sustained for substantial periods of time. In addition to the Protective Measures in the previous Threat Conditions, Federal departments and agencies also should consider the following general measures in addition to the agency-specific Protective Measures that they will develop and implement:

1. Increasing or redirecting personnel to address critical emergency needs

2. Assigning emergency response personnel and pre-positioning and mobilizing specially trained teams or resources

3. Monitoring, redirecting, or constraining transportation systems

4. Closing public and government facilities

Source: excerpt from http://www.whitehouse.gov/news/releases/2002/03/20020312-5.html

**Additional Directions:** Take 10 minutes to answer the following 10 questions without referring to the narrative.

66. What color is associated with the High Terrorist Threat Level?
- ❑ A. Red
- ❑ B. Orange
- ❑ C. Green
- ❑ D. Blue

67. What color is associated with the Guarded Terrorist Threat Level?
- ❑ A. Blue
- ❑ B. Red
- ❑ C. Yellow
- ❑ D. Orange

68. What color is associated with the Elevated Terrorist Threat Level?
- ❑ A. Blue
- ❑ B. Red
- ❑ C. Yellow
- ❑ D. Green

69. What color is associated with a Severe Terrorist Threat Level?
- ❑ A. Green
- ❑ B. Red
- ❑ C. Orange
- ❑ D. Blue

70. What color is associated with a Low Terrorist Threat Level?
- ❑ A. Green
- ❑ B. Blue
- ❑ C. Orange
- ❑ D. Yellow

71. From the choices that follow, choose the one that is not a part of a Low Terrorist Threat Level.
- ❑ A. Ensuring personnel receive proper training on the Homeland Security Advisory System and specific preplanned department or agency Protective Measures
- ❑ B. Refining and exercising as appropriate preplanned Protective Measures
- ❑ C. Institutionalizing a process to assure that all facilities and regulated sectors are regularly assessed for vulnerabilities to terrorist attacks, and all reasonable measures are taken to mitigate these vulnerabilities
- ❑ D. Closing public and government facilities

72. From the choices that follow, choose the one that is not a part of a High Terrorist Threat Level.
   - ❑ A. Restricting threatened facility access to essential personnel only
   - ❑ B. Taking additional precautions at public events and possibly considering alternative venues or even cancellation
   - ❑ C. Closing public and government facilities
   - ❑ D. Preparing to execute contingency procedures, such as moving to an alternative site or dispersing their workforce

73. From the choices that follow, choose the one that is not a part of a Severe Terrorist Threat Level.
   - ❑ A. Closing public and government facilities
   - ❑ B. Turning control of the protection of the country over to the United Nations
   - ❑ C. Increasing or redirecting personnel to address critical emergency needs
   - ❑ D. Monitoring, redirecting, or constraining transportation systems

74. From the choices that follow, choose the one that is not a part of an Elevated Terrorist Threat Level.
   - ❑ A. Increasing surveillance of critical locations
   - ❑ B. Coordinating emergency plans as appropriate with nearby jurisdictions
   - ❑ C. Restricting threatened facility access to essential personnel only
   - ❑ D. Implementing, as appropriate, contingency and emergency response plans

75. From the choices that follow, choose the one that is not a part of a Guarded Terrorist Threat Level.
   - ❑ A. Implementing, as appropriate, contingency and emergency response plans
   - ❑ B. Checking communications with designated emergency response or command locations
   - ❑ C. Reviewing and updating emergency response procedures
   - ❑ D. Providing the public with any information that would strengthen its ability to act appropriately

# Glossary Questions

**Directions**: For this test, spend 45 minutes reading and studying the glossary terms and definitions that follow. The objective is to commit to memory as many of the terms and associated definitions as you can. Do not take notes. For this test, you are to rely entirely on your recall of the terms and definitions that you are able to commit to memory.

## Adultery
*Adultery* is the act of engaging in sexual intercourse with another person and either of the two involved in the act has a living spouse at that time.

## Arson
*Arson* is the act of intentionally destroying or causing damage to a vehicle or building by setting off an explosion or otherwise purposely causing a fire.

## Assault
*Assault* is the act of one person intending to cause a physical injury to another person, and then committing an act that causes such physical injury to that person or another person.

## Bribe Receiving
*Bribe receiving* is the act of a public servant receiving when he or she ask for, or accepts, a benefit on the understanding that his or her official actions will be influenced by that benefit.

## Bribery
*Bribery* is the act of offering or giving some benefit to a public servant with the intent and understanding that the public servant's official actions will be influenced.

## Burglar's Tools
*Burglar's tools* are any instruments that a person uses to facilitate the commission of a burglary, larceny, or theft of services.

## Burglary
*Burglary* is the act of entering or unlawfully remaining in a building or a dwelling with the intent to commit a crime while there.

## Chain of Custody
*Chain of custody* is the witnessed, written record of all individuals who maintained the unbroken control over an item of evidence.

## Citation
A *citation* is an official summons calling for an appearance in court.

## Cite
To *cite* is to summon before a court of law.

### Criminal Contempt
*Criminal contempt* is the act of refusing to be sworn in before a grand jury or a court, or the act of refusing to answer the legal questions of a grand jury or a court.

### Criminal Impersonation
*Criminal impersonation* is the act of pretending to be a police officer, a parole officer, a fireman, or any other public servant with the intent of having someone submit to that authority.

### Criminal Mischief
*Criminal mischief* is the act of intending to damage the property of another and, without the legal right to do so, damaging to that person's property.

### Criminal Trespass
*Criminal trespass* is the act of knowingly entering or remaining unlawfully in a building.

### Criminally Negligent Homicide
*Criminally negligent homicide* is the act of causing the death of another person by engaging in negligent behavior while failing to perceive it as a risk to other people.

### Felony
A *felony* is a serious crime, such as murder, rape, or burglary, punishable by a more severe sentence than that given for a misdemeanor.

### Jostling
*Jostling* is the act committed when, in a public place, a person intentionally places a hand near the pocket or handbag of another person, or unnecessarily crowds another person, while an accomplice places a hand near another person's pocket or handbag.

### Manslaughter
*Manslaughter* is the act committed when one person, with the original intent to cause physical injury to another person, causes that person's death.

### Menacing
*Menacing* is the act of using physical force to place intentionally, or attempt to place, another person in fear of immediate physical danger.

## Misdemeanor

A *misdemeanor* is an offense less serious than a felony.

## Petit Larceny

*Petit larceny* is the act of taking property that belongs to another without that person's consent, with the intent to keep that property—either personally or by transferring it to another person not the owner; in most jurisdictions, this property has a value of $250 or less.

## Probable Cause

*Probable cause* is a protection under the Fourth Amendment, which protects against unreasonable search and seizure and an unfounded issuance of an unfounded warrant. The purpose of probable cause is to protect against the abuses inherent in this kind of power by compelling there be a reasonable belief of the presence of evidence or the commission of a crime before an officer can stop or search a suspect, or obtain a warrant to search a suspect or a suspect's property, or take a suspect into custody.

## Rape

*Rape* is the act of forcing a female to have sexual intercourse against her will, or in any instance when the male is over the age of 21 and the female is younger than 17; different rules apply when the persons are legally married.

## Robbery

*Robbery* is the act of taking the property of another person by the use of or the threatened use of force against that person or another.

## Theft of Services

*Theft of services* is the failure to pay for public transportation.

**Additional Directions**: For questions 76–100, choose the word that follows the definition that matches that definition. Complete these 25 questions in 15 minutes.

76. The act of knowingly entering or remaining unlawfully in a building.
    - ❏  A.  Burglary
    - ❏  B.  Larceny
    - ❏  C.  Criminal trespass
    - ❏  D.  Felony

77. The act of a public servant receiving when he or she asks for, or accepts, a benefit on the understanding that his or her official actions will be influenced by that benefit.
    - ❑ A. Bribery
    - ❑ B. Jostling
    - ❑ C. Theft of services
    - ❑ D. Bribe receiving

78. The act committed when, in a public place, a person intentionally places a hand near the pocket or handbag of another person, or unnecessarily crowds another person, while an accomplice places a hand near another person's pocket or handbag.
    - ❑ A. Larceny
    - ❑ B. Jostling
    - ❑ C. Burglary
    - ❑ D. Petit theft

79. The act of intentionally destroying or causing damage to a vehicle or building by setting off an explosion or otherwise purposely causing a fire.
    - ❑ A. Arson
    - ❑ B. Assault
    - ❑ C. Sodomy
    - ❑ D. Jostling

80. The act committed when one person, with the original intent to cause physical injury to another person, causes that person's death.
    - ❑ A. Felony
    - ❑ B. Negligent homicide
    - ❑ C. Manslaughter
    - ❑ D. Homicide

81. The act of pretending to be a police officer, a parole officer, a fireman, or any other public servant with the intent of having someone submit to that authority.
    - ❑ A. Criminal mischief
    - ❑ B. Criminal impersonation
    - ❑ C. Criminal trespass
    - ❑ D. Theft of services

82. The act of entering or unlawfully remaining in a building or a dwelling with the intent to commit a crime while there.
    - ❑ A. Burglary
    - ❑ B. Larceny
    - ❑ C. Theft of services
    - ❑ D. Criminal trespass

83. A serious crime, such as murder, rape, or burglary, punishable by a more severe sentence than that given for a misdemeanor.
- ❑  A.  Larceny
- ❑  B.  Criminal contempt
- ❑  C.  Felony
- ❑  D.  Misdemeanor

84. To summon before a court of law.
- ❑  A.  Cite
- ❑  B.  Criminal impersonation
- ❑  C.  Probable cause
- ❑  D.  Menacing

85. The act of intending to damage the property of another and, without the legal right to do so, damaging to that person's property.
- ❑  A.  Criminal impersonation
- ❑  B.  Criminal mischief
- ❑  C.  Burglary
- ❑  D.  Larceny

86. The act of refusing to be sworn in before a grand jury or a court, or the act of refusing to answer legal questions of a grand jury or a court.
- ❑  A.  Citation
- ❑  B.  Probable cause
- ❑  C.  Criminal impersonation
- ❑  D.  Criminal contempt

87. Any instruments a person uses to facilitate the commission of a burglary, larceny, or theft of services.
- ❑  A.  Carrying concealed weapon
- ❑  B.  Unlicensed firearm
- ❑  C.  Burglar's tools
- ❑  D.  Citation

88. The protection under the Fourth Amendment that protects against unreasonable search and seizure and an unfounded issuance of an unfounded warrant.
- ❑  A.  Probable cause
- ❑  B.  Chain of custody
- ❑  C.  Menacing
- ❑  D.  Misdemeanor

89. The act of engaging in sexual intercourse with another person and either of the two involved in the act has a living spouse at that time.
    - ❏ A. Sodomy
    - ❏ B. Jostling
    - ❏ C. Adultery
    - ❏ D. Theft of services

90. The act of causing the death of another person by engaging in negligent behavior while failing to perceive it as a risk to other people.
    - ❏ A. Murder
    - ❏ B. Criminally negligent homicide
    - ❏ C. Suicide
    - ❏ D. Manslaughter

91. The witnessed, written record of all individuals who maintained the unbroken control over an item of evidence.
    - ❏ A. Probable cause
    - ❏ B. Suspicious behavior
    - ❏ C. Chain of custody
    - ❏ D. No visible means of support

92. The act of using physical force to place intentionally, or attempt to place, another person in fear of immediate physical danger.
    - ❏ A. Menacing
    - ❏ B. Manslaughter
    - ❏ C. Jostling
    - ❏ D. Chain of custody

93. The act of taking property that belongs to another without that person's consent, with the intent to keep that property—either personally or by transferring it to another person not the owner; in most jurisdictions, this property has a value of $250 or less.
    - ❏ A. Larceny
    - ❏ B. Petit larceny
    - ❏ C. Burglary
    - ❏ D. Theft of services

94. An offense less serious than a felony.
    - ❏ A. Larceny
    - ❏ B. Burglary
    - ❏ C. Misdemeanor
    - ❏ D. Bribery

95. The act of forcing a female to have sexual intercourse against her will, or in any instance when the male is over the age of 21 and the female is younger than 17; different rules apply when the persons are legally married.

&#10065;  A.  Assault

&#10065;  B.  Manslaughter

&#10065;  C.  Jostling

&#10065;  D.  Rape

96. An official summons calling for an appearance in court.

&#10065;  A.  Citation

&#10065;  B.  Probable cause

&#10065;  C.  Jurisdiction

&#10065;  D.  Assault

97. The act of offering or giving some benefit to a public servant with the intent and understanding that the public servant's official actions will be influenced.

&#10065;  A.  Theft of services

&#10065;  B.  Bribery

&#10065;  C.  Jostling

&#10065;  D.  Larceny

98. The act of taking the property of another person by the use of or the threatened use of force against that person or another.

&#10065;  A.  Larceny

&#10065;  B.  Burglary

&#10065;  C.  Robbery

&#10065;  D.  Adultery

99. The act of one person intending to cause a physical injury to another person, and then committing an act that causes such physical injury to that person or another person.

&#10065;  A.  Rape

&#10065;  B.  Assault

&#10065;  C.  Jostling

&#10065;  D.  Manslaughter

100. The failure to pay for public transportation.

&#10065;  A.  Theft of services

&#10065;  B.  Larceny

&#10065;  C.  Burglary

&#10065;  D.  Robbery

# 16

# Answer Key to Practice Test 3

| | | |
|---|---|---|
| 1. D | 19. A | 37. A |
| 2. B | 20. D | 38. C |
| 3. A | 21. B | 39. A |
| 4. C | 22. A | 40. B |
| 5. B | 23. C | 41. D |
| 6. C | 24. D | 42. C |
| 7. D | 25. D | 43. A |
| 8. A | 26. B | 44. B |
| 9. B | 27. A | 45. D |
| 10. D | 28. D | 46. B |
| 11. C | 29. C | 47. D |
| 12. A | 30. B | 48. B |
| 13. B | 31. B | 49. C |
| 14. B | 32. A | 50. D |
| 15. C | 33. C | 51. B |
| 16. A | 34. D | 52. C |
| 17. B | 35. A | 53. A |
| 18. D | 36. B | 54. A |

| | | |
|---|---|---|
| 55. C | 71. D | 87. C |
| 56. D | 72. C | 88. A |
| 57. B | 73. B | 89. C |
| 58. A | 74. C | 90. B |
| 59. B | 75. A | 91. C |
| 60. A | 76. C | 92. A |
| 61. B | 77. D | 93. B |
| 62. D | 78. B | 94. C |
| 63. C | 79. A | 95. D |
| 64. D | 80. C | 96. A |
| 65. C | 81. B | 97. B |
| 66. B | 82. A | 98. C |
| 67. A | 83. C | 99. B |
| 68. C | 84. A | 100. A |
| 69. B | 85. B | |
| 70. A | 86. D | |

1. **Answer D is correct.**

2. **Answer B is correct.**

3. **Answer A is correct.**

4. **Answer C is correct.**

5. **Answer B is correct.**

6. **Answer C is correct.**

7. **Answer D is correct.**

8. **Answer A is correct.**

9. **Answer B is correct.**

10. **Answer D is correct.**

11. **Answer C is correct.**

12. **Answer A is correct.**

13. **Answer B is correct.**

14. **Answer B is correct.**

15. **Answer C is correct.**

16. **Answer A is correct.** Three of the robberies have occurred at, on, or near 9:00 p.m. (2100 hours), and the other occurred at 10:05 p.m. (2205 hours); therefore, only one (answer A) robbery occurred at about 2200 hours.

17. **Answer B is correct.**

18. **Answer D is correct.**

19. **Answer A is correct.**

20. **Answer D is correct.** Answer A (June 13) is the date of the first robbery. No robbery occurred on June 20 (answer B). The second robbery occurred on June 27 (answer C).

21. **Answer B is correct.**

22. **Answer A is correct.**

23. **Answer C is correct.**

24. **Answer D is correct.**

25. **Answer D is correct.**

26. **Answer B is correct.** Answer B is a direct quote from the narrative. Answers A, C, and D contain incorrect information.

27. **Answer A is correct.** Answers B, C, and D are incorrect information.

28. **Answer D is correct.** Answers A, B, and C are mentioned in the narrative; answer D is the one with information not mentioned in the narrative.

29. **Answer C is correct.** Answers A, B, and D are incorrect because they weren't mentioned in the narrative, and because they describe actions that either should not (answers A and B) or will not necessarily (answer D) be performed by the first officer to arrive at a crime scene.

30. **Answer B is correct.** Answers A, C, and D are incorrect because they weren't mentioned in the narrative, and because they describe actions that should not be performed by the first officer to arrive at a crime scene.

31. **Answer B is correct.** *Any observed characteristics* is a critical phrase in this question, therefore, answer B is incorrect because it is not the responsibility of the first officer at the scene to record the

"characteristics" of emergency personnel. Answers A, C, and D are correct because the officer should note and record *any observed characteristics* about any victims, witnesses, or suspects.

32. **Answer A is correct.** Answer A is incorrect because it is not a time the narrative advises the first office at the scene should record. Answers B, C, and D are correct because they describe times that are important and should be recorded.

33. **Answer C is correct.** Answer C is a direct quote from the narrative. Answers A, B, and D contain incorrect information.

34. **Answer D is correct.** Answer D is a direct quote from the narrative. Answers A, B, and C contain incorrect information.

35. **Answer A is correct.** Answer A is a direct quote from the narrative. Answers B and C contain incorrect information. Answer D replaces the important word *diligent* (which means *carried out with careful attention and effort*) with *negligent* (which means *characterized by neglect or carelessness*).

36. **Answer B is correct.**

37. **Answer A is correct.**

38. **Answer C is correct.**

39. **Answer A is correct.**

40. **Answer B is correct.**

41. **Answer D is correct.**

42. **Answer C is correct.**

43. **Answer A is correct.**

44. **Answer B is correct.**

45. **Answer D is correct.** Answer D is a direct quote from the narrative. Answer A is incorrect because it states to establish a command center when the investigation will be completed quickly. Answer B is incorrect because despite the crime center sometimes being used as a information point for the media, that isn't its primary reason for being established. Answer C is incorrect because although the objective of all crime investigations is the eventual charging and prosecution of a suspect or suspects, that isn't the reason for establishing a command center.

46. **Answer B is correct.** Answers A, C, and D have incorrect information; answer D is specifically incorrect because of the word *usually*; fingerprints are *always* unique to a person.

47. **Answer D is correct.**

48. **Answer B is correct.**

49. **Answer C is correct.** Evidence recovered is to be listed in chronological order beginning with the first item recovered.

50. **Answer D is correct.** Answers A, B, and C are all parts of the evidence chain of custody. Answer D, the exact time A crime occurred, cannot always be determined based solely from the evidence collected at the scene.

51. **Answer B is correct.**

52. **Answer C is correct.**

53. **Answer A is correct.**

54. **Answer A is correct.**

55. **Answer C is correct.**

56. **Answer D is correct.** Answer A is incorrect because the bite mark may be on a living victim; even if the victim is dead, the officer in the field is seldom the one to excise skin and the storage method suggested may not be what is required by the crime lab. Answer B is incorrect for the same reasons as A. Answer C is incorrect because the officer in the field would not be the one to excise human tissue nor would human tissue be stored in a paper envelope.

57. **Answer B is correct.**

58. **Answer A is correct.**

59. **Answer B is correct.**

60. **Answer A is correct.** A *fracture match* piece of evidence is one that must be joined with the whole in a jigsaw puzzle–style manner; therefore, answers B, C, and D are correct.

61. **Answer B is correct.**

62. **Answer D is correct.**

63. **Answer C is correct.**

64. **Answer D is correct.**

65. **Answer C is correct.**

66. **Answer B is correct.**

67. **Answer A is correct.**

68. **Answer C is correct.**

69. **Answer B is correct.**

70. **Answer A is correct.**

71. **Answer D is correct.**

72. **Answer C is correct.**

73. **Answer B is correct.**

74. **Answer C is correct.**

75. **Answer A is correct.**

76. **Answer C is correct.** *Criminal trespass* is the act of knowingly entering or remaining unlawfully in a building.

77. **Answer D is correct.** *Bribe receiving* is the act of a public servant receiving when he or she asks for, or accepts, a benefit on the understanding that his or her official actions will be influenced by that benefit.

78. **Answer B is correct.** *Jostling* is the act committed when, in a public place, a person intentionally places a hand near the pocket or handbag of another person, or unnecessarily crowds another person, while an accomplice places a hand near another person's pocket or handbag.

79. **Answer A is correct.** *Arson* is the act of intentionally destroying or causing damage to a vehicle or building by setting off an explosion or otherwise purposely causing a fire.

80. **Answer C is correct.** *Manslaughter* is the act committed when one person, with the original intent to cause physical injury to another person, causes that person's death.

81. **Answer B is correct.** *Criminal impersonation* is the act of pretending to be a police officer, a parole officer, a fireman, or any other public servant with the intent of having someone submit to that authority.

82. **Answer A is correct.** *Burglary* is the act of entering or unlawfully remaining in a building or a dwelling with the intent to commit a crime while there.

83. **Answer C is correct.** A *felony* is a serious crime, such as murder, rape, or burglary, punishable by a more severe sentence than that given for a misdemeanor.

84. **Answer A is correct.** To *cite* is to summon before a court of law.

85. **Answer B is correct.** *Criminal mischief* is the act of intending to damage the property of another and, without the legal right to do so, damaging to that person's property.

86. **Answer D is correct.** *Criminal contempt* is the act of refusing to be sworn in before a grand jury or a court, or the act of refusing to answer legal questions of a grand jury or a court.

87. **Answer C is correct.** *Burglar's tools* are any instruments a person uses to facilitate the commission of a burglary, larceny, or theft of services.

88. **Answer A is correct.** *Probable cause* is a protection under the fourth amendment which protects against unreasonable search and seizure and an unfounded issuance of an unfounded warrant.

89. **Answer C is correct.** *Adultery* is the act of engaging in sexual intercourse with another person and either of the two involved in the act has a living spouse at that time.

90. **Answer B is correct.** *Criminally negligent homicide* is the act of causing the death of another person by engaging in negligent behavior while failing to perceive a risk to other people.

91. **Answer C is correct.** *Chain of custody* is the witnessed, written record of all individuals who maintained the unbroken control over an item of evidence.

92. **Answer A is correct.** *Menacing* is the act of using physical force to place intentionally, or attempt to place, another person in fear of immediate physical danger.

93. **Answer B is correct.** *Petit larceny* is the act of taking property that belongs to another without that person's consent, with the intent to keep that property— either personally or by transferring it to another person not the owner; in most jurisdictions, this property has a value of $250 or less.

94. **Answer C is correct.** A *misdemeanor* is an offense less serious than a felony

95. **Answer D is correct.** *Rape* is the act of forcing a female to have sexual intercourse against her will, or in any instance when the male is over the age of 21 and the female is younger than 17; different rules apply when the persons are legally married.

96. **Answer A is correct.** A *citation* is an official summons calling for an appearance in court.

97. **Answer B is correct.** *Bribery* is the act of offering or giving some benefit to a public servant with the intent and understanding that the public servant's official actions will be influenced.

98. **Answer C is correct.** *Robbery* is the act of taking the property of another person by the use of or the threatened use of force against that person or another.

99. **Answer B is correct.** *Assault* is the act of one person intending to cause a physical injury to another person, and then committing an act that causes such physical injury to that person or another person.

100. **Answer A is correct.** *Theft of services* is the failure to pay for public transportation.

APPENDIX A

# Need to Know More?

## Chapter 1

### Informative magazines

 http://www.policemarksman.com

*Police Marksman*

*Police Marksman* is a monthly magazine and subscription. The magazine contains informative articles on defensive tactics, subject control, and vehicle stops. Additionally, you will find articles on legal issues, law enforcement equipment, and trends.

 http://www.policemag.com

*Police, the Law Enforcement Magazine*

*Police* is also a monthly magazine. It contains current law enforcement news from across the country. You will also find articles on new police products, police resources, and officer safety. There is also a classified section for job openings and products for sale.

### Helpful web sites

 http://www.officer.com

This website is a good source for job leads, current law enforcement news, and products and services. You will also find articles on the police profession, legal issues, and officer safety.

http://www.lawenforcementjobs.com

This website is also a good source of police job openings across the country. You will find links leading to opportunities in police education and training, and a salary guide.

 http://www.grandlodgefop.org

The Fraternal Order of Police (FOP) is the world's largest organization of sworn law enforcement officers, with more than 310,000 members in more than 2,100 local lodges. The FOP is committed to improving the working conditions of law enforcement officers and the safety of those we serve through education and legislation. The FOP also provides legal assistance to its active sworn members in lawsuits against them.

 http://www.cophealth.com

The Law Enforcement Wellness Association is an organization dedicated to the physical and psychological health of police officers. You will find articles on physical and psychological fitness, and how to deal with everyday stress in law enforcement.

# Chapter 2

 http://www.readingcomprehensionconnection.com/

Online lessons to improve reading comprehension.

 http://www.reading.org

Detailed articles about reading and comprehension.

 http://www.hio.ft.hanze.nl/thar/reading.htm

Tips and techniques for improving reading.

# Chapter 3

 http://www.mindtools.com

This site contain articles explaining the mechanics of memory and how you can improve your memory by following a number of mind exercises.

http://www.officer.com

This site contains informative articles on current law enforcement trends and practices.

# Chapter 4

 http://www.multimap.com

Street layout for all the major cities and towns.

 http://www.randmcnally.com

Trip planning guide.

 http://www.mapquest.com/

Street layout for all the major cities and towns.

# Chapter 5

Even though "Need to Know More" resources are limited for this topic, improving analytical skills in general tends to help develop skills needed to process information as a police officer. The following sites are worth checking out as practice on honing your analytical skills.

 http://www.job-interview.net/Bank/QAnalyticalSkills.htm

Site contains general interview guide and tips/essays on improving analytical skills.

 http://www.write-an-essay.com/show-your-analytical-skills.html

Short essay on developing analytical and written communication skills.

# Chapter 6

 http://www.grammarstation.com

Visit this site to explore and learn the English language and understand the correct grammar usage.

http://www.edufind.com

This site, among informative articles about English language, provides a search engine to locate educational and informational resources available on the internet for students and educational professionals.

# Chapter 7

 http://www.cocosheriff.org/recruiting/oral_int_tips.htm

This is a sample interview preparation site. This site contains guide on how to prepare questions and how the interview results are evaluated.

 http://www.parks.ca.gov/default.asp?page_id=21271

Interview preparation site with guide on different interview topics.

 http://www.policeemployment.com/interview/

Sample interview preparation site. This site contains guide on how to prepare questions and how the interview is evaluated.

 http://www.lasd.org/recruitment/Oral_Interview.htm

This site contains guide on how to prepare questions and areas of evaluations.

# Chapter 8

 http://www.ncoer.com/apft/

This site lists useful ideas on how to improve overall fitness by United States Army standards.

 http://www.24hourfitness.com

This site contains articles on improving general fitness and nutrition.

 http://www.bodyworks-nutrition.com/fitar.html

This site contains articles on improving general fitness.

# Chapter 9

 http://www.time-management-tools.com/articles/index.htm

Informative articles with practical advice on how to manage your time to its full capacity.

 http://www.mindtools.com/pages/main/newMN_HTE.htm

Everyday practical tips on time management and goal setting.

# Chapter 10

 http://www.eop.mu.edu/study/

Short practical advice and general test-taking tips.

 http://www.bucks.edu/~specpop/tests.htm

General advice on test taking.

 http://www.questia.com/Index.jsp?CRID=test_taking&OFFID=se1&KEY=test_taking

Online library of test-taking strategies.

# Glossary

## abbreviated notes

A self-created set of abbreviations that help while taking down notes for study. Abbreviated notes are particularly useful during the study period for preparing for the police officer written test. These notes are also helpful in noting down information in the limited time given for preparation just before the test.

## agencies

This term, when referred to in the book, means different police departments.

## consistent pattern

This term is used particularly to help you with your writing skills. Sentences should be written so they should follow a certain pattern or style. This is particularly important in the case of writing reports, and those who want to be in law enforcement must be able to write reports well. This is also related to paragraph writing, which is also part of the police exam written test.

## crime scenes

This is the physical location where a crime has occurred.

## direct routes

This is the shortest way of getting from point A to point B. This is important to you as a police candidate because you must be able to locate the most direct route to the scene of a problem requiring police attention.

## field investigation reports

These are initial investigative reports taken by the uniform officer who is working the district.

## five-minute introduction

A memorized personal statement of introduction to a customer or employer that you can completely recite in five minutes. You will need to prepare this introduction for the oral interview that is part of the police officer selection process.

## flexibility

This is the ability of a joint to move through a normal range of motion of bending and a stretching of the muscles surrounding it. Improving flexibility is important for the physical agility test that is a part of the police officer selection process.

## incident reports

This term is mostly used in police work to refer to a report of an occurrence or incident.

## individual interview

An employment interview with one person; for example, the human resource manager or the chief of police.

## information organization

This term means to be able to categorize information according to its correct themes. Information organization will be required for all aspects related to preparation for the police officer selection, especially for studying and preparing for the oral interview.

## law definitions

These are law summaries written for law enforcement officers to use in the field.

For example: Burglary—A person who knowingly and intentionally enters a residence or dwelling with an intention to commit felony, commits burglary, a Class C felony.

## memorization

Learning in a way so that you are able to recall the information exactly. Some information to be learned for the police officer exam is based on facts and figures and must be memorized.

## negatives

Words that denote something negative, such as *no*, *never*, *not*, and so on. Questions related to negatives might be given in the language section of the police officer written test.

## notes

This term means to jot down brief, summarized accounts. Candidates wanting to take part in the police officer exam should practice taking down notes. This is beneficial both for better study habits as well as for police field work, when you need to take down details and facts at crime scenes or other locations requiring police assistance. Your notes will be critical for creating effective and accurate police reports in the field.

## observation

The act of noticing and paying attention. In police work, it is important that a police officer notices or observes details so that no point escapes him or her.

## oral interview

This is the interview portion of the police selection process. This interview is a significant part of the police officer selection exam that occurs when the candidate is interviewed by a board or the chief of police.

## personal inventory
An essay or list of bulleted items describing personal achievements; that is, those achievements not related to your job. Personal inventory is important when preparing for an oral interview. It allows you to think in advance about what you have accomplished in life and how you will communicate this to the interviewers.

## physical agility standards
This term refers to the score required to pass the physical agility test.

## physical agility test
This is a person's test of physical stamina and endurance. The physical agility test is a part of the police officer selection process in which different tasks are given to candidates to perform in a specific time period.

## police dispatches
This term refers to police communication orders that are intended to call for help when it is needed by district officers.

## prioritize
This term means to place tasks, or any other points, in order of importance. This is an important action to take when planning for study time while you are preparing for the police exam.

## professional accomplishments
This term refers to an essay or list of bulleted items listing work-related achievements. Personal accomplishments are different from a personal inventory. In a personal inventory, you are evaluating whether being a police officer is something for you. Or, if you have the qualities needed to become a good police officer. On the other hand, professional accomplishments are accomplishments in your personal and professional life. Again, making a list of your professional accomplishments will help you successfully answer questions in the oral interview.

## punctuation
Punctuation is the use of commas, semicolons, dashes, exclamation marks, and question marks while writing. You must have solid punctuation skills when taking the writing sections of the written portion of the police exam.

## push-ups
This is a physical exercise that requires the performer to push his body weight using the upper arms, triceps, and shoulder muscles. Push-ups are used to build upper body strength. As a test, push-ups measure the endurance of the chest, shoulder, and triceps muscles.

## qualifiers
These are words that alter a sentence or statement, such as *always*, *most*, and *often*. During the police officer written test, it is important for candidates to recognize qualifiers in order to more accurately understand what a question is asking.

### resist arrest

This term is used for suspects who try to avoid being arrested.

### resume

This is a document that lists goals, education, and employment experience. A resume is mostly used as an introduction to employers.

### retention

This is your ability to remember key points about text and photos given to you during the reading and preparation phase of the exam. It is very important to retain maximum information. During the written test, you will be required to recall a variety of information. Retention is also critical in police work as you will need to remember facts and key points concerning incidents.

### run scenarios

These are situations of short, police-related accounts based on calls for help.

For example: Officer Jones and Officer Smith were dispatched to 987 Main Street to investigate a residence burglary.

### self-discipline

This is the act of controlling yourself. This is a critical task to master as you prepare for the police exam. You need this to establish study times and focus for the content you need to master for the exam.

### sentence structure

This term refers to the way in which a sentence is written and how is it worded. Using correct sentence structure is useful when writing police reports.

### sit-ups

This is a physical exercise that requires the performer to sit up by using his stomach muscles. The exercise is used to build stomach muscles.

### skilled observer

This is a person trained to observe a variety of information. For example, in police work, an officer is required to notice even minor details while recording an account, questioning for information, and performing many other police-related tasks.

### spatial orientation

This refers to the natural ability to maintain the direction your body is facing. Spatial orientation is important and relevant to the physical agility test that is part of the police officer selection process.

### sprinting

This term refers to quick or fast-speed running. This is a requirement of the physical agility test that is a part of the police officer selection process.

### standard operating procedures

This term refers to one way of performing a certain task across the whole police department.

### street grid

This term refers to a square block that is created by intersecting north-, south-, east-, and west-running streets. These are used for map-reading questions in the police officer exam.

### structured oral interview

This is an employment interviewing environment in which all the participating candidates are asked the same questions and their responses are evaluated according to a set standard of answers.

### study area

This is a designated area in your home, away from all distractions, to be used only for studying purposes.

### subject-verb agreement

This term means that there is an agreement between the subjects and verbs you use in writing. Plural subjects require plural verbs and singular subjects require singular verbs. This could be assessed as part of the language portion of the police officer written test.

### suspect

This term refers to a person who is considered to have possibly committed a crime.

### tasks

These are everyday jobs or other responsibilities.

### tense consistency

This term refers to a person's ability to maintain the correct tense while writing. For example, if you're writing a report in the present tense, you should write the *entire* account in the present tense. This is especially important for writing accounts in police reports.

### thank you letter

This is a formal letter of appreciation sent to an interviewer or the interview board by the interviewee after the interview.

### two-minute introduction

This is a memorized personal statement introducing yourself to a customer or employer that you can recite and finish in two minutes. You should prepare this introduction for the oral interview that is part of the police officer selection process.

### vertical jump

This term refers to the ability to reach your highest point vertically using lower-body explosive power. This type of jump is becoming a standard test for the police officer selection process.

# Index

## A

accident reports, 99-102

active learning, 27-28, 175

addresses

    directional attributes, 69

    numbering system, 69

advancement, 12

agility tests, 146

    demonstrations, 153

    events, 147-148

    fexibility tests

        guidelines for, 156

        improving test scores, 159

    push-ups

        guidelines for, 153-154

        improving test scores, 157

    resting, 154-155

    running

        guidelines for, 156

        improving test scores, 158-159

        sprints workouts, 158-159

    sit-ups

        guidelines for, 154-155

        improving test scores, 157

    standards, 148

    strategies for

        early starts, 172

        pacing, 173

        personal limitations, 172

        rehearsals, 173

        stopwatches, 173

analytical skills improvement Web sites, 323

answering

    all questions (oral interview strategies), 172

    reading comprehension questions, 26

answers

    oral interview preparation, 134-135

    predicting (test-taking strategies), 181

    reviewing (test-taking strategies), 169, 185

# D–E

dashes (grammar), 114

data extraction (reading comprehension exam section), 37-41

designated study areas (test-preparation strategies), 167

direct route questions (geographical orientation exam questions), examples of, 71-75

directional attributes (addresses), 69

discipline (test-taking strategies), 166

double negatives (grammar), 114

dressing for oral interviews, 138

drug screening (applicant screening process), 20

dummy dragging, physical agility tests, 148

early starts
  oral interview strategies, 171
  physical agility test strategies, 172

eating habits (test-preparation strategies), 166

educational opportunities, 9

employment applications (applicant screening process)
  fingerprints, 15
  required documents, 15
  required information, 14

employment information websites
  FOP (Fraternal Order of Police), 322
  Law Enforcement Jobs, 322
  Officer.com, 321

evidence inventory and analysis forms, 90

exam formats
  grammar, 110
  memory retention, 48

exams
  formats
    grammar, 110
    memory retention, 48
  geographical orientation section
    direct route questions, 71-75
    follow the path questions, 75-77
    landmark/spatial orientation questions, 77-79
  MMPI, 17-18
  polygraph tests, 18-19
  reading comprehension section
    active learning, 27-28
    answering questions, 26
    data extraction, 37-41
    law definition questions, 29-31
    policy and procedure questions, 32-37
    taking notes, 26-27, 41-42
  written exams (applicant screening process), 14

exclamation marks (!),
grammar, 114

expectations (test-taking strategies),
170

extracting data (reading
comprehension exam section),
37-41

**F**

fingerprints (employment
applications), 15

fitness websites, 324

five-minute introductions (oral
interviews), 131

flashcards (test-preparation
strategies), 167

flexbility tests (physical agility
tests), 147, 156, 159

floor plans, memory retention
exam scenarios, 56-59

follow the path questions
(geographical orientation exam
questions), examples of, 75-77

FOP (Fraternal Order of Police)
website, 322

formatting resumes, 130

forms
accident reports, 99-102
arrest reports, 92-95, 99
charging information, 91
evidence inventory and
analysis, 90
traffic tickets, 96-99

**G**

geographical orientation
beat integrity, 69
direct route exam questions,
examples of, 71-75
follow the path exam questions,
examples of, 75-77
landmark/spatial orientation
exam questions, examples of,
77-79
street layouts, 68-70

global learning styles, 175

grading schemes, knowing
(test-taking strategies), 179

grammar
apostrophes, 112-113
double negatives, 114
exam formats, 110
pronunciations, 115
punctuation, 114-115
sentence fragments, 113
sentence structures, 112
spelling, 115
spelling guide, 118-120
subject-verb agreement, 111
tense consistency, 111
vocabulary
syllable division, 116
word confustion, 116-118
websites, 323

grids (street layouts), 69-70

## H–I

health benefits, 6

highlighting keywords (test-taking strategies), 180

holidays, 6

improving physical agility test scores, 157-159

information organization (memory retention techniques), 49

information retention

exam formats, 48

exam scenarios

building floor plans, 56-59

crime scenes, 50-52

suspect information, 52-56

information organization, 49

notes, 49

interviews

applicant screening process, 14

oral

building confidence, 138

introductions, 131

personal appearance, 138

personal/professional, 128-129

positive statements, 136

preparing for, 133-137

resumes, 129-131

strategies for, 171-172, 176

thank you letters, 138-139

polygraph tests, 18-19

preparation websites, 324

intuitive learning styles, 175

inventories (personal/professional), 128-129

## J–K

job descriptions, 3-4

benefits, 6

advancement, 12

educational opportunities, 9

holidays, 6

lunch breaks, 6

salary, 6

television versus reality, 5

work shifts, 5-6

job information websites

FOP (Fraternal Order of Police), 322

Law Enforcement Jobs, 322

Officer.com, 321

job requirements, 7-8

keywords, highlighting (test-taking strategies), 180

knowing number of questions vs. time alloted for answers (oral interview strategies), 171

## L

landmark orientation questions (geographical orientation exam questions), 77-79

last-minute time management checklist (test-taking strategies), 170-171

# O

obstacle courses (physical agility tests), 148

officer arrest reports, 92
  instructions, 94, 99
  sample questions, 95
  sample scenarios, 93

Officer.com website, 321-323

oral interviews
  applicant screening process, 14
  confidence, building, 138
  introductions, 131
  personal appearance, 138
  personal/professional inventories, 128-129
  positive statements, 136
  preparing for
    answers, 134-135
    power statements, 135
    practice questions, 135-137
    questions, 133
  resumes, 129-131
  strategies for
    answering all questions, 172
    early starts, 171
    knowing number of questions versus time alloted for answers, 171
    listening to questions, 172
    saving questions for later, 172
    sound bites, 176
  thank you letters, 138-139

# P

pacing (physical agility test strategies), 173

pay, 6

performance reviews (test-preparation strategies), 167

personal appearance, oral interviews, 138

personal inventories, 128 129

personal learning styles, 175

personal limitations (physical agility test strategies), 172

personal references (background investigation), 16-17

physical ability (applicant screening process), 14

physical agility tests, 146
  demonstrations, 153
  events, 147-148
  flexibility tests, 156, 159
  push-ups, 153-154, 157
  resting, 154-155
  running
    guidelines for, 156
    improving test scores, 158-159
    sprints workouts, 158-159
  sit-ups, 154-157
  standards, 148
  strategies for
    early starts, 172
    pacing, 173
    personal limitations, 172
    rehearsals, 173
    stopwatches, 173

# Q

qualifiers, identifying (test-taking strategies), 181-182

question marks (?), grammar, 115

questions

answering

all questions (oral interview strategies), 172

maintaining speed when (test-taking strategies), 185

reviewing answers (test-taking strategies), 185

writing legibly (test-taking strategies), 186

listening to (oral interview strategies), 172

negatives, identifying (test-taking strategies), 182

oral interview preparation, 133-137

prioritizing (test-taking strategies), 169

qualifiers, identifying (test-taking strategies), 181-182

reading comprehension questions

answering, 26

law definition questions, 29-31

policy and procedure questions, 32-37

saving for later (oral interview strategies), 172

types of, identifying (test-taking strategies), 183-184

understanding (test-taking strategies)

highlighting keywords, 180

identifying negatives, 182

identifying qualifiers, 181-182

identifying types of questions, 183-184

looking for clues, 181

maintaining speed when answering questions, 185

predicting correct answers, 181

reading questions in detail, 180

reviewing questions, 185

twists in questions, 180-181

writing legibly, 186

# R

ranking structures, 13

reading comprehension section (exams)

active learning, 27-28

data extraction, 37-41

notes, taking, 26-27, 41-42

questions

answering, 26

law definition questions, 29-31

policy and procedure questions, 32-37

websites, 322

reading questions in detail (test-taking strategies), 180

reflective learning styles, 175

If you would like more answer sheets than are available here, visit this book's website at www.examcram.com. You can download and print as many answer sheets as you want.

# Answer Sheet for Practice Exam

**Directions:** Read each question carefully and choose the best answer. Fill in the oval completely with a soft lead pencil.

1. (A) (B) (C) (D)
2. (A) (B) (C) (D)
3. (A) (B) (C) (D)
4. (A) (B) (C) (D)
5. (A) (B) (C) (D)
6. (A) (B) (C) (D)
7. (A) (B) (C) (D)
8. (A) (B) (C) (D)
9. (A) (B) (C) (D)
10. (A) (B) (C) (D)
11. (A) (B) (C) (D)
12. (A) (B) (C) (D)
13. (A) (B) (C) (D)
14. (A) (B) (C) (D)
15. (A) (B) (C) (D)
16. (A) (B) (C) (D)
17. (A) (B) (C) (D)
18. (A) (B) (C) (D)
19. (A) (B) (C) (D)

20. (A) (B) (C) (D)
21. (A) (B) (C) (D)
22. (A) (B) (C) (D)
23. (A) (B) (C) (D)
24. (A) (B) (C) (D)
25. (A) (B) (C) (D)
26. (A) (B) (C) (D)
27. (A) (B) (C) (D)
28. (A) (B) (C) (D)
29. (A) (B) (C) (D)
30. (A) (B) (C) (D)
31. (A) (B) (C) (D)
32. (A) (B) (C) (D)
33. (A) (B) (C) (D)
34. (A) (B) (C) (D)
35. (A) (B) (C) (D)
36. (A) (B) (C) (D)
37. (A) (B) (C) (D)
38. (A) (B) (C) (D)

39. (A) (B) (C) (D)
40. (A) (B) (C) (D)
41. (A) (B) (C) (D)
42. (A) (B) (C) (D)
43. (A) (B) (C) (D)
44. (A) (B) (C) (D)
45. (A) (B) (C) (D)
46. (A) (B) (C) (D)
47. (A) (B) (C) (D)
48. (A) (B) (C) (D)
49. (A) (B) (C) (D)
50. (A) (B) (C) (D)
51. (A) (B) (C) (D)
52. (A) (B) (C) (D)
53. (A) (B) (C) (D)
54. (A) (B) (C) (D)
55. (A) (B) (C) (D)
56. (A) (B) (C) (D)
57. (A) (B) (C) (D)

Answer Sheet

58. Ⓐ Ⓑ Ⓒ Ⓓ          73. Ⓐ Ⓑ Ⓒ Ⓓ          87. Ⓐ Ⓑ Ⓒ Ⓓ

59. Ⓐ Ⓑ Ⓒ Ⓓ          74. Ⓐ Ⓑ Ⓒ Ⓓ          88. Ⓐ Ⓑ Ⓒ Ⓓ

60. Ⓐ Ⓑ Ⓒ Ⓓ          75. Ⓐ Ⓑ Ⓒ Ⓓ          89. Ⓐ Ⓑ Ⓒ Ⓓ

61. Ⓐ Ⓑ Ⓒ Ⓓ          76. Ⓐ Ⓑ Ⓒ Ⓓ          90. Ⓐ Ⓑ Ⓒ Ⓓ

62. Ⓐ Ⓑ Ⓒ Ⓓ          77. Ⓐ Ⓑ Ⓒ Ⓓ          91. Ⓐ Ⓑ Ⓒ Ⓓ

63. Ⓐ Ⓑ Ⓒ Ⓓ          78. Ⓐ Ⓑ Ⓒ Ⓓ          92. Ⓐ Ⓑ Ⓒ Ⓓ

64. Ⓐ Ⓑ Ⓒ Ⓓ          79. Ⓐ Ⓑ Ⓒ Ⓓ          93. Ⓐ Ⓑ Ⓒ Ⓓ

65. Ⓐ Ⓑ Ⓒ Ⓓ          80. Ⓐ Ⓑ Ⓒ Ⓓ          94. Ⓐ Ⓑ Ⓒ Ⓓ

66. Ⓐ Ⓑ Ⓒ Ⓓ          81. Ⓐ Ⓑ Ⓒ Ⓓ          95. Ⓐ Ⓑ Ⓒ Ⓓ

67. Ⓐ Ⓑ Ⓒ Ⓓ          82. Ⓐ Ⓑ Ⓒ Ⓓ          96. Ⓐ Ⓑ Ⓒ Ⓓ

68. Ⓐ Ⓑ Ⓒ Ⓓ          83. Ⓐ Ⓑ Ⓒ Ⓓ          97. Ⓐ Ⓑ Ⓒ Ⓓ

69. Ⓐ Ⓑ Ⓒ Ⓓ          84. Ⓐ Ⓑ Ⓒ Ⓓ          98. Ⓐ Ⓑ Ⓒ Ⓓ

70. Ⓐ Ⓑ Ⓒ Ⓓ          85. Ⓐ Ⓑ Ⓒ Ⓓ          99. Ⓐ Ⓑ Ⓒ Ⓓ

71. Ⓐ Ⓑ Ⓒ Ⓓ          86. Ⓐ Ⓑ Ⓒ Ⓓ          100. Ⓐ Ⓑ Ⓒ Ⓓ

72. Ⓐ Ⓑ Ⓒ Ⓓ

# Answer Sheet for Practice Exam

**Directions:** Read each question carefully and choose the best answer. Fill in the oval completely with a soft lead pencil.

1. Ⓐ Ⓑ Ⓒ Ⓓ   20. Ⓐ Ⓑ Ⓒ Ⓓ   39. Ⓐ Ⓑ Ⓒ Ⓓ
2. Ⓐ Ⓑ Ⓒ Ⓓ   21. Ⓐ Ⓑ Ⓒ Ⓓ   40. Ⓐ Ⓑ Ⓒ Ⓓ
3. Ⓐ Ⓑ Ⓒ Ⓓ   22. Ⓐ Ⓑ Ⓒ Ⓓ   41. Ⓐ Ⓑ Ⓒ Ⓓ
4. Ⓐ Ⓑ Ⓒ Ⓓ   23. Ⓐ Ⓑ Ⓒ Ⓓ   42. Ⓐ Ⓑ Ⓒ Ⓓ
5. Ⓐ Ⓑ Ⓒ Ⓓ   24. Ⓐ Ⓑ Ⓒ Ⓓ   43. Ⓐ Ⓑ Ⓒ Ⓓ
6. Ⓐ Ⓑ Ⓒ Ⓓ   25. Ⓐ Ⓑ Ⓒ Ⓓ   44. Ⓐ Ⓑ Ⓒ Ⓓ
7. Ⓐ Ⓑ Ⓒ Ⓓ   26. Ⓐ Ⓑ Ⓒ Ⓓ   45. Ⓐ Ⓑ Ⓒ Ⓓ
8. Ⓐ Ⓑ Ⓒ Ⓓ   27. Ⓐ Ⓑ Ⓒ Ⓓ   46. Ⓐ Ⓑ Ⓒ Ⓓ
9. Ⓐ Ⓑ Ⓒ Ⓓ   28. Ⓐ Ⓑ Ⓒ Ⓓ   47. Ⓐ Ⓑ Ⓒ Ⓓ
10. Ⓐ Ⓑ Ⓒ Ⓓ   29. Ⓐ Ⓑ Ⓒ Ⓓ   48. Ⓐ Ⓑ Ⓒ Ⓓ
11. Ⓐ Ⓑ Ⓒ Ⓓ   30. Ⓐ Ⓑ Ⓒ Ⓓ   49. Ⓐ Ⓑ Ⓒ Ⓓ
12. Ⓐ Ⓑ Ⓒ Ⓓ   31. Ⓐ Ⓑ Ⓒ Ⓓ   50. Ⓐ Ⓑ Ⓒ Ⓓ
13. Ⓐ Ⓑ Ⓒ Ⓓ   32. Ⓐ Ⓑ Ⓒ Ⓓ   51. Ⓐ Ⓑ Ⓒ Ⓓ
14. Ⓐ Ⓑ Ⓒ Ⓓ   33. Ⓐ Ⓑ Ⓒ Ⓓ   52. Ⓐ Ⓑ Ⓒ Ⓓ
15. Ⓐ Ⓑ Ⓒ Ⓓ   34. Ⓐ Ⓑ Ⓒ Ⓓ   53. Ⓐ Ⓑ Ⓒ Ⓓ
16. Ⓐ Ⓑ Ⓒ Ⓓ   35. Ⓐ Ⓑ Ⓒ Ⓓ   54. Ⓐ Ⓑ Ⓒ Ⓓ
17. Ⓐ Ⓑ Ⓒ Ⓓ   36. Ⓐ Ⓑ Ⓒ Ⓓ   55. Ⓐ Ⓑ Ⓒ Ⓓ
18. Ⓐ Ⓑ Ⓒ Ⓓ   37. Ⓐ Ⓑ Ⓒ Ⓓ   56. Ⓐ Ⓑ Ⓒ Ⓓ
19. Ⓐ Ⓑ Ⓒ Ⓓ   38. Ⓐ Ⓑ Ⓒ Ⓓ   57. Ⓐ Ⓑ Ⓒ Ⓓ

Answer Sheet

58. Ⓐ Ⓑ Ⓒ Ⓓ    73. Ⓐ Ⓑ Ⓒ Ⓓ    87. Ⓐ Ⓑ Ⓒ Ⓓ

59. Ⓐ Ⓑ Ⓒ Ⓓ    74. Ⓐ Ⓑ Ⓒ Ⓓ    88. Ⓐ Ⓑ Ⓒ Ⓓ

60. Ⓐ Ⓑ Ⓒ Ⓓ    75. Ⓐ Ⓑ Ⓒ Ⓓ    89. Ⓐ Ⓑ Ⓒ Ⓓ

61. Ⓐ Ⓑ Ⓒ Ⓓ    76. Ⓐ Ⓑ Ⓒ Ⓓ    90. Ⓐ Ⓑ Ⓒ Ⓓ

62. Ⓐ Ⓑ Ⓒ Ⓓ    77. Ⓐ Ⓑ Ⓒ Ⓓ    91. Ⓐ Ⓑ Ⓒ Ⓓ

63. Ⓐ Ⓑ Ⓒ Ⓓ    78. Ⓐ Ⓑ Ⓒ Ⓓ    92. Ⓐ Ⓑ Ⓒ Ⓓ

64. Ⓐ Ⓑ Ⓒ Ⓓ    79. Ⓐ Ⓑ Ⓒ Ⓓ    93. Ⓐ Ⓑ Ⓒ Ⓓ

65. Ⓐ Ⓑ Ⓒ Ⓓ    80. Ⓐ Ⓑ Ⓒ Ⓓ    94. Ⓐ Ⓑ Ⓒ Ⓓ

66. Ⓐ Ⓑ Ⓒ Ⓓ    81. Ⓐ Ⓑ Ⓒ Ⓓ    95. Ⓐ Ⓑ Ⓒ Ⓓ

67. Ⓐ Ⓑ Ⓒ Ⓓ    82. Ⓐ Ⓑ Ⓒ Ⓓ    96. Ⓐ Ⓑ Ⓒ Ⓓ

68. Ⓐ Ⓑ Ⓒ Ⓓ    83. Ⓐ Ⓑ Ⓒ Ⓓ    97. Ⓐ Ⓑ Ⓒ Ⓓ

69. Ⓐ Ⓑ Ⓒ Ⓓ    84. Ⓐ Ⓑ Ⓒ Ⓓ    98. Ⓐ Ⓑ Ⓒ Ⓓ

70. Ⓐ Ⓑ Ⓒ Ⓓ    85. Ⓐ Ⓑ Ⓒ Ⓓ    99. Ⓐ Ⓑ Ⓒ Ⓓ

71. Ⓐ Ⓑ Ⓒ Ⓓ    86. Ⓐ Ⓑ Ⓒ Ⓓ    100. Ⓐ Ⓑ Ⓒ Ⓓ

72. Ⓐ Ⓑ Ⓒ Ⓓ

# Answer Sheet for Practice Exam

**Directions:** Read each question carefully and choose the best answer. Fill in the oval completely with a soft lead pencil.

1. (A) (B) (C) (D)
2. (A) (B) (C) (D)
3. (A) (B) (C) (D)
4. (A) (B) (C) (D)
5. (A) (B) (C) (D)
6. (A) (B) (C) (D)
7. (A) (B) (C) (D)
8. (A) (B) (C) (D)
9. (A) (B) (C) (D)
10. (A) (B) (C) (D)
11. (A) (B) (C) (D)
12. (A) (B) (C) (D)
13. (A) (B) (C) (D)
14. (A) (B) (C) (D)
15. (A) (B) (C) (D)
16. (A) (B) (C) (D)
17. (A) (B) (C) (D)
18. (A) (B) (C) (D)
19. (A) (B) (C) (D)

20. (A) (B) (C) (D)
21. (A) (B) (C) (D)
22. (A) (B) (C) (D)
23. (A) (B) (C) (D)
24. (A) (B) (C) (D)
25. (A) (B) (C) (D)
26. (A) (B) (C) (D)
27. (A) (B) (C) (D)
28. (A) (B) (C) (D)
29. (A) (B) (C) (D)
30. (A) (B) (C) (D)
31. (A) (B) (C) (D)
32. (A) (B) (C) (D)
33. (A) (B) (C) (D)
34. (A) (B) (C) (D)
35. (A) (B) (C) (D)
36. (A) (B) (C) (D)
37. (A) (B) (C) (D)
38. (A) (B) (C) (D)

39. (A) (B) (C) (D)
40. (A) (B) (C) (D)
41. (A) (B) (C) (D)
42. (A) (B) (C) (D)
43. (A) (B) (C) (D)
44. (A) (B) (C) (D)
45. (A) (B) (C) (D)
46. (A) (B) (C) (D)
47. (A) (B) (C) (D)
48. (A) (B) (C) (D)
49. (A) (B) (C) (D)
50. (A) (B) (C) (D)
51. (A) (B) (C) (D)
52. (A) (B) (C) (D)
53. (A) (B) (C) (D)
54. (A) (B) (C) (D)
55. (A) (B) (C) (D)
56. (A) (B) (C) (D)
57. (A) (B) (C) (D)

Answer Sheet

58. (A) (B) (C) (D)      73. (A) (B) (C) (D)      87. (A) (B) (C) (D)

59. (A) (B) (C) (D)      74. (A) (B) (C) (D)      88. (A) (B) (C) (D)

60. (A) (B) (C) (D)      75. (A) (B) (C) (D)      89. (A) (B) (C) (D)

61. (A) (B) (C) (D)      76. (A) (B) (C) (D)      90. (A) (B) (C) (D)

62. (A) (B) (C) (D)      77. (A) (B) (C) (D)      91. (A) (B) (C) (D)

63. (A) (B) (C) (D)      78. (A) (B) (C) (D)      92. (A) (B) (C) (D)

64. (A) (B) (C) (D)      79. (A) (B) (C) (D)      93. (A) (B) (C) (D)

65. (A) (B) (C) (D)      80. (A) (B) (C) (D)      94. (A) (B) (C) (D)

66. (A) (B) (C) (D)      81. (A) (B) (C) (D)      95. (A) (B) (C) (D)

67. (A) (B) (C) (D)      82. (A) (B) (C) (D)      96. (A) (B) (C) (D)

68. (A) (B) (C) (D)      83. (A) (B) (C) (D)      97. (A) (B) (C) (D)

69. (A) (B) (C) (D)      84. (A) (B) (C) (D)      98. (A) (B) (C) (D)

70. (A) (B) (C) (D)      85. (A) (B) (C) (D)      99. (A) (B) (C) (D)

71. (A) (B) (C) (D)      86. (A) (B) (C) (D)      100. (A) (B) (C) (D)

72. (A) (B) (C) (D)

# Answer Sheet for Practice Exam

**Directions:** Read each question carefully and choose the best answer. Fill in the oval completely with a soft lead pencil.

1. Ⓐ Ⓑ Ⓒ Ⓓ
2. Ⓐ Ⓑ Ⓒ Ⓓ
3. Ⓐ Ⓑ Ⓒ Ⓓ
4. Ⓐ Ⓑ Ⓒ Ⓓ
5. Ⓐ Ⓑ Ⓒ Ⓓ
6. Ⓐ Ⓑ Ⓒ Ⓓ
7. Ⓐ Ⓑ Ⓒ Ⓓ
8. Ⓐ Ⓑ Ⓒ Ⓓ
9. Ⓐ Ⓑ Ⓒ Ⓓ
10. Ⓐ Ⓑ Ⓒ Ⓓ
11. Ⓐ Ⓑ Ⓒ Ⓓ
12. Ⓐ Ⓑ Ⓒ Ⓓ
13. Ⓐ Ⓑ Ⓒ Ⓓ
14. Ⓐ Ⓑ Ⓒ Ⓓ
15. Ⓐ Ⓑ Ⓒ Ⓓ
16. Ⓐ Ⓑ Ⓒ Ⓓ
17. Ⓐ Ⓑ Ⓒ Ⓓ
18. Ⓐ Ⓑ Ⓒ Ⓓ
19. Ⓐ Ⓑ Ⓒ Ⓓ

20. Ⓐ Ⓑ Ⓒ Ⓓ
21. Ⓐ Ⓑ Ⓒ Ⓓ
22. Ⓐ Ⓑ Ⓒ Ⓓ
23. Ⓐ Ⓑ Ⓒ Ⓓ
24. Ⓐ Ⓑ Ⓒ Ⓓ
25. Ⓐ Ⓑ Ⓒ Ⓓ
26. Ⓐ Ⓑ Ⓒ Ⓓ
27. Ⓐ Ⓑ Ⓒ Ⓓ
28. Ⓐ Ⓑ Ⓒ Ⓓ
29. Ⓐ Ⓑ Ⓒ Ⓓ
30. Ⓐ Ⓑ Ⓒ Ⓓ
31. Ⓐ Ⓑ Ⓒ Ⓓ
32. Ⓐ Ⓑ Ⓒ Ⓓ
33. Ⓐ Ⓑ Ⓒ Ⓓ
34. Ⓐ Ⓑ Ⓒ Ⓓ
35. Ⓐ Ⓑ Ⓒ Ⓓ
36. Ⓐ Ⓑ Ⓒ Ⓓ
37. Ⓐ Ⓑ Ⓒ Ⓓ
38. Ⓐ Ⓑ Ⓒ Ⓓ

39. Ⓐ Ⓑ Ⓒ Ⓓ
40. Ⓐ Ⓑ Ⓒ Ⓓ
41. Ⓐ Ⓑ Ⓒ Ⓓ
42. Ⓐ Ⓑ Ⓒ Ⓓ
43. Ⓐ Ⓑ Ⓒ Ⓓ
44. Ⓐ Ⓑ Ⓒ Ⓓ
45. Ⓐ Ⓑ Ⓒ Ⓓ
46. Ⓐ Ⓑ Ⓒ Ⓓ
47. Ⓐ Ⓑ Ⓒ Ⓓ
48. Ⓐ Ⓑ Ⓒ Ⓓ
49. Ⓐ Ⓑ Ⓒ Ⓓ
50. Ⓐ Ⓑ Ⓒ Ⓓ
51. Ⓐ Ⓑ Ⓒ Ⓓ
52. Ⓐ Ⓑ Ⓒ Ⓓ
53. Ⓐ Ⓑ Ⓒ Ⓓ
54. Ⓐ Ⓑ Ⓒ Ⓓ
55. Ⓐ Ⓑ Ⓒ Ⓓ
56. Ⓐ Ⓑ Ⓒ Ⓓ
57. Ⓐ Ⓑ Ⓒ Ⓓ

Answer Sheet

58. Ⓐ Ⓑ Ⓒ Ⓓ

59. Ⓐ Ⓑ Ⓒ Ⓓ

60. Ⓐ Ⓑ Ⓒ Ⓓ

61. Ⓐ Ⓑ Ⓒ Ⓓ

62. Ⓐ Ⓑ Ⓒ Ⓓ

63. Ⓐ Ⓑ Ⓒ Ⓓ

64. Ⓐ Ⓑ Ⓒ Ⓓ

65. Ⓐ Ⓑ Ⓒ Ⓓ

66. Ⓐ Ⓑ Ⓒ Ⓓ

67. Ⓐ Ⓑ Ⓒ Ⓓ

68. Ⓐ Ⓑ Ⓒ Ⓓ

69. Ⓐ Ⓑ Ⓒ Ⓓ

70. Ⓐ Ⓑ Ⓒ Ⓓ

71. Ⓐ Ⓑ Ⓒ Ⓓ

72. Ⓐ Ⓑ Ⓒ Ⓓ

73. Ⓐ Ⓑ Ⓒ Ⓓ

74. Ⓐ Ⓑ Ⓒ Ⓓ

75. Ⓐ Ⓑ Ⓒ Ⓓ

76. Ⓐ Ⓑ Ⓒ Ⓓ

77. Ⓐ Ⓑ Ⓒ Ⓓ

78. Ⓐ Ⓑ Ⓒ Ⓓ

79. Ⓐ Ⓑ Ⓒ Ⓓ

80. Ⓐ Ⓑ Ⓒ Ⓓ

81. Ⓐ Ⓑ Ⓒ Ⓓ

82. Ⓐ Ⓑ Ⓒ Ⓓ

83. Ⓐ Ⓑ Ⓒ Ⓓ

84. Ⓐ Ⓑ Ⓒ Ⓓ

85. Ⓐ Ⓑ Ⓒ Ⓓ

86. Ⓐ Ⓑ Ⓒ Ⓓ

87. Ⓐ Ⓑ Ⓒ Ⓓ

88. Ⓐ Ⓑ Ⓒ Ⓓ

89. Ⓐ Ⓑ Ⓒ Ⓓ

90. Ⓐ Ⓑ Ⓒ Ⓓ

91. Ⓐ Ⓑ Ⓒ Ⓓ

92. Ⓐ Ⓑ Ⓒ Ⓓ

93. Ⓐ Ⓑ Ⓒ Ⓓ

94. Ⓐ Ⓑ Ⓒ Ⓓ

95. Ⓐ Ⓑ Ⓒ Ⓓ

96. Ⓐ Ⓑ Ⓒ Ⓓ

97. Ⓐ Ⓑ Ⓒ Ⓓ

98. Ⓐ Ⓑ Ⓒ Ⓓ

99. Ⓐ Ⓑ Ⓒ Ⓓ

100. Ⓐ Ⓑ Ⓒ Ⓓ

# Answer Sheet for Practice Exam

**Directions:** Read each question carefully and choose the best answer. Fill in the oval completely with a soft lead pencil.

1. Ⓐ Ⓑ Ⓒ Ⓓ    20. Ⓐ Ⓑ Ⓒ Ⓓ    39. Ⓐ Ⓑ Ⓒ Ⓓ

2. Ⓐ Ⓑ Ⓒ Ⓓ    21. Ⓐ Ⓑ Ⓒ Ⓓ    40. Ⓐ Ⓑ Ⓒ Ⓓ

3. Ⓐ Ⓑ Ⓒ Ⓓ    22. Ⓐ Ⓑ Ⓒ Ⓓ    41. Ⓐ Ⓑ Ⓒ Ⓓ

4. Ⓐ Ⓑ Ⓒ Ⓓ    23. Ⓐ Ⓑ Ⓒ Ⓓ    42. Ⓐ Ⓑ Ⓒ Ⓓ

5. Ⓐ Ⓑ Ⓒ Ⓓ    24. Ⓐ Ⓑ Ⓒ Ⓓ    43. Ⓐ Ⓑ Ⓒ Ⓓ

6. Ⓐ Ⓑ Ⓒ Ⓓ    25. Ⓐ Ⓑ Ⓒ Ⓓ    44. Ⓐ Ⓑ Ⓒ Ⓓ

7. Ⓐ Ⓑ Ⓒ Ⓓ    26. Ⓐ Ⓑ Ⓒ Ⓓ    45. Ⓐ Ⓑ Ⓒ Ⓓ

8. Ⓐ Ⓑ Ⓒ Ⓓ    27. Ⓐ Ⓑ Ⓒ Ⓓ    46. Ⓐ Ⓑ Ⓒ Ⓓ

9. Ⓐ Ⓑ Ⓒ Ⓓ    28. Ⓐ Ⓑ Ⓒ Ⓓ    47. Ⓐ Ⓑ Ⓒ Ⓓ

10. Ⓐ Ⓑ Ⓒ Ⓓ    29. Ⓐ Ⓑ Ⓒ Ⓓ    48. Ⓐ Ⓑ Ⓒ Ⓓ

11. Ⓐ Ⓑ Ⓒ Ⓓ    30. Ⓐ Ⓑ Ⓒ Ⓓ    49. Ⓐ Ⓑ Ⓒ Ⓓ

12. Ⓐ Ⓑ Ⓒ Ⓓ    31. Ⓐ Ⓑ Ⓒ Ⓓ    50. Ⓐ Ⓑ Ⓒ Ⓓ

13. Ⓐ Ⓑ Ⓒ Ⓓ    32. Ⓐ Ⓑ Ⓒ Ⓓ    51. Ⓐ Ⓑ Ⓒ Ⓓ

14. Ⓐ Ⓑ Ⓒ Ⓓ    33. Ⓐ Ⓑ Ⓒ Ⓓ    52. Ⓐ Ⓑ Ⓒ Ⓓ

15. Ⓐ Ⓑ Ⓒ Ⓓ    34. Ⓐ Ⓑ Ⓒ Ⓓ    53. Ⓐ Ⓑ Ⓒ Ⓓ

16. Ⓐ Ⓑ Ⓒ Ⓓ    35. Ⓐ Ⓑ Ⓒ Ⓓ    54. Ⓐ Ⓑ Ⓒ Ⓓ

17. Ⓐ Ⓑ Ⓒ Ⓓ    36. Ⓐ Ⓑ Ⓒ Ⓓ    55. Ⓐ Ⓑ Ⓒ Ⓓ

18. Ⓐ Ⓑ Ⓒ Ⓓ    37. Ⓐ Ⓑ Ⓒ Ⓓ    56. Ⓐ Ⓑ Ⓒ Ⓓ

19. Ⓐ Ⓑ Ⓒ Ⓓ    38. Ⓐ Ⓑ Ⓒ Ⓓ    57. Ⓐ Ⓑ Ⓒ Ⓓ

Answer Sheet

58. Ⓐ Ⓑ Ⓒ Ⓓ          73. Ⓐ Ⓑ Ⓒ Ⓓ          87. Ⓐ Ⓑ Ⓒ Ⓓ

59. Ⓐ Ⓑ Ⓒ Ⓓ          74. Ⓐ Ⓑ Ⓒ Ⓓ          88. Ⓐ Ⓑ Ⓒ Ⓓ

60. Ⓐ Ⓑ Ⓒ Ⓓ          75. Ⓐ Ⓑ Ⓒ Ⓓ          89. Ⓐ Ⓑ Ⓒ Ⓓ

61. Ⓐ Ⓑ Ⓒ Ⓓ          76. Ⓐ Ⓑ Ⓒ Ⓓ          90. Ⓐ Ⓑ Ⓒ Ⓓ

62. Ⓐ Ⓑ Ⓒ Ⓓ          77. Ⓐ Ⓑ Ⓒ Ⓓ          91. Ⓐ Ⓑ Ⓒ Ⓓ

63. Ⓐ Ⓑ Ⓒ Ⓓ          78. Ⓐ Ⓑ Ⓒ Ⓓ          92. Ⓐ Ⓑ Ⓒ Ⓓ

64. Ⓐ Ⓑ Ⓒ Ⓓ          79. Ⓐ Ⓑ Ⓒ Ⓓ          93. Ⓐ Ⓑ Ⓒ Ⓓ

65. Ⓐ Ⓑ Ⓒ Ⓓ          80. Ⓐ Ⓑ Ⓒ Ⓓ          94. Ⓐ Ⓑ Ⓒ Ⓓ

66. Ⓐ Ⓑ Ⓒ Ⓓ          81. Ⓐ Ⓑ Ⓒ Ⓓ          95. Ⓐ Ⓑ Ⓒ Ⓓ

67. Ⓐ Ⓑ Ⓒ Ⓓ          82. Ⓐ Ⓑ Ⓒ Ⓓ          96. Ⓐ Ⓑ Ⓒ Ⓓ

68. Ⓐ Ⓑ Ⓒ Ⓓ          83. Ⓐ Ⓑ Ⓒ Ⓓ          97. Ⓐ Ⓑ Ⓒ Ⓓ

69. Ⓐ Ⓑ Ⓒ Ⓓ          84. Ⓐ Ⓑ Ⓒ Ⓓ          98. Ⓐ Ⓑ Ⓒ Ⓓ

70. Ⓐ Ⓑ Ⓒ Ⓓ          85. Ⓐ Ⓑ Ⓒ Ⓓ          99. Ⓐ Ⓑ Ⓒ Ⓓ

71. Ⓐ Ⓑ Ⓒ Ⓓ          86. Ⓐ Ⓑ Ⓒ Ⓓ          100. Ⓐ Ⓑ Ⓒ Ⓓ

72. Ⓐ Ⓑ Ⓒ Ⓓ

## Arrest Form

| | | |
|---|---|---|
| 1. Arresting Officer | 2. ID Number | 3. Badge Number |
| 4. Transporting Officer | 5. ID Number | 6. Badge Number |

| | | | |
|---|---|---|---|
| 7. Arrestee | 8. DOB | 9. Age | |
| 10. Address | 11. City | 12. Zip Code | |
| 17. S.S.N. | 14. H. Phone | 15. W. Phone | |
| 16. Height | 17. Weight | 18. Hair | 19. Race | 20. Sex |

## Traffic Ticket

| 1. Date | 2. Time | 3. Location | |
|---|---|---|---|
| 4. Officer | 5. ID Number | | 6. Badge Number |
| 7. Assisting Officer | 8. ID Number | | 9. Badge Number |
| 10. Driver | 11. DOB | 12. Age | |
| 13. Address | 14. City | 15. Zip Code | |
| 16. S.S.N. | 17. H. Phone | 18. W. Phone | |
| 19. Vehicle Make | 20. Model | 21. Lic. | |

| 22. Charge | 23. Traffic Code |
|---|---|
| 24. Fine | 25. Due Date |

**Accident Report**

| 1. Investigating Officer  King, R | 2. ID Number  K-0221 | 3. Badge Number  844 |
|---|---|---|
| 4. Assisting Officer  Jones, B | 5. ID Number  J-2231 | 6. Badge Number  932 |

| Location  1512 E. Lawrence Street | Date  4-3-04 | Time  4:15 PM |
|---|---|---|

| 7. Driver 1  Smith, Michael | 8. DOB  9-22-80 | 9. Age  24 |
|---|---|---|
| 10. Address  1152 E. 16th Street | 11. City  Indianapolis | 12. Zip Code  46256 |
| 13. S.S.N.  314-06-9932 | 14. H. Phone  317-598-2241 | 15. W. Phone  317-632-1991 |
| 15. Vehicle 1  Green | 17. Make  Toyota | 18. Model  Corolla | 19. Lic.  34F7890 |
| Striking Vehicle | | | |

| 20. Driver 2  Kennedy, David | 21. D.O.B.  11-11-79 | 22. Age  25 |
|---|---|---|
| 23. Address  6332 W. Horseshoe Ln | 24. City  Indianapolis | 25. Zip Code  46232 |
| 27. S.S.N.  312-86-2219 | 28. H. Phone  317-635-7381 | 29. W. Phone  317-925-6619 |
| 10 Vehicle  Red | 17. Make  Jeep | 18. Model  Wrangler | 19. Lic.  63A5253 |

# Accident Report

| 1. Investigating Officer *Smith, D* | 2. ID Number *5-2241* | 3. Badge Number *2367* |
|---|---|---|
| 4. Assisting Officer *Gannon, D* | 5. ID Number *6-3546* | 6. Badge Number *914* |

| Location *5600 N. Washington Blvd.* | Date *9-1-2003* | Time *7:00 PM* |
|---|---|---|

| 7. Driver 1 *Major, John* | 8. DOB *4-4-62* | 9. Age *42* |
|---|---|---|
| 10. Address *2345 W. Michigan Street* | 11. City *Indianapolis* | 12. Zip Code *46222* |
| 13. S.S.N. *216-09-2114* | 14. H. Phone *317-623-7741* | 15. W. Phone *317-925-1732* |

| 15. Vehicle 1 *Black* | 17. Make *Olds* | 18. Model *Delta 88* | 19. Lic. *32J6623* |
|---|---|---|---|

Striking Vehicle

| 20. Driver 2 *Rogers, Anthony* | 21. D.O.B. *6-3-70* | 22. Age *34* |
|---|---|---|
| 23. Address *9935 Six Point Road* | 24. City *Plainfield* | 25. Zip Code *46237* |
| 27. S.S.N. *346-28-9876* | 28. H. Phone *317-839-9913* | 29. W. Phone *317-235-1125* |

| 10 Vehicle *Blue* | 17. Make *Honda* | 18. Model *Accord* | 19. Lic. *68T2957* |
|---|---|---|---|